Invisible Warfare

Invisible Warfare

Mona Miller

| WARNING: |
| This book could change your life. |

COMMUNICATION ARTS PRESS
SHERMAN OAKS, CALIFORNIA
2006

Editors: Adryan Russ, Roger Wolfson
Cover collage and graphic designer: Doug Haverty/Art & Soul Design

Communication Arts Press
15030 Ventura Boulevard, Suite 19–884
Sherman Oaks, California 91403

http://www.communicationartscompany.com

ISBN-10: 0-9786652-0-1
ISBN-13: 978-0-9786652-0-3

I dedicate this book to my son, J.J.,

my family,

my clients,

their friends.

~

My son has been my inspiration to know myself inside and out, to go beyond what I know.

To my mom for her unbelievable strength and depth, my dad for his charisma and play, and for letting me be and supporting me. To my sister Pam who listens and plays with every crazy voice I've ever had. Who laughs and cries with me always. To my brother Eddie who had to walk with me as I challenged his every step. And Johnny who I always thought was my child. I give this book to all of you with so much appreciation and love.

As for my first client, Amber, and the clients that followed, I watched them change themselves and affect so many around them. As I sit, tucked away in my mountain, they soar. This book is for them to take for themselves and whomever they wish. It is a result of our think tank—right, Cathi? You encouraged and helped me start it all.

Acknowledgments

For all of you I am so grateful.

First, to Berni, for letting me be and do whatever I had to do and be. I thank you for your spiritual, mental, and financial support.

To J.J. and Nicole, who in the last three years of writing this book have not once complained. Any pressure or guilt put on me for the time and work it took to finish this project was self-induced. You all have backed me 100% and I thank you and love you with all my heart and soul.

To my typesetter and assistant, Jennifer De Haven, who was and is irreplaceable. No job was too big or small. This book would not have been finished if not for you. We made it come alive, Jennifer!

My editor, Adryan Russ, what a sweet and patient soul. Thank you for your commitment, endurance and enjoyable company.

My clients for their encouragement that really pulled me through times of exhaustion and also to those clients who have donated their stories. Your bravery kept me raw, open and honest. I respect each and every one of you.

And of course, my friends, those who have not seen me and those who have sat with me, listening to many of these chapters as my captive audience.

Contents

Preface

If I were to venture into a jungle for the first time, I would want a map or a guide who lived in that jungle, someone who knew it from the inside out. Never having been there, I might get lost. While I'm willing to explore the jungle, I want to be able to enjoy it and learn a few things on the way.

This book is your guide. Like a map, it is a way in and out of the jungle of your own ego, spirit, logic and feelings. I cannot make you lose your fear of this journey through the jungle. I cannot make you change. You are the only person who can do these things. But I can help you get there. I have many beliefs, but one of the strongest is: Find the fear and know the truth and you're halfway home.

The world in which we live today is a manifestation of our own internal misunderstandings. How many of us truly understand ourselves, let alone others? Our intellect judges too easily, and judgments crush feelings and creativity. The intellect, while crucial for our development, is just a piece of our brain. To be whole, we need to know our whole selves. The difficulty comes when different parts of our selves battle each other because of the lack of self-understanding and the need to develop processing skill. This book offers you a way to do both.

Understanding our invisible wars is the way to create visible peace. The goal is to consciously understand the subconscious—our subliminal mind—which is so powerful that it can take us on a trip through our past, present and future in less than a second, stimulating us emotionally, creatively and chemically, causing mood swings that range from depression to brilliance.

This book is the road to owning up to your depression so that you can find your brilliance. Everyone is brilliant. We just can't see it sometimes.

—Mona Miller

P.S. Do not rush through this book. Take a section at a time. Feel free to do it with others and share what you're writing and learning. Meet weekly or monthly. Let's grow together.

Before you begin this book you will need:

1. A sense of humor

2. An open mind

3. A notebook—a journal

4. A pen or pencil

5. An old tennis racket, whiffle bat, or mallet

6. Old vinyl pillow or your bed

7. You may also use a punching bag with gloves

8. Your commitment not to quit before you have completed this book even if it upsets you

9. Some tissues (hopefully)

10. Movies (can be rented or found in most libraries):
    Mystic River (Chapter 8)
    A Christmas Carol (Chapter 11)
    Sybil (Chapter 14)
    What the Bleep Do we Know? (Chapter 15)
        (to order: www.whatthebleep.com)
    The Karate Kid (Chapter 16)

Invisible Warfare

1 Am I My Worst Enemy?
Self-Judgment Is Killing Me!

A few years ago my mother sent me a picture of myself from when I was three years old. As soon as I looked at it, I wanted to throw it out the window. I felt so much rage and pain towards this cute little girl in the picture! Who was this girl I knew was me?

What was happening to me? What was I feeling? When I write music, poems, or stories I always talk about being a little girl of three. Why? Why do I keep seeing a little girl of three?

I look at that little girl in the picture. And I see through judgmental eyes. I see an ugly, fat girl with crooked eyes, fuzzy hair, wearing a stupid dress and a phony smile. When I show it to others, they see a sweet, huggable girl with bright eyes, curly hair and a loving smile. Why do we see the same picture so differently?

And where did I learn to see myself like that?

This perception didn't go away. I feel it as I write this book. When I was little, learning in school was very difficult. The other kids called us the "dummy class." It wasn't until fifth grade—just when I was getting the hang of finger painting—that someone finally decided to transition me into an upper class.

So, at the age of ten, my world had changed.

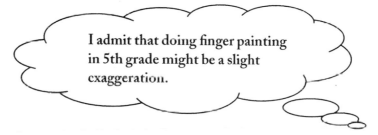

I admit that doing finger painting in 5th grade might be a slight exaggeration.

Leading a Double Life

The low expectations from school and the simultaneous high expectations outside school are conflicting judgments I still struggle with today.

Am I smart or stupid? Am I a blessing or a mistake? Good or bad, talented or insane? Why must I see myself in judgmental dichotomies?

In order to be able to understand and process my life's traumas, accomplishments, confusions, and clarities, I had to begin by comprehending the power struggle between positive and negative opinions. I needed to explore new ideas so my judgments could turn into wisdom and understanding. My judgments were blocking my mind and heart. I was not able to see myself differently. Stuck inside judgment's prison, all we can do is stand still. When we judge ourselves, we are unable to grow.

I had been leading quite the double life. In school, having no "comprehension capability," I had no responsibilities. Back home, where no one was smart enough to figure out I was "limited," I had to cook, clean, baby-sit and do the laundry. I also performed as an actress, pianist and singer. In elementary school I was introverted; outside school, you couldn't shut me up.

In my new class I noticed how many people behaved just like me. Meaning, they acted a certain way in one environment, and differently in another. Even back then I wondered: why do people do this? Why don't we act the same—all the time, in all situations? Why can't we just be who we are, no matter *where* we are? How do I learn to understand myself?

The process of trusting myself didn't begin until years later, when I learned how to CHECK IN to my thoughts and feelings. I somehow understood that I needed to learn how to hear and understand my own thoughts and feelings before understanding those of others.

If you're like me, you probably edit yourself. This type of editing often made me lie or alter the truth in some way. You know, it's all because of "The Inner Editor," who interrupts and alters whatever you might be saying—especially the truth if the truth is judged as upsetting or embarrassing.

That's why I'm going to ask you to CHECK IN and write your answers to the questions in this book. Writing thoughts or feelings about any question can make you so much more aware. As you will see, as we move forward, this book isn't about me *teaching* you lessons; it's about you *integrating* them into your life. Writing things out is a type of visualization, which stimulates feelings. Feelings ignite subconscious thoughts and feelings, causing subliminal pictures that stimulate the memory. And it is the motion in the word emotion that causes subconscious and conscious change, allowing us to integrate what we learn.

Please stay open to these ideas, even if they make you uncomfortable. Let's start with a practice round! Take out some paper or, if it helps, you can use your computer to get started. If you want, answer your own questions or mine on a recorder or answering machine to practice listening to yourself.

 "Stop" means STOP! Question yourself! Take the time to answer the questions (in any way you will) and do the exercises!

1. What happens to a child who is told he or she is stupid or brilliant?

2. What is an example, from your life, of how someone "saw" you? How did this judgment or perception affect what you believed about yourself?

You'll see that sometimes in this book when I ask a question, I'll answer it myself, and sometimes I won't. Please know that our answers may differ; and that's fine. We are different people. Sometimes I use humor to describe things, especially about myself. Humor helps me digest information with less difficulty. Back to my story.

When I was a kid:

• Part of me believed I was stupid, and part of me believed I was smart.

• Part of me believed I was inadequate; part of me, that I was talented.

• Because I was in the "dummy" group, the part of me that thought I was dumb and inadequate often *won*.

The thought that I was dumb became what I *believed*. Notice how much the truth mattered. I would have sworn these judgments and perceptions were true. But a belief is not necessarily a fact. Sometimes things that we believe all of our life are not true.

1. Have you ever discovered something you had always believed to be true—isn't?

What Is a Belief?

> **BELIEF:** A belief is a thought or feeling you deem true and therefore real. Because you believe it is true you have manifested it as real. Just as we can program a computer to run a certain way, we can program what we think and feel. Over time, programmed thoughts and feelings become beliefs—regardless of whether they're true. What we believe affects the way we live. Our beliefs become our reality.

This becomes a problem when we realize that many of us look at ourselves through others' judgments and perceptions. Why do we need to see our struggles and mistakes so negatively?

1. Is there something negative you believe about yourself that may not be true?

2. Write that negative belief.

3. Now write what you feel may be the truth.

4. Can you come up with any reasons why you adhere to that negative belief, even when the truth tells you otherwise?

5. Did you teach yourself to believe that negative thought, or is it a judgment someone else taught you?

Most of us believe something negative about ourselves that isn't true. In so doing, we make our reality just a little worse. There is danger in believing things without finding out whether they are true. Even if they are true, we need to understand why and work on them. When your truth doesn't matter to you, then neither does your reality.

Like many children struggling to learn, I had a different way of learning than my teachers did. Therefore, I perceived them judging me and my ways as inferior. As a result, I adopted their opinions or beliefs, which became my beliefs, and therefore, my reality.

> **You create and become what you
> subconsciously believe, whether or not it is true.**

Your past is a collection of recordings stored in your subconscious mind. These recordings play on the hard drive of your mind—and sometimes make you act like someone you aren't and make you do things you may not like or want to do.

That's why this book encourages you to think about, and understand, what has been said and done to you in your life.

1. Do you sometimes do things you don't like to do or want to do? Like what?

2. When you do those things, whose voice do you hear in your head? What is this person saying inside your head?

The Difference Between Judging and Understanding

Judgments and opinions are confusing, because they are inconsistent and do not represent the truth. And yet, people with strong judgments believe their opinions to be fact. Why are we so closed-minded to seeing and accepting people and things that are different? Why must we be right? Judgments and opinions vary for a variety of reasons—some of them come from racial, cultural, family, or religious beliefs. How could differences of opinion not occur? But why does this result in us having to fight, go to war, and even die?

Opinions with no openness to differences can seriously block our ability to find understanding in all truths. In the midst of strong judgment, there is no room for understanding another point of view. Gossip is judging with no understanding. How does this kind of communication about others feel to them and to you later? How can we find peace without understanding?

The question many of us face in any fight or disagreement is: Who is the "good" guy and who is the "bad" guy? But is there really a good guy or a bad guy? And if so, are good and bad guys really that different? Could all of us have core beliefs that are really similar, but expressed with different words and/or stories?

Pull out the pen or the keyboard...

1. When you are with someone who is different from you, is your goal to *judge* that person, or is your goal to *understand* that person and his or her differences? (Think a minute!)

2. What's the difference between judging and understanding? (Don't worry about "right" or "wrong" answers. Just write what you think and feel!)

3. *Judging is...*
   Judging feels...
   Judging creates...

4. Most of us have a strong judgmental reaction to someone or to some type of person. Who do you judge?
   A person I judge is...
   The reason I judge this person or type of person is...
   This person makes me feel...
   And this person reminds me of (who in your past)...
   I am different from this person because...

5. Again, just write what you think and feel.
   Understanding is...
   Understanding feels...
   Understanding creates...

6. Most of us believe we understand someone or a certain type of person. Who do you understand?

> *The person I understand is...*
> *The reason I understand this person or type of person is...*
> *This person makes me feel...*
> *And this person reminds me of (who in your past)...*
> *I am different from this person because...*

Are you checking in? Here are a few more questions!

1. Most religions say: "Do not judge." Why do you think they say this? If you judge others, will your inner judgmental voice turn on you and judge you as well? How could this happen?

2. How understanding are you toward yourself?

3. How judgmental are you toward yourself?

4. Do you call yourself negative names? If so, what names? Why? When?

These may not be easy questions to answer. But if you take the time to answer them honestly, you'll see more clearly.

---

5. If you are a parent, teacher or coach do you judge your children? Do you judge your parent(s)? Be honest, please... C'mon, it's common in many cultures to name-call. What do you "call" your parent or children when you judge them (judging counts whether it is said out loud or stays in your head)?

6. Did your parents, teachers or coaches call you those names? What do you remember?

7. How did that make you feel?

You Are on an Exciting Journey! Stop and remember to answer *all* questions in writing!! This is how you *personalize* this book and

make it about *you*! Writing helps you really *see* what you are thinking and feeling. Instead of just reading through the questions, be sure to write your answers, and keep what you write! If you stick with this book, you'll want to look back on what you've written to discover what has and has not changed. This can be an exciting new journey—if you remain open to new and different perceptions!

I'm going to start focusing on the word *see.* I want the word to register subconsciously, to create a subliminal message for you. The goal is to *see* beyond, to go underneath the surface—yours, and that of others.

> If inspiration lives in our *subconscious* mind, and our "will" lives in our *conscious* mind, then we need a process that shows us how to recognize when we are in one or the other. Inspiration connects to our essence and comes from inner truth. Our will connects to our "drive," which is derived from a low- or high-ego state of mind. We need a way to move back and forth between them to create differently. To do this, we must change the way we think, which will change the way we feel—and act.

New Thoughts Create New Feelings and New Behavior

Why do people avoid evolving? Has our world made it so difficult to recover from mistakes because the universe tells us it is only through our mistakes that we can learn? What a setup for depression. Any mistake has brilliance in it. It is through the mistake we shall see what isn't true, which is invaluable in showing us what is true. All I need now is a wish!

It all begins with a wish.

Do you wish for someone or something outside you? What about a better job, a bigger house, a new lover, a child?

Although these are wonderful things, you must still think, feel and act like *you*, but who are you? You are the only one who can change your life! This may sound like a curse, but it is a blessing once you realize its power.

How can we complain and say the world is an awful mess and needs change if we don't even know a formula for change within ourselves?

> **Do you want to change the world?**
> **Then change you!**

Because I was convinced as a child that I was a "dummy," teaching today is a life experience I never dreamed possible. When I changed my perception of myself, I began to change my choices and behaviors. First my thoughts changed, then my feelings changed, and then my beliefs changed.

Today, my struggles are as crucial to me as my accomplishments. The understanding of my struggles took me out of a place of judgment and into a place of understanding—myself as well as others. I am comfortable knowing that, down deep, I still am "stupid." All this means is I can always learn. It keeps me from thinking I'm finished. It keeps me open to myself as well as other people. Life has a purpose. We are never finished!

We all can be smart *and* stupid. This duality keeps us open to "seeing" the good, the bad, the beautiful, and the ugly—without hurting ourselves or others.

When people move from judging themselves or others to understanding themselves and others, their lives begin to change in miraculous ways, one miracle at a time.

> **Judging causes me to quit—**
> **on others as well as on myself.**
>
> **Understanding opens my heart and mind and helps**
> **me be creative—with others as well as myself.**

1. Can you "see" how understanding other people seems to be something you are doing for them, but it really is something you are doing for you? Explain in your own words.

2. When in the process of understanding someone, is it better to react emotionally or try to logically "fix" that person?

3. What does listening in an understanding way really mean?

4. What does listening in understanding create?

5. What does listening in judgment create?

6. How would you describe your state of mind when you are just listening?

Chapter Review

I just learned…
And I feel…

Summary

When we lack self-awareness, we judge others and ourselves as good and bad, "better than" or "less than." These judgments, taught to us during our early development, subconsciously control our minds, hearts, and bodies.

Either you go after your thoughts, feelings, and memories, or they come after you. Writing out my inner voices helps me "see" my thoughts and feelings—and understand them in a non-shameful way.

Belief is a choice. We all have the ability to de-program the beliefs that were fed to us before we had a developed sense of self. We are all a mixture of good and bad, right and wrong, strong and weak, smart and ignorant, winner and loser. By accepting our dichotomies, our minds open, and we are able to "see" what we subconsciously already know: We are human beings who have the capability to change our lives.

2 Loving My Neighbor as Myself, I Killed Him

We've talked about how judgment is different from understanding, and how judging ourselves makes us judge others. We've talked about how self-judgments can make us beat ourselves up (self-beats) and self-beats can spiral into depression (spins). The way we treat ourselves has a very real impact on those around us.

If we repeat such actions, we beat ourselves up more and more. Can you see how the self-beat is trying to send us a message, and if we're not listening, we don't get the message, so we spin and repeat the same thought, feeling and behavior over and over again? If we don't change our behavior, it can get worse. We can even start feeling crazy. We lose touch with our thoughts and feelings—with ourselves. If our thoughts and feelings get stuck with no understanding or way out, we become an "Emotional Person" instead of a "Feeling Person," as Julie explains.

As I Hurt, Do I Hurt You?
by Julie

I am a lunatic.

I have always been afraid of seeing a therapist because I've thought that the therapist would lock me up and drug me right away.

I have so many voices inside that scare me. These voices sound like my mom, my brother, teachers, and the kids from my childhood. Back then I was so sensitive and scared I took everyone's words to heart. Their voices still ring in my ears, and have become my suicidal thoughts. Although I now know that these voices are really just me, my own self-beat/judger out of control, I still feel worthless and unimportant. These voices run my life and my belief system of who I am.

So I get bored and frustrated with myself. If I am bored, I know I am really just suffering from so many emotions in conflict that my energy has shut down. Sometimes the voices in my head make me hurt myself. I am what's called a "cutter"; sometimes I cut my skin because it makes me feel better. That means I've internalized the voices of the people who have mentally and physically injured me since I was a little girl—my parents and brother. They used to hurt me. I live in fear that they will hurt me again. So I hurt myself, to be prepared.

I chant on Mona's answering machine, in my writings and in my head: "I'm a fat, ugly loser who needs to die! Die, Julie! Die! Die! Die!" Then I stab myself with a pair of scissors or a sharp object. This is how I make the pain visible. "It's true, Mom! He did hurt me!" Then I scream hysterically and have an asthma attack. Is it them or me who is not listening to me?

The self-beat begins as just a voice in my head. The voices of the doctors and my parents, telling me that I am sick, "I'm going to die," spins in my head. "So get it over with and die, Julie!" So I stab myself again. Then I hide under a table waiting for the murder voices to stop! I usually fall asleep there.

I can say this so clearly now because I am conscious of it. The real scary part is how many times I did this, not conscious of it.

I have become my own abuser. I do not want to deal with the anger that I feel towards my family and then the guilt for being angry. Because of my guilt, I take my anger out on other people, sometimes strangers, and situations or myself that have nothing to do with my true anger. This cycle keeps my anger and me from attacking my family, which is where my anger really belongs.

It is like a ride I can't get off. I want to believe in myself but if I do, I feel I will be molested, hit, attacked physically or verbally! Everyone is better than me. I'm a loser! My experiences from my past are now my fear for my future. I am scared to death of being hurt by others, so I attack them or me first.

And so the spin… spins on…

Can you see how Julie got herself into a Spin Game? Every time a feeling comes up, she shuts herself down from fear. And when she shuts down, she disconnects from her logical mind and her honest thoughts and feelings. Julie is an emotional person rather than a feeling one. Sensitive, feeling people, who have no processing skill, give feelings a bad rap. Who wants feelings if they are going to be hysterical, crazy or out of control? But this is about more than feelings. This is what happens when feelings are judged and are not understood and processed.

Now, how do you think Julie affects the people around her? Do you think they are untouched by what's going on in her head? Are you?

The See-Saw Games We Play

Every thought and feeling has a particular energy—a "vibe," or vibration. This energy moves back and forth between us, and carries energetic information. Whether we're aware enough to interpret this information or not doesn't stop the vibes from existing. But I guarantee you—whether you know it or not, you are sending out vibes all day long. And your subconscious is receiving vibes, and acting on them.

Let's look at Stephanie and Debra.

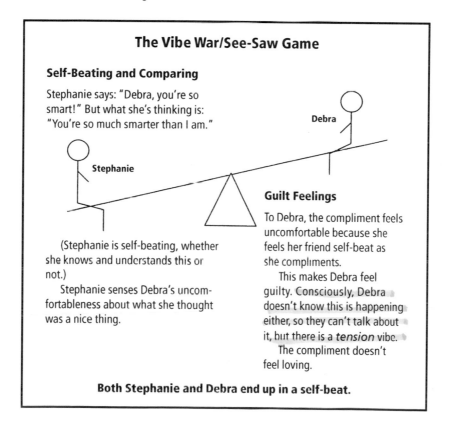

The Vibe War/See-Saw Game

Self-Beating and Comparing

Stephanie says: "Debra, you're so smart!" But what she's thinking is: "You're so much smarter than I am."

Debra

Stephanie

(Stephanie is self-beating, whether she knows and understands this or not.)

Stephanie senses Debra's uncomfortableness about what she thought was a nice thing.

Guilt Feelings

To Debra, the compliment feels uncomfortable because she feels her friend self-beat as she compliments.

This makes Debra feel guilty. Consciously, Debra doesn't know this is happening either, so they can't talk about it, but there is a *tension* vibe.

The compliment doesn't feel loving.

Both Stephanie and Debra end up in a self-beat.

SELF-BEAT: Every thought or feeling that is topped by judgment creates a self-beat. The self-beat voice is telling you to become aware and to understand something. If the self-beat is not heard and understood, it can manifest self-hate, insecurity, depression, addiction, mutilation, suicide, insanity or criminal act-outs. You don't fight or try to get rid of the self-beat; you go to it, understand it and open your mind to new thinking, feeling and behavior. A self-beat keeps us in a spin of self-judgment.

If you are self-beating or in a spin, this book will help you reach an understanding of why this is happening.

Piranha Self-Beat

"You bitch!"

"You loser!"

"Kill yourself!"

"You're so stupid!"

Then I respond with a shut down of, whatever!

SPIN: A thought, feeling or behavior that repeats with no change of thought, feeling, belief or behavior, topped by a self-beat that spirals uncontrollably. A spin happens when you put anger, fear, guilt, shame or hurt on someone or something and repeat those thoughts, feelings or behaviors with no change. You are in a spin because you are not understanding the lies and truths of the situation. There is no owning here. If no awareness or behavior comes, you can begin to feel crazy. If you get stuck in one thought, feeling or belief with no processing or understanding, your spin will turn you into a shut down or depressed, out-of-control, emotional person rather than a sensitive, feeling person.

Stephanie and Debra are both in "ego mode." You end up in a self-beat only if you are in ego whether it's high or low ego. The three primary states of mind are: High Ego (arrogance), Low Ego (insecurity), and Spirit or Essence (a state of self-love, truth, and understanding).

HIGH EGO: The false god we read about. It is an arrogant perception of being superior to others. It is a survival skill for blocking one's shame and guilt. It does not own or understand. It is a state of condescending control and arrogance, created from a lack of acceptance due to painful and embarrassing truths. When a part of you feels injured, the high ego arises to dominate and save you. The goal is to be powerful.

LOW EGO: The concept of slavery that develops from a feeling of insecurity, worthlessness and failure. It is a perception of being inferior to others. It is a survival skill, for protection, to remain invisible or to obey others in order to not be judged as wrong. It is a camouflage of weakness so dominators will not notice you and will leave you alone. Full of self-beat and personalization this is created from a lack of self-responsibility and effort for painful and embarrassing truths. When a part of you feels injured, the low ego suppresses your inner strength to hide you and keep you safe. The goal is to be powerless.

SPIRIT or ESSENCE: "What is." It represents the understanding of all truth and struggle. It knows the importance of flipping to the high and low ego to develop understanding. Before you can experience a balance from the middle, you need to be able to recognize the opposite energies on each side. Spirit sees all as equal and full of purpose. Spirit is the perception of truth and lies with love for both. It is your own personal Higher Power or God energy of awareness. It speaks to you through the intuition, which reveals truth. It shines its light through the understanding of your confusions and mistakes. It does not push or control; it listens with wisdom and compassion. Of an age beyond Earth years, it is faith. Faith that when you are ready, you will come to it and listen. It waits patiently for you to not project the judgments learned from this planet onto this energy. It is here to heal, through deep understanding, the injuries of pain and embarrassment, as it already knows why these injuries exist. It knows your magic and talents and is there to remind you of who you are, if you choose to remember. Reaching this understanding is where the struggle stops. This is empowerment!

Now let's look at Buddy and Joe.

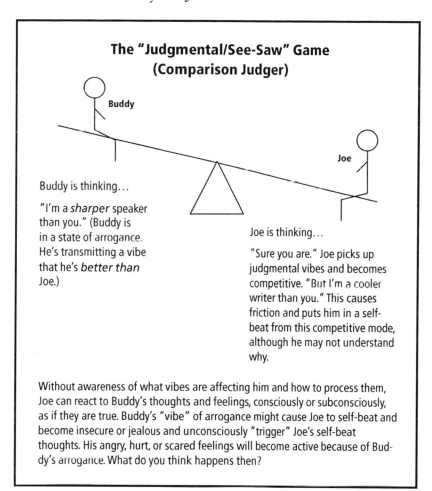

The "Judgmental/See-Saw" Game
(Comparison Judger)

Buddy

Joe

Buddy is thinking...

"I'm a *sharper* speaker than you." (Buddy is in a state of arrogance. He's transmitting a vibe that he's *better than* Joe.)

Joe is thinking...

"Sure you are." Joe picks up judgmental vibes and becomes competitive. "But I'm a cooler writer than you." This causes friction and puts him in a self-beat from this competitive mode, although he may not understand why.

Without awareness of what vibes are affecting him and how to process them, Joe can react to Buddy's thoughts and feelings, consciously or subconsciously, as if they are true. Buddy's "vibe" of arrogance might cause Joe to self-beat and become insecure or jealous and unconsciously "trigger" Joe's self-beat thoughts. His angry, hurt, or scared feelings will become active because of Buddy's arrogance. What do you think happens then?

1. When you are aware of someone else's arrogance or insecurity, how does that make you feel?

2. Do you think it's possible to be affected by someone else's vibes if you have not consciously stated to yourself, "That person is vibing me"? If so, how?

3. Do you think that, when you think these kinds of thoughts or have uncomfortable feelings, other people can feel or react to you whether they are conscious of these or not? What do you think? It's okay to guess.

4. When you are aware that someone is self-beating, how do you feel? Does this trigger you? In what ways?

5. If you self-beat, how does that affect others?

Here are a few more See-Saw Games...

1. Have you ever played the Vibe War or Judgment See-Saw Game? In what way?

2. Have you ever picked up on a vibe that did not feel comfortable?

3. What kind of vibes do you usually pick up on easily? Happy/sad? Angry? Sexually charged? Depressed?

4. Can you write about when this happened to you? I remember when... and I felt...

5. Can you see how it's possible to hurt yourself even while "complimenting" others? Explain.

6. Can you see how it's possible to hurt the person you are "complimenting" as well? Explain.

7. Is it possible to compliment another person without comparing yourself to that person, without self-beating yourself? If so, how?

> ### Seeing What You Like and Don't Like
>
> If you put yourself down while complimenting others, you don't feel loving. Can you be loving and truthful with yourself and with others—without self-beating? Without comparing? The only reason to compare yourself with another person is to "see" what you like and don't like—not to be "better than" or "less than." The truth, positive or negative, is just the truth, plain and simple.

Will you judge, or will you understand?

Just as you cannot breathe and swallow at the same time, you cannot judge and understand at the same time. The moment you judge, your ability to understand disappears. The moment you understand, judgment disappears.

Pick one!

The War Inside Us

This book is called *Invisible Warfare* because invisible wars go on inside and outside us every day. These are fights inside our head that we have with ourself and others. These judgments in our head and within our relationships create confusion and pain in our everyday lives.

I want you to know that my fear of judgment from others—and from myself—almost stopped me from writing this book. How has your fear of judgment stopped you from your wishes?

Someone putting a gun to your head can create visible fear. But *invisible* fear is the kind we don't always notice. We may not be consciously aware that we're afraid. Did you know that we can live in a state of fear and suffer insanity or paralysis without any conscious awareness that this is happening!?

Being emotionally shut down is the stopping of thought and/or feeling altogether. We do this as a way to protect ourselves from having out-of-control, misunderstood, emotional, "big" feelings. This creates more invisible warfare. When I'm shut down, I don't have to hear anyone, see anything, as I do nothing. Hysteria is the flip side of being shut down. And yes, they are the same thing. A shutdown is hysteria on the inside and hysteria is a shutdown on the inside. These personal inner wars can create temporary or permanent insanity or depression.

If the truth upsets us, or we don't like it, we subconsciously or consciously start changing and/or blocking it. We twist and turn the truth in order to suit our will or ego so that we'll feel more comfortable. We delude ourselves into thinking that if we don't feel, we won't experience pain.

When we are shut down we are in a state of self-manipulation of the truth. How can we become evolved and balanced spiritually, mentally, emotionally, physically, sexually and financially if we are shut down?

We continue to want what we want. But what we want could be based on defenses, insecurity, addiction, and/or obsession. Still want what you want? Better know yourself before you go after something!

We twist and spin the truth until we are so confused, inside and out, that we're not even consciously aware that our pain is still there. We are not confused beings, we are manipulators! And confusion is just the changing of truth to make it an acceptable lie! Welcome to the Spin Game of Confusion!

Here is a definition of a word used a lot in this book. Since my client Jenni uses it in her story below, about her involvement in the Confusion/ Spin Game, have a look before reading her story.

> **RINSE:** A technique and processing of our thoughts, feelings and memories—spiritually, mentally, emotionally, physically, sexually, financially and psychically—by writing things down, or physically processing.

To Keep the Peace, I Spin in Confusion
by Jenni

Until recently, I was practically dead inside. I discovered that I was suffering from some very deep and unaddressed traumas. As a result, I behaved sometimes like an adult, and sometimes like a four-year-old. Part of me had emotionally stopped growing. I had developed a "shadow image" of myself, which I held up as real, but which blocked the "light" and kept me from seeing my "true" self. This shadow part I developed helped me survive everyday life. But, surviving life is much different from living life.

I got involved with a man who was stuck and hurt like my inner four-year-old self. His "little boy" also had a "shadow" self. His experiences growing up traumatized him. This scared little boy became a scared and scary man. But he denied he was scared, just as did I.

As we dated, this man showed himself to be an alcoholic, arrogant jerk. He was big, aggressive and emotionally abusive. He was a perfect match for the frightened and scared four-year-old girl inside of me. He helped me create a relationship just like the ones I knew when I was growing up. My husband was like my father and brothers. As crappy as it was, my inner four-year-old was very comfortable with my new husband's behavior. Although I may have hated his behavior, I still accepted him. Comfort won over truth.

So what did I do? I married him. I went off and repeated the same life I hated as a child.

I still remember our wedding. It was amazing. It seemed perfect and beautiful. The honeymoon was fun and romantic. I went right into La La Land. Once we got home and settled in, things went from bad to worse. We both lied about our logical truths and definitely lied about our emotional truths.

We were both so far away from having "self love" that it was impossible to love and understand each other. I was ready to leave him after a few weeks of marriage.

But then I started learning about feelings and how to identify and process them. I realized that I couldn't possibly communicate thoughts and feelings I couldn't understand. Feelings are different than thoughts and logic. I used judgment words and called them feelings.

I had to find, feel and understand all my truths, the truths about who my family is and was for generations. I had to understand my culture and my female-gender judgments. These understandings helped me establish boundaries and develop a loving, strong voice.

Now, a year later, I am still working hard to continually rinse the rubble away so that I stay in my "true self." My inner four-year-old is smart, funny, loving and loveable. She is outgoing and decisive.

Some days, I fall back into my old behaviors. I am usually somewhere between my "true self" and my "shadow self." But on those days that I have rinsed and done my "anger work" and owned, I'm back to my "true self," and I shine!

My goal is to not get confused in an image or what I think others want me to be. I do not keep the peace by lying anymore to others or myself. I'd rather tell the truth and be upset for a while. After all, I know how to "rinse" my upsets. By "rinsing" I stay clear and am forever developing into the person I am meant to be. Even with my trauma memories. I am now stronger than the traumas!

I "see" me as a beautiful person—now with a beautiful daughter—and, yes, with a beautiful husband. That is not how I used to feel about my husband or myself. My husband "rinses" too. I have broken out of my dark hole by using tools to rebuild my life the way I truly want it. I'm not repeating what my past taught me.

I have the tools to find truth, set boundaries and most importantly to have a loving voice—a voice that is me. I have learned to love, feel and understand myself and I can love my husband and daughter without spiritually and emotionally killing them or me.

I needed to learn how to not be confused, in fear, and I believe I have.

How do you think that Jenni's self-love affected the people around her, such as her husband? Her daughter?

Judgment Words Create Imbalance

The words below are words we hear or use every day. How many times a day do you judge something as good or bad? Right or wrong? Best or worst? Stupid or smart?

Good   If I call something good, that means I am holding up an image of what I think I or someone else "should be." What pressure! What happens if I or others can't live up to that image? Are we bad, and what are the chances of a self-beat here? Good can put you in high ego. Good is not necessarily a good word. Good doesn't necessarily mean truth. In fact, to be good, people often lie and omit the truth to appear good.

Bad   Bad is a word perfectly designed to send someone into a self-beat. Bad puts you in low ego. How does a dog look when you cry out, "Bad dog!"? That's how we look, inside, when we judge ourselves or our actions as "bad."

Right   If I am "right," then I am better than everyone else. I am one-dimensional, closed-minded and self-righteous. High ego again. Who likes the person who is "right" all the time? How many relationships have been destroyed because both people are determined to be "right"?

Wrong   If I judge myself to be "wrong" I am "worse" than others. Low ego. Then I must self-beat. No pain, no gain, right? I must be punished. Does punishment breed truth?

Smart   "Smart" creates comparisons of how I am "better than" or "more than" other people. "Smart" leads to high ego and pressure.

Stupid   This is a self-beat word that can cause horrible self-hate and a helpless hopelessness leading to depression.

Other judgment words to be aware of are: Best, Worst, Greatest, Failure, Beautiful, Ugly...the list goes on.

Listening with knowledge of your strengths and weaknesses and no self-beat means learning to love through understanding with no good, bad, right or wrong. This is how you live a life of unconditional love.

My Personal Judgment Words!

What are the judgment words *you* use? Write them down!
As you write them, think about *why* you use them.
I'll start you off with one.

My Judgment Words	Why I Use Them
Dumb	To put myself, or someone else, down.
Inferior	*lower then others*

Understanding the Feeling Words That Cause Us to Judge!

Feeling words describe feelings we experience every day. But the problem is, most of the words that we use often don't mean what we think they mean.

Example: **Anger**

If I accept that my anger is just anger, then all I will be prompted to ask of myself is "Who am I angry with?" Or "Why am I angry?" This process will be very simple, and I might get some understanding out of it, and be able to go deeper but…how?

If I understand that *anger isn't just anger*—anger is *hurt* mixed with *fear*—I will learn far more, and develop a deeper understanding of myself if I ask myself, "How am I hurt?" And "What am I afraid of?"

Example: **Shame**

Shame isn't just shame. Shame is a self-beat. It happens when I blame myself for something, and I try to hide from myself and others. Although shame is a self-beat, it ignites fear and anger as well. To ask myself why must I beat myself up or punish myself can lead to self-compassion, wisdom and then change.

Example: **Guilt**

Guilt isn't just guilt. Guilt blocks our awareness of hurt and sadness. Sad and mad get stuck in the judgment word "bad." I did something or felt something that was judged wrong, stupid or hurtful. Or I was blamed for something. "Guilt" points the finger first at me and then towards others. Guilt says the same thing as shame: You're "bad"; now be sad and regretful so you will want and accept punishment. Where's the understanding? Does this really work or do we start lying and denying and shut down and get depressed?

Please note, no one can make us accept guilt. Guilt is a perception. It is a way of seeing, thinking and believing. But only through understanding the thought, feeling or behavior that triggered the guilt can we let go of guilt once it enters our mind.

So many of our misunderstood emotions boil down to anger and fear. Understanding is the cure for change. If we're in a place of understanding, we have no anger, fear, guilt, or shame, no matter what we have done.

Words Without Judgment

Now that we've looked at judgment and misunderstood feeling words that mislead us, let's look at the world from the other side and focus on words that change our perception and teach wisdom.

Understanding Understanding has no anger, fear, guilt or shame in it. If I can "see" all of myself—the good and the bad and everything in between then I can "see" and feel the same in other people.

Patience When we understand, with no judgment, we become patient. We don't feel pressured by time. There are no false expectations, and no active self-beats. Patience is not tolerance; it is complete acceptance.

Compassion When we are compassionate, we are open to processing and owning our sadness and passion with empathy—no thought of anger, fear, guilt or shame. If we can stand in our own shoes without jumping out of them, we can put ourselves in the shoes of others, as well. We "see" and feel others and can relate to them because we are able to understand our own perceptions and experiences.

Belief   Belief is a perception. What we believe is what we portray. The truth of who we are may not show itself in this lifetime without a desire for inner truth. Everything we experience is meant to teach us to understand what we are as well as what we are not.

Faith   When we have faith, we believe and love the truth whether we like the truth or not. Faith in truth replaces fear of judgment.

When we are connected to all the above words, we depart from a place of judgment, and enter a place of wisdom. We open ourselves to our selves, and to the world of differences.

Crazy Voices and How To Rinse Them

As we've briefly discussed, we all have crazy voices that speak to us inside our head: "Do this! Don't do that!" These are controlling voices derived from judgmental beliefs. They are often illogical and emotional. They fill us with partial truths, anger, fear, guilt, shame, hurt, confusion and lies. To pretend they don't exist or try to shut them down makes life feel like a bad dream.

The way to process these voices is to not *ignore them.* The way to understand them is to listen to them, get to know them. They represent the people, places and things in your past and present that have affected your life.

Once the information these voices give you is conscious and out in the open, you can understand the voices and end their influence over you.

When you give yourself a Crazy Voice Rinse, you *listen* to what your half truths, illogical or insane voices are saying and allow yourself to *see* and *feel* them—without shame, without judgment.

Everyone has crazy voices. Trying to convince yourself that these voices don't exist or matter can create addictive "act-outs," depression or worse. Accept and be free with "what is"—with no shame! To pull a weed, you have to "see" the weed. Then you can remove it and plant a new flower! Don't forget to pull the root (from the past)!

Crazy voices can create invisible warfare in your life. As you already know, what you think and what you feel affect how you behave. That's why these voices need to be "seen" and allowed to escape. Many times crazy voices are voices you logically disagree with, but they come from information you've heard, repeated over and over again, or a big feeling attached to information that affects your mental, emotional, physical, financial and psychic states. These voices often enter with no permission from you.

Mona's "Crazy Voice" Rinse
Crazy Voice 1: I have no professional training, just life experience.
Rinse Voice: There I am, self-beating.

Crazy Voice 2: Suppose these books are successful and I get famous, and every mistake or personal issue of mine ends up publicized, and my family and I get hurt.
Rinse Voice: Oops, there's fear of judgment again!

Crazy Voice 3: Suppose I get rich! I've never studied accounting. What if I make a mistake? I could lose it all! That's what happens sometimes when athletes, trust fund people, and performers get rich quick. They didn't grow up with money, so they don't understand its boundaries or pitfalls.
Rinse Voice: Uh-oh! Fear of the unknown! I am self-beating because if those famous athletes and performers messed up, what hope is there for someone like me?

Crazy Voice 4: My mother is going to kill me for not getting approval, from her, in advance, for writing this book.
Rinse Voice: Please read with the appropriate amount of guilt in your voice so you feel what I feel. Yuck. Love those guilt spins!

Crazy Voice 5: I will overshadow my son's life and ruin his growth as a separate individual.

Rinse Voice: This is fear, but what kind? Where is my faith in my son? Aren't I arrogant here?

Crazy Voice 6: I want to die. Now I can die without guilt because my thoughts and feelings are out in the book.

Rinse Voice: This is a mental and emotional suicide voice not to be taken *literally*, but nonetheless, it's real. Not true, but real.

My crazy voices highlight my *vulnerabilities, insecurities and arrogances.* They lay out many of the thoughts and feelings that make me feel insecure and helpless. They are the voices of friends, family, coaches, my perceptions, and others who have influenced my life, and they have become my self-beats as well as examples of my arrogance.

When I do a Crazy Voice Rinse, I remember *not to judge* my crazy voices. They are there, and they are what they are. If I share my thoughts and feelings with you, I don't want you to judge me as crazy or stupid, so I'm not going to judge myself that way either. Why should I judge myself for having thoughts and feelings that lots of people have? Judging myself would cause me to shut down or become hysterical and no longer look and "see" inside myself and others.

Let's use the lawmaking process of the United States as a metaphor for how conflicting voices work. The House and the Senate go through separate decision-making processes before the President signs a bill into law. The House is larger, more representative of the people, more feeling. The House could represent the right brain. The Senate is smaller, more detached from the public, more theoretical. The Senate would represent the left brain. The two bodies have to reconcile in order for laws or boundaries to be made.

In the same way, our *feelings* are just as important as our *thoughts—* we have to listen to both sides if we want to make clear decisions in our lives.

Let me give you one more example. Do you remember the old TV show "Star Trek"? Mr. Spock was a classic left-brainer: logical, distant, and unfeeling. Dr. McCoy was right-brained: emotional and sympathetic. Spock and McCoy drove each other crazy. It was up to Captain

Kirk, who balanced his left and right brains, to discern the logical and emotional truth. Since Captain Kirk loved them both, he was capable of listening to each of them, in turn, with no judgment. The love created understanding. Only after he processed all their information would he make a decision.

> **Listening to all sides, with no opinions or judgments, creates clarity!**

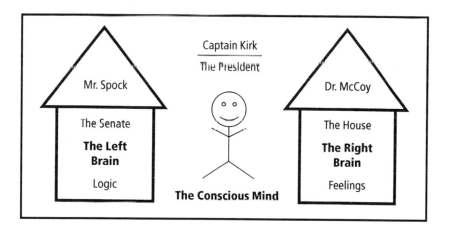

Even though your feelings and your logical mind rarely agree, all your voices, including crazy voices, need to be heard and understood. They are important messengers of information! They convey to us which of our past and present hurts and celebrations, traumas, shames, and talents need attention. Once we "see" these experiences for what they are—a path to learning—we can begin to do something about them. It's amazing how well this works. Want to give it a shot?

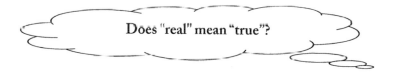

Does "real" mean "true"?

1. Even if they don't make any sense to us, even if they are totally illogical, are our feelings real?

2. How do feelings become vibes?

3. If feelings are real, should we process them? Why?

4. Are feelings always true? Why?

5. Can you identify the "crazy voices" in your head? Can you give me an example of which are "crazy" and which are "true?"

Write yours, and have fun. Are you ready?

My "Crazy Voice" Rinse
Crazy Voice 1: Sometimes, I can be so...
Rinse Voice: I see what this voice is trying to do to me! It's trying to make me... (Self-beat? Judge? Fall prey to shame? Tell me here...)

Crazy Voice 2: I am afraid of...
Rinse Voice: You know what? This is really just a fear of... (Being judged? Of failure? Of the unknown? Tell me here...)

Crazy Voice 3: Suppose that (name a scary scenario) happens. That would mean...
Rinse Voice: Uh-oh! What I really fear is...

Crazy Voice 4: What if (another upsetting situation) were to occur. I would...
Rinse Voice: I "see" that I'm truly thinking and I'm feeling...

Crazy Voice 5: Here I go again! (Name something you are angry with yourself for). I do this every time. I am so...
Rinse Voice: This feels real, but is it true? I think that what is truly going on here is....

Thoughts and Feelings Each Get a Turn!

We are all *made* of thoughts and feelings and insanities. All perceptions affect how we believe and behave. It's important, then, to give our thoughts and feelings equal time and look at them separately. If our feelings and logic interrupt each other, they cannot be heard and definitely cannot be understood. Picture several children talking to you at one time.

What can you possibly comprehend? Your head does the same thing when juggling thoughts and feelings. The thoughts and judgments stimulate or shut down feelings, causing insanity or depression. If you attempt to just follow one side, your ability to perceive grows cloudy. If you attempt to "see" all sides at once, it's like trying to follow two or more conversations at once.

The Damage Crazy Voices Can Do

We all are left-brained and right-brained. But some of us use the left brain more than the right; others use the right more than the left. Both sides, on some level, judge and dismiss the other. Like two children disagreeing, both sides want your full attention and both sides want to be "right."

The goal is to not dismiss information from either side of the brain. That's why letting crazy voices surface helps *balance* your thoughts and feelings, so you can "see" your judgments and craziness.

If you experience a trauma—and your left and right brain do not know how to process it—you can get lost and stuck in judgment and in beliefs from the past! No matter how willful you are, your intelligence may pit your inner judger against your thoughts and feelings, because an opinion or judgment may surface before your thoughts connect to feelings. If thoughts connect to feelings first, the intuition awakens your conscious awareness. If the process is interrupted, you can destroy clarity, wisdom and understanding—the very things you want!

As soon as a judgmental voice kicks in, the self-beat starts. When the self-beat begins, both your feelings and your logical mind (depending on which is the underdeveloped side of your brain) can get blocked. If you've been upset or hurt, you'll become confused, and perhaps feel crazy. That's the time to start processing

Processing our feelings and logical thoughts is something we rarely learn at home, in school, or in houses of worship. So, we have to learn on our own!

Dana' s Story

Dana's mom was in a car accident on Dana's birthday. Dana's illogical, crazy voice said, "She missed my birthday on purpose."

If you judge this as a "silly" thought or feeling because it is literally untrue, sparks can fly internally or externally. Once you can open Pandora's box and a thought, judgment or feeling becomes active, it is now real but not necessarily true! If Dana doesn't get this crazy voice out of her head, part of her heart can shut down and affect the way she thinks, feels and behaves in her life. She'll shut down the part of her heart that's angry and the fact that she is taking her mother's accident personally. And her ability to love herself and others will weaken.

So Dana writes down the crazy voice. Perhaps she cries, self-beats or even laughs at it, but seeing it in black and white, in front of her, allows her to recognize that she has created illogical thoughts and feelings that make her feel like a victim. She can now ask herself, "How did I come up with this?" "What triggered this?" Dana needs to check her past rejections and abandonments.

Something else is active from her past. She could ask, "How have I been abandoned in the past? How do I really "feel" about my mother? What is truly going on?"

Can you "see" the emotional murder or internal suicide that comes from ignoring a crazy voice? Love is the understanding of *all* thoughts and feelings. How can Dana love if she goes to guilt or shame for her crazy voice and doesn't understand all of her mixed thoughts and feelings?

Blocked hurt and fear keep our hearts from being open!

PERSONALIZATION: Personalization has two processes. One is a perception of how to see and feel someone or something and use it as an example and picture, to see an aspect of yourself. This type of personalization is an ingredient for owning, as a way to teach yourself about yourself, as a reflection of others.

The second is to personalize through judgmental eyes, you will see someone or something as your reflection as a way of blaming yourself or others for your thoughts and feelings, creating paranoia. This causes a negative self-perception that will trigger anger, fear, guilt or shame, causing self-beat and self-abuse internally or externally. This type of personalization creates a low- or high-egotistical perception, resulting in a negative self-absorption or a projection of your denied thoughts and feelings and life experiences onto others. This causes you to view everything in fear, which causes you and others pain.

If Dana doesn't know how to process a crazy voice, a voice like that will sit inside her and play with her subconscious mind. She'll still feel that feeling and a part of her will feel guilty for thinking and feeling it. A self-beat voice inside her will say, "I'm a terrible daughter for feeling this way," and she could get caught up in a Confusion/Spin Game. Then her logical mind will say, "What's wrong with me?" Such a question never leads to an answer, does it? This type of question is full of pain and judgment and goes nowhere. She will probably shut down or become hysterical because she has decided that she is "wrong" and "bad." How do you recover from these self-misunderstandings?

You are not exempt from having illogical, crazy thoughts and feelings. Just because you are not consciously aware of them doesn't mean you don't have them! We all have crazy voices. Find them before they find you!

1. How do suppressed crazy voices affect your behavior and your
   life?

2. If you are in a bad mood, and someone cuts in front of you in
   a line, do you think you'll be able to understand that person
   patiently—or would you lash out, at least in your head?

3. Suppose that person took offense at the tone in your voice
   and gave you a "dirty look," do you think you would explode
   or implode? Would you shut down with embarrassment?
   Can you think of an example? What is it?

I Loved My Neighbor As Myself...So I Killed Him!

It doesn't take much to "set off" someone who feels
shame or guilt, especially if that person doesn't even
know he or she feels shame or guilt. This person is missing a crazy voice rinse. Stuck in our "bad" thoughts and
feelings, we attack ourselves as well as others. Sometimes,
when we love our neighbors as ourselves, we treat them
the way we treat ourselves.... Is that what you want to
pass on to others?

When a guilty person lashes out, most of the time no one—not even
the guilty person—understands what just happened! People who experience guilt and shame from self-beats react quickly and personalize
situations due to negative perceptions. A negative perception creates
self-absorption and the belief that "everything and everyone is about
(poor) me." Guilt-ridden people who personalize "emotionally" spin in
unprocessed and misunderstood thoughts and feelings because they
are judging nightmares! They continually judge themselves and others.

When you allow thoughts and feelings of guilt and shame to go
unprocessed, you put yourself in a "self-pity" mode. Your sadness is not
"rinsed" and dealt with because there is a judgment on the sadness.
This type of sadness shuts down your talents and more often than not
you will wait for someone or something outside you to rescue you and

make you better. But *you* are the only person who can rescue, understand, and change you. *you* are the only person who can *make* you save yourself or hurt yourself!

If someone else tries to help or change you, you will feel controlled or manipulated even if they don't want you to feel that way. This can shut you down in so many ways—spiritually, mentally, emotionally, physically, sexually, financially and psychically. You will either blindly follow that person or you will attack! You are in charge of you!

Many people caught in such a spin either cannot cry, or cry endlessly. They spin in their sadness with no relief because they refuse to own their sadness and change themselves from the inside out.

Think about it! Somewhere deep inside, are you violently beating yourself about something, right now?

1. When your thoughts or feelings are illogical, what do you say to yourself, inside your head?

2. How does it make you feel when you say those things to yourself?

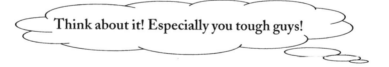

Think about it! Especially you tough guys!

This is me!

I Am A Victim
Help! I can't get up!

I Self-Beat
I'm so stupid! I'm an idiot, a loser!

My Logic Awareness
Why can't I get up while this self-beater is killing me?

You see you are not me, you are you.
Even if you get surgery to look like me,
    you are still not me, because I am me.
So here I am, and say you are me.
Well, how can that be?
We have similar understandings, but
    my molecular make-up still is
    uniquely me and yours molecularly
    you.
You can be an imposter of me, but I am
    still me, see?

You need to write for a reason!

If I know how to put water in a pot to cook but
do not understand how to work the stove, who
cares if my recipe for spaghetti is the greatest?
That water's never going to boil! So, those of
you who still are not writing, let's light that fire
and heat the stove!

Chapter Review

I just learned...
And I feel...

Live long and accept your "wrongs!"

Live in light and keep all truths in sight!

Summary

We come into this life perfectly imperfect. We are all unique and yet all created equal. Society teaches us to compare ourselves within ourselves and then with others. This can shut down our talent or swing our moods up and down in a see-saw game.

There is an advantage to comparing ourselves with others, because it helps us "see" what we want to be or not be. But if we use the terms "better than" and "worse than" when making these comparisons, then we end up arrogant or self-beating.

Understanding brings wisdom and magical developments. Understanding cures insanity and prevents self-sabotage. If we cure the wars inside us, then and only then can we cure the wars outside us.

Everyone has thoughts and feelings! To live "shut down" or to be continually emotional is miserable. If we all are a little crazy, why fear or judge this? Why not "see" and understand it before we are totally psychologically gone! **Real is what we believe. True is what is!**

The left and right brain provide us with checks and balances, not internal adversaries. They are often contradicting, but that has a purpose. Be who you want to be, and how you want to be. When you understand yourself, others will learn to understand you. You create you, no one else.

**Make your choice:
No pain, no gain,
or more pain just to stay the same
or be sane by living with no blame?**

The way we view and treat ourselves is definitely linked to the way we affect other people. And vice versa. But the only person we can truly "change" is ourself! So the only way you can make this planet better is to make you better.

3 Shame:
Fungus Only Grows in a Dark Swamp

Learning to Break the Silence
by Mike

Some people remember a childhood of nurturing bedtime stories on a comfortable armchair near a roaring fire, safely held in the arms of a mom or dad.

For me, it's a toss-up whether I remember that marvelous bouquet of cigarette ashes and empty beer bottles wafting from the trash I was required to take to the curb, or perhaps my mom's great moments of tenderness followed by the unexpected left hook.

Pain and love—perfect together. I was the fourth child of five. My parents just weren't equipped to raise a family. Like many baby boomers, they came out of the Vietnam War making babies, buying over their head, drinking Cutty Sark, and smoking Lucky's. Toss in re-possession, alcoholism, diet pills, the tragic death of one of their children, and bam, you've got my family!

I lived in a state of equal terror from the taxman, my cocktailing parents, and the Grim Reaper. I ate to escape. No "Crazy Voice" rinsing here. Food was my lover and love. I learned to "hide" my shame behind a veil of sarcasm.

During my forties I was—shock of shocks—single, shut down, disallowing of all feelings and truth. I couldn't support myself, I was overweight, a slug. That's what shame looks like on me!

As I neared fifty, I developed a split personality "survivor" skill. I became dynamic at work—a big earner, charismatic, and an industry leader. But at home, I was still alone, afraid, and out of touch. Balance, you ask? Hell, I was all over the road—my yin was yangin' me all over the damn place.

So, there I was with this infrastructure of fear! In the biggest city in America, with work pressure bearing down on me. My shut-down, shame life at home couldn't help but seep into Mr. Personality at work. Just like a leaky basement, I couldn't keep out the dampness of fear.

My artificial foundation began to tumble. The weakness of my "survival" skill was starting to show!

My trainer at the time, Andy, who was physically in great shape, had a girlfriend, a business, and good hobbies, often talked about his "life coach" who helped him. Damn, why does this guy need someone like a Mona Miller? What possibly could be wrong with his life? I was desperate enough to take the plunge, myself.

My first encounter with Mona had me smashing a tennis racket against a "60's" naugahyde couch cushion. Inside I said, "This is nuts." I must be in California! But as I slapped away at that damn cushion, Mona introduced me to the truth.

I'm still a slow learner because my truth has shame all over it. Shame will kill you inside. It slows you down, and the fear just plain stops you from everything! To feel that you're the worst piece of shit alive—no good, fat, ugly, a loser... shame is my "voice" and fear is my heart! Shame chased me everywhere I went.

I now know my shame just means that I'm "in ego mode." Specifically, low ego. And that everyone in low ego flips to high ego, at least every now and then. If not every other minute...

And it's true. At work, I think I am exceptional, better than anyone. Of course, the moment someone makes me believe that I am wrong, then, bam, back to low ego. So, ego either puts me up in arrogance or down in shit!

So how do I get out of it? Well, the first thing I do to keep me on the growth curve is to make the appointment, meet and talk about me each week. Shame does not like consistency or responsibility. So, the more consistent and responsible I am, the less shame I feel.

One of fear's favorite reinforcers is procrastination. So, keeping consistent with myself really helps. If nothing else, I set aside one hour for me. Mona and I have conquered so much, but there is so much more to go. Mona has taught me that, like the great explorers Lewis and Clark, at first glance the truth of my life is not just a parcel of land, west of the Mississippi—but a boundless frontier. Simply, the more I learn, the more there is to learn. How have I changed? How about this—I'm actually excited that my learning about me will never stop. I have a new hobby—me.

～

> *Shhh!*
> **What shame needs to survive is silence.**
> **The cure for shame?**
> **Break the silence!**

1. Think of a truth you're afraid to say, and write it down.

2. Read your truth to someone who will not judge you as good, bad, right, wrong or crazy. Please, don't be afraid to yell your truth out loud—alone, or with an unconditional friend.

Now, let's go a little deeper.

The Truth About My Shame

I am most ashamed of....   *for work*
What I am ashamed of makes me feel...   *bad, powerless*
I remember feeling shame when...   *with family*

In his story, Mike used sarcasm to hide his shame and block his truths, but it didn't help. Blocking techniques jam your tears and anger so shame can keep marching on! Finish the sentences below as quickly as possible so you don't over-think!

I block my shame by...
I do this because...
And it makes me feel...
And then I behave like...   *eat bonn*

> **Mona's Blocks**
>
> My blocks are... I crack jokes, withdraw, or shop. Shame hides my anger, hurt, and insecurity.

> ### Mona's Breaks
>
> I break my shame by writing down what shames me; by going into a quiet room and yelling out loud, by squeezing a pillow and rocking back and forth, by yelling or crying into a pillow, by calling my own answering machine and letting it rip, then listening back to it later when I will be open and not self-judgmental, calling someone I've hurt or upset and telling on myself. Owning my end of a situation releases anger, fear, guilt and shame. Whatever it takes to get my crazy-voice thoughts, judgments and feelings released, that's what I do so my mind and body can clear up.

How We Play the Shame Game

Does admitting your shame and facing your truths scare you? If so, why?

> A type of "passive shame lie" happens anytime you omit or silence a thought, judgment, feeling, or truth.
>
> When you have the strength to question fear, shame—which is fear's ally—will call you "bad" names and use your fear against you. Shame helps fear survive by keeping you away from the truth. Fear can't live in the acceptance of truth. It melts away, just like the wicked witch in *The Wizard of Oz*.
>
> Feel the freedom from guilt and shame by owning up to a mistake, even if it scares you to do so. If you let yourself be "imperfect," without guilt and shame, mistakes will lead to wisdom instead of more shame!

Keep in mind that fear and shame are messengers. They may seem "real" if you are truly in a "bad" situation. But often they have little to do with the present. They are there to remind you of something that

affected you in the past. They are wake-up calls to help you move forward energetically in your life.

> **REALM:** A circle of self-processing. Used as a road
> map, it shows us where we are and where we are lost. It
> is a direction for self-awareness of our different aspects
> of self. There is an order to the realms for our align-
> ment like a spinal column. If the spine is out of order it
> needs an adjustment and a re-alignment. The order
> is... spiritual, mental, emotion, physical, sexual and
> financial.

All of our fears relate to at least one of our realms: spiritual, mental,
emotional, physical, sexual, or financial. Whenever you feel afraid, ask
yourself, "From which of these realms is my fear emanating?" Then,
instead of reacting, you'll already be on the road to processing.

The Shame Game

Shame needs silence. In silence, you continue to self-beat and internally attack yourself—spiritually, mentally, emotionally, physically, sexually, and/or financially, whether it comes from truth or not.

Shame needs stubbornness. When we choose to be stubborn, our stubbornness creates what we believe is the power and strength of self. But, in fact, it is just creating a false sense of stability because truth and love are not the goals of stubbornness. Instead, protection from truth and powerful righteousness are the goals.

Shame needs lies. We lie and withhold information (omissions are lies, too). And when we do so, we have succumbed to believing in our fears as life's leader, as we speak with no voice or the voice of our anger.

Shame suffocates love. Shame feeds on silence and suffocation of truth, therefore blocking understanding. Without understanding, there can't be true love. A life with no love of truth brings a powerful or powerless struggle from the fear that comes from lies and manipulation of self and others.

Shame fears the truth! Unearthing the truth with understanding creates wisdom and, therefore, the dissipation of shame.

Do you play the shame game? Shame's job is to make sure that your fear is never approached, never understood! If your fear comes out in the open, shame knows that its days are numbered!

If you let your shame live, you will move farther and farther away from the original, upsetting truth, the one that gave birth to the fear and shame in the first place. Instead of focusing on what you can do to move forward in your life, your shame and self-beat will become your focus—which can bring new stories and situations, but the same pain.

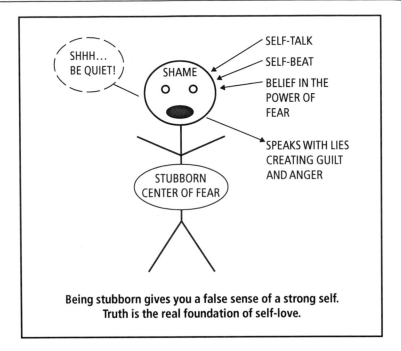

Being stubborn gives you a false sense of a strong self.
Truth is the real foundation of self-love.

If shame becomes your self-talk,
shame becomes your belief.

If shame becomes your belief,
it creates self-doubt.

Self-doubt creates fear, which turns into anger.

Anger turns inward,
creating self-hate and self-beating.

The result of this self-beat is more hatred,
toward yourself and others.

Are you ready to write about *your* shame game? Let's go!

I won't speak about...
I won't speak about it because...
I'm stubborn when...
I'm stubborn at those times because...
I lie (or omit the truth) about...
I do this because...
I suffocate love by...
I do this because...
I fear...
I fear this because...
This makes me angry because...
My anger looks like and acts like...
My self-beat says...
My self-beat feels...
I hurt others with this because...
and this makes me feel...

Secrecy vs. Privacy
Shame vs. Boundaries

Keeping secrets breeds shame; but having self-boundaries is being private.

Secrecy is full of guilt and shame.

Privacy is full of understanding self-awareness
and boundaries with no "care" or "worry!"

First: a preview of the words "care" and "worry"

Care and worry are words that have more than one meaning. Care and worry can mean to control, to personalize, and to take charge of anyone or anything you like, under the guise of love.

If you want to create anxiety, just care and worry about something or someone! Care and worry are not spiritual or love words. Care implies control and worry implies a lack of faith.

The cure for care is *love*, which is deep *understanding* of how and why you (and others) are the way that you (and others) are. To get care in balance, you let go of control, and you choose to understand with no projection of your beliefs or judgments. To cure worry, you have *faith* in truth, whether you like the truth or not.

How Sneaky is Shame?

Secrecy *versus* *Privacy*

SHAME	BOUNDARIES
1. I am not speaking because I am feeling guilt and shame.	1. I'm *choosing* to not speak. I have no shame or guilt regarding my information and feelings.
2. Whatever awareness I have of myself makes me self-beat.	2. What I know of myself, I own. I have no anger, fear, guilt or shame.
3. I have unclear and uncomfortable feelings and judgments about my information and truths.	3. I don't "*care*" or "*worry*" (create anxiety) that someone else knows my information, because I've processed and accepted my truths.
4. I judge my information about myself as good, bad, right, wrong, stupid or smart.	4. I know and accept my boundaries and limits through my strengths and weaknesses.
5. I let people hurt me or I hurt others, because I haven't processed, rinsed, owned, forgiven and understood the information and feelings yet.	5. I understand myself, which creates self-respect and has led to self-confidence, not arrogance. I do not take it personally if other people judge or attack me. I de-personalize while allowing myself to be myself.
6. You can hurt me, especially if I am self-beating and hurting myself. I'll eventually teach you to feel bad about me too.	6. I can say no without shame or guilt.
7. I am deflecting my truth and feelings onto others. I am defensive and I'm blocking information about myself.	7. I do not hide information about myself behind anger or sarcasm. If I choose not to share information, it's not because I'm embarrassed or scared of their reaction.
8. I am image based. I "care" and "worry" what I look like and what people think of me. I also judge others, either out loud or in my head, creating fear and pressure.	8. I don't accept false images. I accept and process "what is"—the truth—whether it's negative or positive

1. What about yourself would you like to change?

2. What new thoughts, feelings or behaviors would you like to have?

3. Do you fear being "wrong," as you're "trying" to grow and change? What can happen if you let yourself be wrong?

4. Can you change while you're afraid of being "wrong?" Explain, even if it sounds illogical.

Shame kills uniqueness and self-love. If shame walks in and calls my unique thoughts and feelings "bad" names, I shut down spiritually, mentally, emotionally, physically, sexually, or financially, which is the death of my positive or centered energy. This death can create a sabotage or suicide voice that may or may not manifest itself physically.

Shame causes a short circuit. Thoughts and feelings feel "crazy" when they are judged and shamed. I have a choice. I can either get stuck in self-pity, as I judge my thoughts and feelings stupid or ridiculous and become a "victim" of myself, or I can write down my thoughts and feelings, process them, and understand them.

REMEMBER!

Shame causes you to self-beat.
Write the first thing that comes to mind:

I feel ashamed because...

NOTE: Because shame attacks inside, towards your-self, you can become very passive. These inner attacks create:

Flat energy	Self-hate
Heaviness	Low self-esteem
Depression	Physical illness
Uncontrollable crying	No sense of self
Codependency	A need to be a follower

Although your parents, teachers, religion, or society may not have meant to make you feel shame, what they said or did triggered it, and now the shame is yours, not theirs.

If you don't own your shame, it grows. If shame stays quiet, inside you, you end up more and more stuck in self-beat, self-pity and depression.

Shame is hidden, suppressed and passive, whereas guilt can be more overt and aggressive.

You can't change other people, but you can change yourself! Changing yourself will change the shame dynamic, forever.

No Shame Means...No Judging What We Think and Feel!

As we discussed in the last two chapters, if you feel angry, scared, guilty, ashamed or sad and you add a *judgment* of good, bad, right, wrong, stupid or smart on top of it all, you become stuck in **suppressed** anger, fear, guilt, shame or sadness. Suppressed thoughts and feelings put you into a spin of self-beat and shame, which can lead to depression.

You need to separate your judgment from your thoughts and feelings—quickly!

Example: If you are "sad" and pile *judgment* voices on top of your sadness, the judgment voices may say something like...

> *I'm being a baby.*
> *Get over it! I'm so ridiculous!*
> *It's no big deal. Whatever!*
> *People are staring, so drop it!*

Now "sad" has turned to "bad," because you *judged* your sadness. Now "sad" is stuck in sadness and can't turn into compassion. What happens next? Self-pity is coming, and victimhood! All because you *judged* your sadness. This is why crying and owning are crucial. They help you release the sadness and clear your mind. Then you can take action to heal the sadness.

Example: If you are angry and allow your *judgment* voice to sit on top of your anger, the judgment voice might say something like...

> *Everyone's an idiot!*
> *Everyone's a selfish asshole!*
> *I'm a piece of trash!*
> *I'm a complete moron!*

Now, your anger turns to blame and then shame. Blaming others and yourself is the outcome of you *judging* your anger as if you are bad for being angry or deflecting your anger and blaming others for it. Now, your anger is stuck in meanness and can't turn into passion. If you judge your anger, it stays there, and never leaves! Is anger bad or is unprocessed and not owned anger that is bad?

Example: If you feel "fear" and your inner voices judge the fear, your judgment voices might say something like...

> *I can't because I'll screw it up.*
> *I'm not good or smart enough.*
> *What will my family and others say?*

If I do this, I could get hurt.
I'm scared, so I can't.
I don't know. I can't remember.

Now, fear turns to insanity or attacks, and eventually becomes paranoia, a phobia or projection because you *judged* your fear as stupid or ridiculous. Your fear, far from truth and understanding, is shut down inside depression, maybe even insanity. Fear can't turn to peace and wisdom, because it has not been processed!

Stuck in depression, you will begin to disconnect. You'll shut down from yourself and disengage from your truth, logical mind and feelings. You may become cold, easily upset, and insist on living inside old memories.

Lost in the fear, you have no *awareness* of the truth of the past or present. You still have thoughts and feelings, but you don't understand them. You are disconnected from the understanding of your thoughts, feelings and truth! All this, because you judged your fear. You judged it, so the fear stays—and grows.

Do you really want to keep judging your thoughts and feelings, knowing that these things can happen?

Your Self-Beat Has a Message for You

Do you ever feel "down" or "tired" for no apparent reason? Guess what? That means a self-beat is active inside you.

When your self-beat is alive, it takes over your thoughts, feelings and memories. It doesn't think of itself as a "bad" guy. It thinks it's teaching you a lesson, something you need to know! All you have to do is stop and understand that there's a message there for you.

If you ask questions of the self-beat in writing, you will start to "see" what is happening. If you're not sure what questions to ask, take any information in your head and start a question with words such as who, what, where, when, why, how, could or would. Questions will start to come to you. Don't forget to answer any questions that are in your head. Give it a shot, below. Write the first thing that comes to mind after each phrase:

Check-In
Questions to Ask in Order to Understand a Self-Beat:

1. Who is on my mind?
2. What is disturbing me?
3. Where is this pain coming from?
4. When did it start?
5. Why do I feel this way?
6. Could I do (something—fill in this blank) about this?
7. How can I change my behavior?

Make up your own questions!

8. _____
9. _____
10. _____

Questions for Me to Ask You:

1. Does learning have to hurt for us to be motivated to "see," feel or change?

2. What's the purpose of getting to the understanding of a self-beat?

3. When ignored, do self-beats go away, or do they come back with friends? Explain.

An Important Note!

No feeling is "good" or "bad."

Feelings need understanding.

Once understood, their energy can be released.

Understanding the messages of your feelings and your self-beat will make you more aware.

Feelings are not necessarily truths or facts. They are just messengers that need to be understood.

Let's do an experiment! Write a self-beat to yourself! If you write one now, you'll be _aware_ of what it feels like. Are you ready?

_Dear _____ (your name)_

I am stupid, because...

I make myself sick, because...

I hate me, because...

I self-beat, because...

And this makes me feel...

To create a different outcome and learn, I must self-beat, because...

And if I don't self beat, I'm afraid that the following will happen...

Now, let's find out if we "see" a message from your self-beat.

1. In your self-beat, above, does your fear or pain motivate you to be more, to be better? If so, how?

2. Where did you learn this "technique," and from whom?

3. Does your self-beat shut you down as you freeze and do nothing? Is this positive? Why is this positive? If you don't move, are you safe and not wrong? Explain.

4. If your feelings are energy that's always moving, can your feelings work like gasoline in a car—give you the energy to get into motion? Explain.

5. Do you think that negative feelings motivate change more than positive feelings? Explain.

6. What does negative motivation create—in the long run?

7. Do your self-beat, fear and pain affect you in a depressive or sabotaging way? Explain.

Handling Your Negative and Positive Thoughts and Feelings

I believe anger, fear, guilt, shame, punishment and pain are sometimes used to motivate us because negative energy uses fast impulses, and *fast* impulses create quicker and stronger movement to create fast results. Negative energy can be stronger than positive energy.

Controlling people use anger, fear, guilt, shame, punishment and pain as motivators because they can "see" rapid results in the people they want to control.

Remember! When you are in the midst of anger, fear, guilt or shame, you may be in too much pain to "check in" with yourself to find your own thoughts, feelings and truths. You can easily lose yourself. You can be controlled or controlling. This is why it's so important to learn how to handle your negative and positive thoughts and feelings! You become more aware of yourself and therefore others.

If negative feelings are stronger than positive ones, and if I'm a parent, teacher or coach, I could choose to use negativity to get you to do what I want you to do. For example, if I whip a horse, how fast will the horse move? If that horse fears me, can I train it to do what I want faster and faster? In the end, what will this horse look like and feel like? How long will this horse live? Could this horse push itself to self-injury? How many fear tactics would it take to get this horse to obey? Would I trust my relationship with this horse and turn my back on it?

Now, how much time and patience would it take to lovingly train this horse? Would it take longer than using the whip technique? Would you be able to turn your back on this horse if you used boundaries, love and patience? How does this horse look, feel and run in the long run now?

Maybe I believe that I motivate you faster if I'm negative! Negative feelings ignite mine and other's feelings. And if feelings create actions, what's wrong with a little negative reinforcement?

Fungus can only grow in the dark. Light kills it. Negativity, likewise, can only survive in the absence of light, which is truth.

What "fungus" are you growing in your life?

1. How would you change your world if you used wisdom, questions, and understanding as motivators instead of anger, fear, guilt, shame, punishment, and pain?

2. Who, from your past, sounds most like the shame/self-beat voice in your head? Is it your mom, dad, grandparent, teacher, coach, sibling, religious leader?

3. How did or does that voice influence you and your life today?

Don't Skip the Self-Beat Voice!
It will eat you up!

I call the Shame/Self-Beat Voice "the piranha."

If the piranha runs your life, you're stuck in a version of hell, creating fear, chaos, and insanity instead of truth, understanding, and love!

ARE YOU OUT OF CONTROL?

Why do you feel the need to self-beat? If you would just deal with and process your anger, fear, guilt, shame, sadness, beauty, talents and sensitivities— you would be able to move on with your life, and grow!

Shhh... Shame needs you to be quiet and keep your thoughts and feelings a secret and stay stuck and depressed.
Shame only grows in the dark.
Turn out your light.

Chapter Review

I just learned…
And I feel…

Summary

If shame's goal is to block truth and keep your essence down so you can be "good" and follow others or live up to an image, won't this enable fear to live to its full capacity? Imagine how much shame echoes through your mind and/or falls out of your mouth every time you desire, love, grow, tell the truth and question yourself and others. Is this what we are afraid of or anxious about? How many lies, shutdowns, stubborn thoughts and behaviors control your senses? The more stubborn you are, the more you stay in the power of fear and continue to experience guilt and shame. Free will? *What* free will?

Are you shaming yourself and others by holding secrets in, or do you understand your thoughts and feelings?

4 Guilt:
I Will Never Surrender

While shame is a *passive/aggressive* form of *self-beat*, pointed inward, guilt is an *aggressive/passive* form of shame that stabs inward at you *and then* outward, toward others.

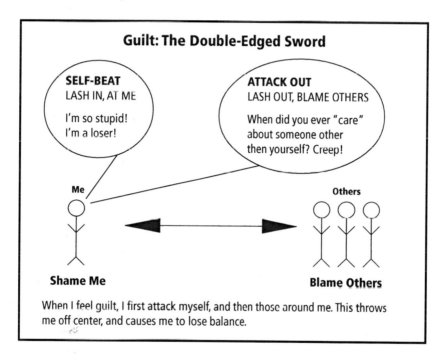

Guilt: The Double-Edged Sword

SELF-BEAT
LASH IN, AT ME

I'm so stupid!
I'm a loser!

ATTACK OUT
LASH OUT, BLAME OTHERS

When did you ever "care"
about someone other
then yourself? Creep!

Me

Others

Shame Me

Blame Others

When I feel guilt, I first attack myself, and then those around me. This throws me off center, and causes me to lose balance.

> ## REMEMBER!
> ### My Guilt Creates Chaos!
>
> **Guilt causes you to self-beat and lash out.**
> **Write the first thing that comes to your mind:**
>
> *I feel guilty because...*
>
> **NOTE: Because guilt attacks inward within yourself,
> and outward, at others, you can become very aggressive,
> which creates:**
>
> | | |
> |---|---|
> | Egomania | A bad attitude |
> | Bitchiness | Aggressiveness |
> | Righteousness | Know-it-all behavior |
> | Addiction | Physical Illness |
> | Rage | Bossiness |
> | Desire to create control battles | |

Invisible Guilt

Guilt can be tricky to recognize—in ourselves, and in others. Sometimes the guilt we feel is obvious; it walks in the front door of our lives, and we "see" it. Front-door guilt is a feeling of remorse because we were not acting out of truth and love. Other times, the guilt we feel is invisible. It slips in through the back door and takes hold of us when we're not aware of it. Back-door guilt is a heavy feeling. It is an overly responsible feeling of hopelessness that comes from carrying others' thoughts, feelings, judgments and truths while holding love for them with no self-boundaries. How can guilt be so tricky? Because back-door guilt is often hard to detect. Back-door guilt is not based on truth. Here's how it happens.

1. People in your life who have not "owned" may have put their thoughts, feelings and issues, verbally or behaviorally, on you as a way of blaming you for their thoughts, feelings and actions.

2. You accept this blame, which keeps you from being self-aware and responsible. Once you accept someone's blame as your truth, personal "owning" becomes impossible. To not agree with someone, especially if they are angry with you, could spin you into a guilt state of mind so fast, you won't know what hit you. But you must either let them be angry and not personalize it, or sit in invisible guilt with no guidance from truth.

3. If you develop invisible guilt, your ability to "see" the truth of yourself or others is damaged.

4. How many things have you taken on as your fault? How many of these things are truly even an issue for you? Do any of these guilts have anything to do with you? Does this guilt shut you down or make you hysterical? Back-door guilt will influence every decision you make.

5. If you do not know where truth belongs, how can you set boundaries? If you have trouble experiencing your own thoughts and feelings without guilt, care and worry, how are you going to see and understand the thoughts and feelings of others?

My Back-Door Guilt
by Andy

When I first met Mona, I attended one of her group classes. At the time, I looked confident, poised, strong, and successful. If you looked at me (as some of the others did in the class), you'd think I had it all.

Yet there was this "thing" nagging at me somewhere deep inside. Something told me I was "off." I was uncomfortable in my own skin. I felt like a robot—doing the things that everyone else had taught me how to do! My whole life up to that point had been about "fitting in," trying to "do" and "be" whatever I thought anyone wanted me to be.

My parents are very successful and accomplished people. I felt like I had to start where they ended up. I was never "good" enough, or "smart" enough with this false image in my head. There was a sense I could always be more. I had to be what they needed me to be so they could feel good through my accomplishments. No surprise that in high school I was dying for social acceptance from my "friends." This continued in college, when I joined a fraternity, and upon graduation, when I was commissioned as an officer in the Marine Corps. Talk about "looking good"—the Corps literally gave me a manual on how to behave. It was perfect! If I lived by these rules, I'd be "good" and "look good" too. Aah, this was what I was looking for.

Please remember, none of this was conscious. I was on autopilot. But certain situations, in retrospect, were red flags. When I got pulled over by a cop for speeding—I trembled inside for hours after. When meeting a girl in a bar I would feel like my tongue had swollen three sizes too big. When I got out of the USMC there was a banquet in my honor, and I tried to stand up and talk. Not only couldn't I remember the names of my best friends, I couldn't remember my *own* name! Whenever something fell outside the parameters of what I had been taught, forget it…I was lost. I could spit out rules, regulations and how things are "supposed to be" done, but if I had to do any creative thinking or feeling of my own, I was finished.

I'll never forget my first private session with Mona. The first thing she did was tell me that I needed to cry. That sent me into a tailspin. "What, *me*, cry?! I'm a man, I don't cry since crying makes you weak!" Boy was I wrong! When I started to allow myself to feel through "anger work" and writing, I found tears, *big* tears.

In that first session, she also read to me from her friend's thesis on cults. I had no idea why she was reading this to me, since I had never been a member of a cult—in fact, I thought she was a bit out of her mind. What she knew, that I didn't, was although I was never part of a cult, I had "cult thinking" and "behavior" left over from a socially acceptable cult called the Marine Corps.

What I've learned since then is, the teachings of the Marines have their place, especially in times of war. Actually, many of the leadership qualities I learned while serving, I still cherish. However, I allowed the rules and regulations to take the place of me generating my own thoughts, feelings and creations. This is why I felt like a walking zombie and why I would get so thrown "off" by anything that fell outside the box. There is a lot of preparing and training to become a Marine but there was no program at the time to adjust your thinking or release feelings from any traumatic experience to re-enter into "everyday living." The Marines are about how to "survive"—not "live!"

Notice, the Marines were just a manifestation of what I had learned and believed from my parents and aunt. How did I become a follower, when I thought I was a leader? The "Back Door Guilt" twisted everything up with no awareness. My family, my friends, and the Marines imposed their judgments of "good" and "bad" onto me and controlled me with guilt. Guilt stemmed from a self-pressure now.

I'm happy to say that, after years of self-exploration and hard work, I'm more complete. Of course, I'm in no way perfect (my wife continuously reminds me of this), but I've integrated many of the missing parts of my personality and life. I now feel grounded, balanced, and assured. I get thrown "off" less and less when faced with a situation. My tongue doesn't swell in a conversation with a stranger. I can remember my own name, and I can have meaningful conversations about life and feelings with just about anyone. I no longer try to take responsibility for others; I just stay inside my own mind and body. I've released a lot of invisible guilt—but there's still more to go…

∽

1. Do you have anything that is nagging at you, the way that Andy did? Do you feel "off?" In what way?

2. Do you ever feel like your thoughts, feelings or behaviors are on autopilot? Explain.

3. How do you handle things that are "different" from what you've been taught?

4. Do you cry? If the answer is no, why not? If the answer is yes, how often? How easily? Do you cry a for a specific reason? What reason?

5. Is there any part of your life-school, groups you've belonged to, religious training, sports, patriotic endeavors—that you think might have involved elements of "cult thinking?" Explain.

Back-Door Guilt
from Mary

Dear Daddy,

When you are "in your ego," you treat me differently than when you are in a state of understanding and love. When you are inside your low or high ego, you trigger "guilt" in me.

I know it's a choice to receive the guilt. But you send me such mixed messages! You tell me I'm "not good enough." And then you feel bad and give me a sincere, heart-felt gift. It's infuriating! You mix guilt and control with love...and it makes me feel "stuck" inside. I get so confused. It's as if I am "wrong" for being me. So, I start self-beating.

I know I'm supposed to feel good and be grateful for your gift and your love, but inside I'm really just twisted, angry and resentful. To put me down, and then give something to me with love energy and no understanding, makes me hysterical. The mixing of guilt with love hurts me, Daddy. Help me!

Love,
Mary

High ego—I am "it"

Low ego—I am "nothing"

Centered or Spirit—I am what I am and what is, "is."

If you were raised by a parent, teacher, religion, or society that did not understand you, and consciously or subconsciously processed their thoughts and feelings by blaming you, you are probably walking this Earth laden with invisible back-door guilt.

Almost all of us are raised with the concept of "fault." Fault is blame laden with shame. If you try to reject this energy, whether it's back-door guilt or front-door guilt from an actual mistake, you may become defensive and aggressive or shut down in depression. Fault has such pain from the shame in it, many of us fight taking responsibility for whatever the fault is. Certainly, our political, legal, criminal, religious, and ethical systems are laced with it. When a mistake happens, society teaches us that someone is at fault and punishment will follow. The problem is that the more we believe we are at fault, the more we lie, self-beat, deny and deflect.

I have changed my perception of fault. I do not see someone as a "bad person," even if he/she did something bad. If you believe you are bad, you cannot recover and will continue to be bad out of a helpless/hopeless point of view. The bad thing does not go away once it has been done. It can haunt you forever. Many give up and hurt themselves "badly," becoming addicts or criminals or killing themselves. Their pain could spill onto others and they could keep being bad because bad is what they now believe they are. The psyche will create what you believe: You've already screwed up, so it's too late anyway. The lack of recovery from the word "bad" is what continues the cycle of "bad." How do we accept our mistakes, and take responsibility, without hurting ourselves or others, and break the bad/fault cycle?

How can you own with self-awareness and accept self-responsibility when you are feeling the powerlessness of shame and guilt? In reality, mistakes happen. Can fault and blame enable truth to be seen and owned without tremendous fear of pain? Isn't protecting yourself a survival mechanism and reflex? It takes a long time for us to feel safe enough to see imperfection in ourselves and tell the truth. This process is scary. There has got to be another way.

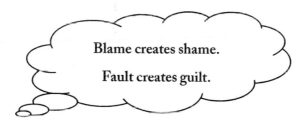

Blame creates shame.

Fault creates guilt.

To Take Responsibility Is to Own

Just as blaming and finding fault lead to shame and guilt, owning and taking responsibility lead to clarity and wisdom. If you are looking to blame someone (or yourself) for something, you are really trying to judge and to punish. If you are looking to own, then you are understanding (without care or worry), taking responsibility (without guilt or shame), and changing your behavior (with truth and love).

> **COMING INTO YOUR OWN**: Happens when we begin to open up and see ourselves and the world through self-awareness and self-responsibility. When we come into our "own," we have *learned* to own our truth and change our lives.

Many of us think that owning and apologizing involve other people. In fact, owning and forgiving involve personal beliefs. They are a way of thinking and processing. Sometimes it is very healing to go to others and tell them, with compassion, what you have learned from a mistake, but you cannot force people to hear and forgive you if they choose not to. Owning and self-forgiveness are elements of a very deep and personal journey. They process in the same way.

You can approach the other person or people involved (assuming this is possible) and ask to share your process and revelation from your owning or forgiveness. But the issue is yours, not theirs, so the responsibility to own or forgive is yours. Do not approach them with a need for approval or validation. You approach them clean, holding your center of truth no matter their reaction.

Once you have owned or forgiven, your beliefs will change. You will move from a state of anger, fear, guilt and shame, to a state of clarity, wisdom and love.

Remember the term "love means never having to say you are sorry"? Sorry has shame and guilt in it. If you can't process yourself out of the shame and guilt, you cannot grow and change with clarity, wisdom and love. If you understand and own, you create a miracle that changes your patterns. You begin to understand your truths and lies, so you behave differently.

When do you approach others with an own or forgiveness? Once you have truly processed, learned, and changed your behavior and they have given you permission to approach.

"I'm sorry" and/or "it's okay" infuriate people more than if you did nothing at all. Why? If little is learned, and even less is changed, how can people possibly trust? We will just wait for you to do "it" again. To say you're sorry and then own and change may still cause people to hesitate because there has been no consistent change yet, but they will feel hope and a sense of healing. Now, you have touched me, meaning your truth has given my heart a chance to hear truth inside of me as well. Everyone and everything is your path to empowerment if you can see, own and take responsibility by changing.

How to Own and Forgive

Owning and forgiving together means taking responsibility by understanding everyone's point of view without judging anyone's thoughts, feelings, and actions, and learning to grow. Owning and forgiving require the following steps. Do them yourself, first!

Only when you have fully processed on your own can you consider approaching others and sharing this with them.

Admit the truth to yourself. Write out and know what happened without self-beating, without care, and without judgment. No victim or blaming allowed.

Understand why it happened. Find a place to rinse and write. (Rinse paper will follow later). Ask yourself and others questions concerning present, past and future experiences. Remember to understand one person's view at a time. Understanding may not mean agreeing, just seeing different perceptions without judgment.

De-personalize the situation. This means understanding that your actions, and the other person's actions, are separate from each other. Look at the circumstances from every angle, without becoming reactive. Understand yourself and then the person who upset you. Whoever was upsetting you was an off-center person. Do not disconnect from your truths, thoughts, feelings and intuition in the process. Stay aware and connected to yourself and maintain an understanding of the people involved. Hold on to the truth that belongs to you and let go of the rest.

Empathize with how you and other people are affected. See yourself and others and how you truly feel, without a judgmental attack. Imagine how it feels to be the person or people you affected or who have affected you.

Prevent and Act. Come up with new behaviors that prevent repeating upsetting actions, and create actions that are positive. If they don't work, try again. (This step might involve finding books, programs, support groups, and others who understand).

Celebrate the learning and the growth, in a healthy (not addictive) way. When we speak of what a "mistake" has taught us, we experience wisdom, and that's something to celebrate!

There are limits to owning and forgiving. Own everything you can—but stop owning/forgiving when it turns into an attempt to control others or hurt you. Stop when you've reached the limits of your true responsibility or the person you are forgiving. At that point, just let go and be comfortable with the truth. Let people be angry or hate you. Hold your center and give them time. Owning or forgiving beyond your truth is just another form of care, worry and control that can cause angry, fearful, or shameful patterns to continue.

Owning and forgiveness comprise being humble, which means handling mistakes, hurts and celebrations with intuition, awareness and wisdom. There is no shame or hierarchy. Shame turns humility into humiliation. Careful! Being humble does not put anyone above or below anyone else.

If we don't have the ability to "own," two outcomes are possible. Either we become insecure and full of self-doubt, or we become a self-righteous, know-it-all, fixer of others. Fixing others is not fixing ourselves. Rather than preach, be what you want others to be. Not taking responsibility for ourselves can cause us to become irresponsible, or overly responsible for things that aren't our responsibility. We lose our sense of boundaries. Can you see how we are constantly trying to balance? The issue is, we are trying to counter imbalances with their opposites. But an opposite just causes an imbalance in the other direction. You have to own opposite sides to see the middle view, which is where true balance occurs.

Believe it or not, you can never truly be "wrong" or "bad."

Your invisible guilt often stems from others' thoughts, feelings and issues that were put on you, and *you* accepted them as your own!

Your visible guilt comes from thoughts, feelings and behaviors that you are not owning or forgiving.

MISTAKE: An experience that happens when truth is not clear.

Practicing Owning and Forgiveness
There are few skills more vital than learning how to own and to forgive. This section shows you how to do it.

Step One: Admit the Truth
When you own or forgive, and describe what has happened, be aware when you use the term "I'm sorry" more than once. Repeating "I'm sorry," even to yourself, can easily trigger shame, self-beating and guilt. Furthermore, judgmental words such as "bad," "wrong," and "sorry"

can spin and go nowhere, unless you process the attached anger and sadness to achieve compassion.

For example, write out your process the way you see and feel it. Then return and substitute those judgment words with the feeling word "sad."

| sad | sad | sad | sad |
| ~~bad~~ | ~~wrong~~ | ~~sorry~~ | ~~mad~~ |

So, when you own what you have thought, felt, or done, rather than saying "I feel bad because…," you'll say "I feel sad because…" Whereas judgments spin and get stuck, feelings expressed help us achieve wisdom.

Step Two: Understand

This is the "why" step (why you have the issues, why you said or did what you said or did). Understanding means understanding the who, what, where, when, how, and why it happened, and the impact it had on you and others. It means understanding your thoughts, feelings and history of your life and that of others involved. Asking yourself when you have experienced situations like this before will help you reach even more subconscious clarity. We are creatures of habit. Check the past whenever possible.

Step Three: De-personalize

To de-personalize means to see yourself separate from other people and events. To understand *how* you and others come to your present thoughts, feelings or behaviors is the goal. Sometimes you may know the truth of how some people became the way they are and sometimes you may need to guess what "could have" happened to them that caused their behavior today. Everything happens for a reason. If you do not understand their story, you can remain a victim and stuck in the pattern caused from these people or memories. Anyone or anything that reminds you of the one(s) who hurt you, or whom you hurt, will put you back in time. You will repeat the behavior with that original person or event and re-create your issues—over and over again.

Step Four: Empathize

Once you can feel *you*, you can then have feelings while listening to others. Empathy creates layers of understanding and compassion while sympathy is feeling care and worry. We are separate energetically, yet feeling in understanding together. Empathy does not mean liking or agreeing—it just means reaching a point of understanding for all perceptions and accepting them.

Step Five: Prevent and Act

Create ideas and decide to do things differently, to break patterns and habits so you can change outcomes. Stimulate your creativity. You can write out a "wish" paper to find creative ideas. For example I "wish" I'd been treated like…I "wish" I could say…write your wishes in pictures or picture words, to see and feel. You can pretend you are your best friend or loved one and write out what you think they could do and then insert your name where their name is and re-read what you wrote.

Don't be afraid to get help from a twelve-step program, therapy, and support group. Do your best to break as many thoughts, feelings and behavioral patterns as you can. Don't worry if they are right or wrong. You won't know until you do something if it works for you or not. You are in charge of you. If something doesn't work, do something else until you find the approach that does. Just don't quit! Creation is infinite.

Step Six: Celebrate

Celebrate the learning process with energy, action, and words. (This doesn't mean engaging in addictive behavior!) Celebration is not about deserving a reward. Deserving a reward means you also believe in deserving a punishment. Celebration means remembering where you came from. Your history has become your ticket to wisdom. This is your chance to love and appreciate every little mistake and change. This gives you energy to continue owning and growing on this path called life.

Let's own and forgive something we've done to ourselves or to someone else. Pick something that you have done recently to upset or hurt yourself or someone else. Now own and forgive it, step by step.

1. *I'm sorry because...(remember to use "sad" after writing "bad" or "wrong," and only use "sorry" once) or I admit...*

2. *This happened because... This made me feel... And this reminds me of...*

3. *I will retell and de-personalize the experience by telling a story of how I or others got this way, whether it is fictional or historically true. Here's how I envision what happened...*

4. *This made me feel...and this is how it would make me feel if I were the other person or people involved...*

5. *My prevention(s) is (are)...*

6. *I am so excited because... I've learned...I feel... and I am grateful for...*

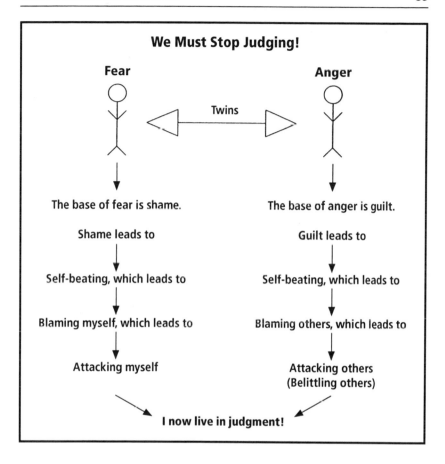

We Must Stop Judging!

Fear

Twins

Anger

The base of fear is shame.

The base of anger is guilt.

Shame leads to

Guilt leads to

Self-beating, which leads to

Self-beating, which leads to

Blaming myself, which leads to

Blaming others, which leads to

Attacking myself

Attacking others
(Belittling others)

I now live in judgment!

From Blaming to Owning

You can do this exercise with someone or as a writing exercise by choosing someone in your head to blame and list the "You are..." For example, You are beautiful. You are a liar. Etc.

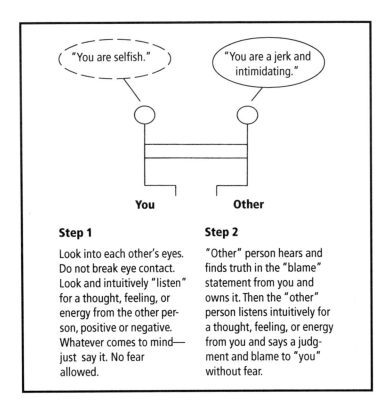

You   **Other**

Step 1

Look into each other's eyes. Do not break eye contact. Look and intuitively "listen" for a thought, feeling, or energy from the other person, positive or negative. Whatever comes to mind— just say it. No fear allowed.

Step 2

"Other" person hears and finds truth in the "blame" statement from you and owns it. Then the "other" person listens intuitively for a thought, feeling, or energy from you and says a judgment and blame to "you" without fear.

Part of what's going on here is that whoever is speaking is actually "reading vibes," and feeling the energy that the other person is giving out. That's why you can do this exercise with a complete stranger. Also realize, since we are all the same (yet different) the one speaking is projecting as well. Everything from everyone gets owned eventually.

"Vibe reading" others is often a projection of our own issues or life awarenesses. We can see in others what we know is true in ourselves. We all have an inner intuitive sense that feels energy coming from others and from within ourselves as well. This exercise is an amazing way to see ourselves if we know how to own. Vibe reading can be dangerous and incorrect if you can't own because you could be feeling your disowned thoughts and feelings while looking at someone else. This is disconnected blaming from your blocked truths in a judgmental attack. This is a pure projection with all your self-beat regurgitating on someone else. That is why knowing how to see yourself without judgment, control or fixing is crucial before seeing and speaking with others. We still have a free-will choice to "see" ourselves in others and admit whether something is our issue or not. Everyone is a reflection of ourselves in one way or another. And the more you own when you "see" others, the more you will be able to "see" and know yourself and others.

OWN: To admit and understand with feeling what happened or is happening and find a prevention or new behavior that will change your path for your future. Owning is remembering the past and understanding why and where something originally happened. Owning leads you to truth and understanding of the past, present and truth for the future. Owning is taking responsibility for pain and wishes, no matter who is at fault.

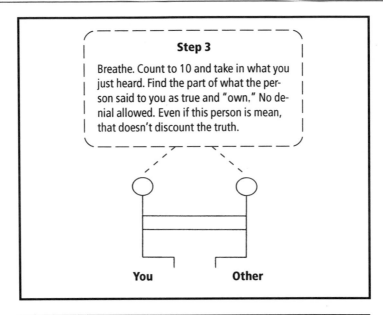

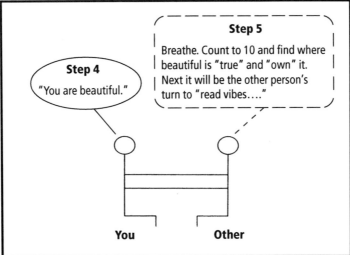

Keep holding hands and continue until you run out of things to say.

Remember: Both positive and negative truths are important!

Which is more difficult for you to hear— the positive or the negative?

From Guilt and Shame to Owning

Now, the "I am" part of the vibe-reading exercise has a different purpose than the "You Are" part of the exercise. You can write out this part as well, in the "I am" fashion. This time, you're practicing owning your own vibes, your own innermost self. When you say "I am…" now, it's a reading of your own thoughts, feelings and energy. When you are listening, you are also practicing how to listen without judgment or fixing. It's about you…seeing and owning yourself. No judgment allowed!

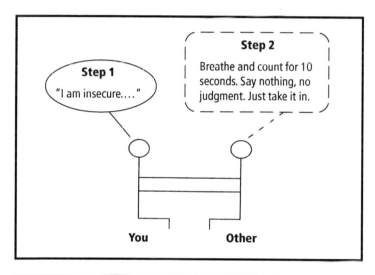

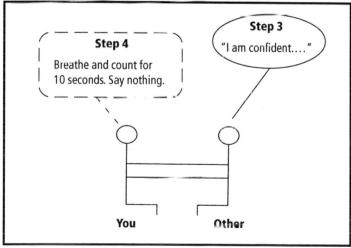

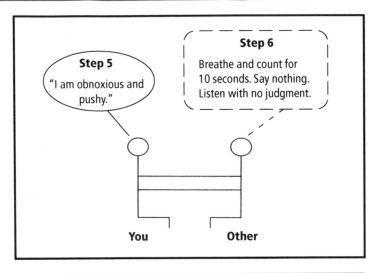

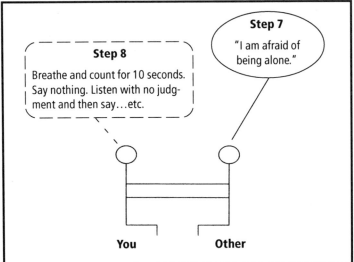

Keep holding hands.

By owning ourselves, we change our lives.

Check-In

Are you self-beating? Getting "stuck"?

Go back and write the "*You are*" to someone you know and then write the "*I am.*" Own and see your good/bad and ugly, or be arrogant and insecure.

We are *all* everything—good and bad. Get used to *hearing* all these perceptions without getting upset or angry.

No one can hurt you but your own thinking!

When you can own everything about yourself, with no self-beat… how can anyone *get* you?

People can still judge you, but you will be able to hear the judgment, own, understand it and de-personalize all at the same time.

There are two kinds of people in the world—those who own and those who *don't*. We are either open or closed, not perfect. Which are you?

When this exercise gets easy for you, no one will be able to hurt you, because no one will have anything "on you" that you haven't already accepted! Owning your truths will wash the shame and guilt off you! And remember that during this process, you can learn without hurting yourself. No guilt or shame is allowed while you are admitting and finding truths.

Once you get used to hearing positive and negative truths and crazy voices without shutting-down, self-beating or becoming defensive and righteous—you will actually understand the meaning of "choosing" who you want to be.

Practice! Practice! Practice!

If it doesn't get easy to do the
You are/I am exercise,
you will struggle and be a
Blocker of Truth.

If it gets easy to do the
You are/I am exercise,
you will be a
Welcomer of Truth.

The Blocker of Truth vs. The Welcomer of Truth

BLOCKER OF TRUTH	WELCOMER OF TRUTH
1. I feel anger, fear, guilt and shame, and do not welcome truth. I judge and attack truth!	1. I feel peace, let go of care, worry and control. I accept all truths, without judgment. I am patient.
2. I am a "know-it-all." I don't ask questions; I tell people what I think I know. I stopped learning, which has killed my growth.	2. I know that to question is to understand, and this gives me the *wisdom* to know that with every answer there are more questions. I can now *grow* beyond what I "know."
3. I do not question. I speak in answers, opinions and statements, to ensure my righteous outcome.	3. I don't "care" or "worry" about the outcome. I stay in the present and trust the process of listening while owning.
4. I show no understanding.	4. I understand and "own" myself and therefore others.
5. I am defensive, and I argue.	5. Instead of blaming myself or others, I own myself and understand others.
6. I self-beat and personalize everyone and everything to make it about me.	6. I do not personalize or self-beat what is not my truth, but I do personalize to see and own what is my truth.
7. I cover myself in guilt. I use guilt, care and worry as "love" to control others, without truth, without owning.	7. I love by understanding all perceptions because I have faith in the truth.
8. I quit and "shut down," which creates depression.	8. I "rinse," processing my thoughts, feelings, and judgments to remain open.
9. I use control and fixing to disguise lack of intimacy.	9. I am comfortable with mistakes because I know how to process and recover from them and therefore freely see and connect to others.
10. I judge everything and everyone.	10. I can "own" and set boundaries within myself.
11. I *trust* no one, including myself.	11. I have *faith*—in myself, and others. I trust in truth and have faith in who you and I truly are inside.

Chapter Review

I just learned...
And I feel...

Summary

I wish that I had understood the concept of invisible guilt and self-beating before the age of forty. If only I had understood the concept of feeling shameful and guilty when I did something "bad," versus feeling "sad" for a mistake that was inevitable on the human journey of life! I didn't know how to own and understand the guilt I experienced for just living. I was living and caring about what everyone else was thinking, feeling and doing. I felt so overly responsible for them that I could not have found and owned a truth if my life had depended on it, and in many ways my life did.

Are back-door guilts and self-beat shame how "good" people get twisted?

If fear and anger are twins and if fear's base is shame and anger's base is guilt, is it any surprise that addiction, murder, divorce, and child abuse are rampant?

Judging is a mental war game all in itself. Fear of judgment is what creates major lies, denials, and mental disorders. But still, we do it. Here in America we think it is our inalienable right. Look at our institutions—the judicial system, the educational system, our religious systems.

The You are! I am! exercises help you get used to owning without judgment. "Seeing" yourself through others definitely helps you "see" imperfections without so much guilt and shame. It makes you more compassionate. You will "see" unbelievable worth in being a **welcomer of truth** versus a **blocker of truth**. You will be able to listen from within—and truly hear.

5 Self-Pity:
Stuck in Sadness; Let's Have a Pity Party!

All of us have within ourselves a little child. This child represents the essential part of us that existed before society began to socialize, define, and control us. Our inner child can be playful, funny, sad, wise, needy—just like our adult self can be. But the more we understand our inner child, the more we understand who we are, where we came from, and why we are truly here. The child part of us is the energy in all of us that is most capable of remembering why we are here in the first place. It is said, through the child you will know your purpose.

Your inner child experiences are crucial because they affect your thoughts, emotions and belief systems that are very real to your psyche and subconscious mind. If your inner child, for example, feels sad about something that your judger judges ridiculous, you may feel a deep, bizarre sadness that seems totally unrelated to life in present time. You may say, "I shouldn't feel that way!" And you then condemn yourself for being so foolish. This can cause a shutdown. So now you are ignoring the sadness altogether. Did that make the sadness go away?

Soon your inner child shuts down, throws temper tantrums, gets high or drunk as a way to release the blocked sadness without understanding or owning it. We adults can be so childish, but do you know why? Being childish means I am stuck in an immature or young child's thoughts, feelings or judgments with no sense of personal responsibility or adult awareness. Being childlike is different. It is being an aware adult, with childlike energy. If the inner child's feelings are judged and not understood, the inner child and your adult self are stuck in this sadness. Your inner child knows it has been ignored, but the adult doesn't. The two have separated from each other. If the child is acting out, you will feel out of control; if the adult is acting out alone with no connection to the inner child's sadness because the sadness was judged, you will feel depressed inside and indifferent on the outside. This can often look like a logical person with little or no feeling. This blocking of the inner child or adult's hurts can cause the sadness to turn into shame. And when shame blocks and suffocates sadness, you end up stuck in self-pity. Now you are depressed because your truth and feelings are suppressed and you probably don't know why.

The truth is, everyone experiences self-beats and self-pity. The question is, why do so many of us deny it? Denial gets us nowhere. Is it really sadness that makes us weak, or the denial of it? Sadness is a feeling and messenger. Where did we get that sadness is weak? Only through the understanding of our sadness can we release ourselves of denial, self-pity, depression and act-outs. Since we can't love others any better than we love ourselves—understanding our sadness and self-pity is essential to living in peace or joy.

Getting to Know Your Inner Child

Do you have a picture of you as a child? If you can, find one of yourself between the ages of two and four. Make copies and put them in your wallet, on your desk, in this book, and anywhere else you can. Little by little, your subconscious mind will start to remember things, just by looking at these pictures. Don't worry if you can't remember anything, yet. If you don't have a picture, draw one of yourself—even a stick person representation is okay.

Your *inner* child is that part inside of you that holds your memories, your soul, and your deepest thoughts and feelings—good and bad. Understanding this part of your childhood and history will help you understand where your sadness and self-pity come from.

Self-pity makes you a victim. It is full of trapped hurt, anger, guilt, shame, fear, and sadness. Unless you release the anger, fear and sadness, change your behavior, or make a move, you will stay "stuck" in this sadness. This is what "feeling sorry" for yourself means. Since self-pity and depression are there whether you admit it or not, you might as well admit it. Then, you'll be on your way to feeling lighter and clearer about yourself.

PITY/SYMPATHY: Feeling sorry *for* yourself or some-one else, not processing and taking an action for the an-ger and sadness concerning you or someone else. You're carrying yours or others' sadness with no self-responsi-bility and no change. Others' sadness does not belong to you; yours does. Therefore, it can become very heavy, like a weight, and cause depression! Sympathy is feel-ing *for someone*, not to be confused with empathy, feel-ing *with* someone.

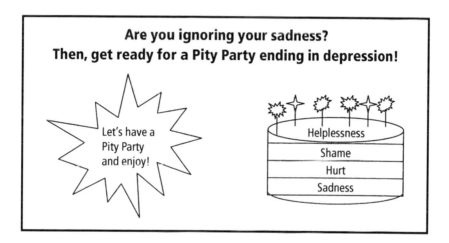

Mona's Pity Party

Sometimes, when teaching from a loving and giving place, I feel my inner child (little Mona) feeling sorry for myself. Why? Because she wants some of the love and learning my adult Mona is giving to every-body else. In fact, I can hear the baby voice in my head right now, as I'm writing.

So, to understand my inner neediness and self-pity, I write a letter from my adult self (Big Mona) to my inner child (Little Mona).

> *Dear Little Mona:*
> *What are you thinking and feeling? How old are you?*
> *What do you remember? What do you wish?*
> *Signed, Big Mona*

Next, I look at my picture. I hold the pencil differently or I slouch like a little girl. I answer in little Mona's voice, the way I would have answered as a child.

> *Dear Big Mona:*
> *I miss my sister. I miss my family. I want to go back home to them. I am eight years old… (Hold on, I'm already crying). I wish I could be understood and play with people while being silly, deep, fun, weird, and free to cry as much as I wanted.*
> *Signed, Little Mona*

Now, when I write as if I'm Little Mona, do I sound ridiculous, with an immature voice and irrational frustration? According to a judgmental, big Mona, yes. So what! I "see" it, "feel" it, "write" it, "read" it. And the feelings from the letter open up my creativity to see where I could take action. I then find an action to release my sadness. For example, I call my sister and give myself a talk and some attention like the attention I had been giving others. And then I start to feel better. What's wrong with that? Now it's your turn.

My Pity Party

Dear Little _____, (Your name)

What are you thinking and feeling? How old are you? What do you remember? What do you wish?

Now, put yourself in the mind of your inner child. Listen deep within yourself. Talk in your child's voice, sit like a child, be like a child, and answer:

Dear Big _____,

_____

_____

_____

What are some actions you can take to release the powerlessness of the sadness and change it to empowerment?

Signed, _____

Now how weak is sadness? Did you learn anything? Try this:

I just learned...
And I feel...

The Difference Between Self-Pity and Sadness

When we sit in self-pity, we are looking to be rescued by someone or something other than ourselves. When we are sad, it's not about "others," it's about us figuring ourselves out and taking action—even if others have upset us. We are simply experiencing our feelings. We are not waiting to be saved. We own our sadness and, on some level, we celebrate sad's message. The understanding of sadness brings compassion, wisdom and patience. If you are impatient, you are not dealing with some type of sadness. Don't wait for the past, a parent, a friend, lover or God to come and fix it *for you*. If finding your sadness is difficult, picture the last person you can think of who was sad. Was that person sad or in self-pity? Can you "see" the difference? If you can't find your sadness you're probably stuck in a judgment of sadness which lands you in a pool of self-pity.

A sad person is easier to comfort than a self-pity person because he or she isn't consciously or subconsciously drawing you in to fix anything. The sad person is just feeling sad. And, let's face it. We've all been both of these people before. Which would you rather be?

Waiting for a rescuer cripples us. As long as the rescuer is "outside us," we are not really in "sad," we are in "self-pity," and we are paralyzed and depressed from the suppression of it.

This angry, helpless, hopeless, suffocated sad energy sets up many control battles. The only real rescue is to change your thinking and your behavior through understanding your rational and irrational feelings. Many times we are remembering things from our past that are sad at the same time we are feeling sad in present time. That's why the sadness can feel so big and overwhelming sometimes. That's why we must not judge sad. It will grow into a big energetic monster inside if it builds with no release. You can easily be controlled by a fixer person operating under the guise of care and worry. You will explode or implode. If you want to be saved, your hero has to be you.

Mona's Story
by Mona

When I was in my mid-twenties, I was very sick. For a while, I lived in a wheelchair. I wanted to like myself and be my true self so much, but I didn't know how.

One day, it was an ordinary day in Mona's wheelchair. I rolled myself past a mirrored building, and suddenly paused and looked at myself.

For some reason I decided to wink at myself in the mirror. This made me smile. So I didn't stop. I started playing with myself in the mirror. Laughing, having fun.

Suddenly, I looked behind me and saw that a man had been watching me the whole time. Before I could get embarrassed, he said, "Don't worry, you are very cute."

I said, "Thank you. I just didn't want to miss my cuteness, in case it went away." He laughed and we talked for a minute. He then gave me his card and said to call him if I ever needed anything.

Did one honest, sweet, playful, pretend egotistical moment, with no shame, get me some compassion?

What does this say about the energy we put out into the world when we "see" and own ourselves without shame or self-pity? Was I being childish or childlike? I felt like I was just playing with my inner child and adult self at the same time. What do you think?

～

The Mirror Game

Your turn. Get in front of a mirror and say, in a playful or humorous way, yet being honest at the same time, things like, "Oooo, to be you!" Wink at yourself. Play energetically with yourself. Smile at you. Charm you. Maybe you'll like you too. Don't judge the inner child who is playing with your adult self. Aren't we all still children in a grown-up body?

Try it for a week. Every time you pass by a mirror smile, wink and talk to yourself. This isn't as easy as it looks if you are a judger/self-beater.

This game kept me from hating me in that wheelchair. But doesn't everyone own a wheelchair, metaphorically? What's yours?

My handicap literally or metaphorically is...
This makes me feel...
This creates the following in my life...

Maybe you, too, will become your own best friend at the end of this exercise. Most pain is derived from self-disgust anyway. Anytime we're cute or fun with ourselves, watch that judger come out with a vengeance!

Cinderella's Story

Remember Cinderella? She was trained perfectly to be an old-fashioned princess. She learned to obey, to play a part, to be poised, not to speak up, and to please other people rather than herself. Was her role as a stepdaughter perfect training to be a poised princess?

Have you ever wondered what happened after the Prince rescued Cinderella? What the "happily ever after" might have been like?

Let's think about it. Was Cinderella sad while living with her stepmother? Did Cinderella rescue herself from her sadness? Did Cinderella own the hurt, sadness and shame that she might have felt? Could this behavior prepare her to be a dressed-up prisoner? Or a wise, aware, compassionate leader of people?

If Cinderella didn't process and understand her inner child's thinking and feelings, she could still end up the same person she was when she lived with her stepmother. Cinderella had three choices—to remain the same, become just like her abuser or become "her true self." She would have had to de-program herself from her experiences and own her sadness by rinsing, understanding and then changing her thoughts, feelings and behaviors to not repeat what she knew. We can create only from what we know unless we process and turn our pain, sadness and mistakes into wisdom.

Be A Creative Writer and Imagine

1. How much sadness and shame did Cinderella have? (Remember her sisters, too?)

2. If Princess Cinderella never learned to process her thoughts and feelings, in what ways might she continue to be the same?

3. Now how about if she learned to go through her sadness, rescue herself, and process her feelings? What kind of princess could she become?

4. What do you want to be rescued from?

5. How can you change you and your thinking?

6. Is there one thing that you can do differently in your situation to break a pattern? What could that be?

A Story of Two Criers

Remember the difference between the sad person and the self-pity person?

What does **the self-pity crier** want to do? Sleep, eat, self-medicate somehow? Why? Could the self-pity crier be energetically tired from waiting and feeling so helpless? If he or she will not "own" and self-rescue, this crier will not feel, understand, or change personal beliefs or behavior and is likely to be taken over by a caring, controlling person. Self-pity criers do not take responsibility for their own sadness. They become heavy from carrying suppressed sadness around. Their lack of self-responsibility causes other people to feel responsible and sorry for them. So energetically people in self-pity are asking for someone to take them over and to "fix" or "take care" of their cries.

Sometimes fixers have no interest in fixing, and don't even understand how this dynamic came about. Other times, fixers don't want to deal with their own sadness, so they fix or control someone else who is stuck in sadness as a way of fixing themselves without owning their feelings. This can start many invisible and visible control battles.

Can you "see" how this control battle gets confusing? Fixers start out trying to be "good." Can you "see" why "good" can be confusing and "trying" can be controlling? Fixers feel they have to help the helpless self-pity criers who will not "fix" themselves.

Self-pity criers block change by not understanding or taking action to heal their own sadness. They want someone to sympathize with them.

Sympathy **will make someone else feel for them and take responsibility for their sadness.**

Pity causes someone sad to become a victim of their own sadness, only to feed the sadness.

This victim energy ticks people off!

Fixers aren't sure why they're angry with Self-pity criers, which makes them feel back-door guilt.

The **sad crier** is an entirely different story. Although, on the surface the two criers may look the same, they don't feel the same.

Sad criers want a supportive person, someone who may give some help and empathy, not sympathy.

Empathy **is experiencing feelings *with* someone who is taking responsibility for personal sadness without needing to be fixed or controlled.**

Sad criers do not have to be saved, rescued or fixed by someone else.
They take responsibility.
People want to help and give a hug to sad criers.

> When you are sad—who is the rescuer?
>
> Is it you, or is it someone or something other than you?
>
> This simple "check-in" will let you know if you are wallowing in self-pity, or if you are feeling sad.

Creative Writing Is Welcome

1. How could self-pity lead you into lying and denying? Why?

2. Have you ever been a Fixer? Why?

3. Do you think the Fixer is someone who needs to be needed? Explain.

4. Do you think neediness stems from an "inner child" craving? Explain.

5. Does the need to be needed come from low self-esteem? Explain.

6. How does self-pity lead to depression and victimization?

7. How can sadness lead to wisdom and change?

Gratitude—The Path Out of Low Ego, Pity/Self-beat Hell!

We've all heard the term "count your blessings." Sometimes recounting what we see as our blessings is enough to take us out of a low ego state, such as self-pity, and place us in a state of feeling gratitude.

But sometimes recounting blessings doesn't seem to help. It might give us a momentary high, but it doesn't really create a miracle (a true change in perception). Could it be such gratefulness is coming from high ego and not a centered balanced perception?

I am grateful for... (list ten things, people, or events)

And I feel...

Blessings do not judge, nor compare. Blessings are not about low or high ego gratification!

"Blessings" examples:

- *I'm grateful that I don't have acne like my brother.*

- *I'm grateful that I am stronger than most people my age.*

- *I'm grateful that I still have a career, not just a job like my friends.*

- *I'm grateful that I got into a prestigious college because my dad couldn't.*

- *I'm grateful that I'm not nuts like my ex-lover.*

- *I'm grateful not to be living in a poor neighborhood, like those uneducated people.*

- *I'm grateful that I'm not stupid like the professors at school.*

Having been raised in an ego-dominant culture, most of us look at the world through the filter of the ego. This experience is not spiritual. Putting yourself or others above or below each other is not being truly grateful. Such ups and downs are egotistical judgments. When you process from the ego, you stir up anger, fear, guilt and shame.

The person who is grateful not to have acne is living in fear of being unattractive. That's not gratitude. The person who is grateful for his or her strengths over someone else is fearing his or her weakness. Same with the person who feels powerful from something external, like a job. The person proud of his or her college just wants prestige to feel superior because he or she feels inferior inside. This is all ego and pride. It is the "See-Saw Game"—not gratification.

Take another look at the blessings list above. Do you see how any of your listed blessings might relate to feeding ego glorification based from conscious or subconscious fears, instead of spiritual gratitude?

So, let's try again! Count ten more blessings; but look at your life from the perspective of your essence and spirit. Look for blessings that come from within you, that help you see your world and its lessons more clearly. Blessings that center you and remind you of your truth; blessings that help you understand and love yourself and others.

If this seems challenging to you, let me give you a hint: look at everything and everyone around you as a teacher. Pick someone or something or an event in your life that taught you something. Try this: *"I'm grateful for…"* (someone, something, or an event) *"I'm grateful because…"* (descriptive term). *"This makes me feel…"* and *"I just learned…"*

Many people who count their blessings without an ego may say something like:

- *I'm grateful for my mistakes, because they teach me wisdom. You couldn't pay me a million dollars to take away what I have learned. My understanding makes me clear and not feel crazy.*

- *I'm grateful for my friends, because they taught me how to see and understand myself unconditionally. They are there for me more than I have ever been there for myself.*

- *I'm grateful I can sit up in bed by myself because I have experienced what it is like to not have basics and this has taught me I can never fail because my only expectation is to get up without help. I am a success every day for that.*

If there is no ego, these are true blessings.

The way to turn hurtful mistakes into blessings is to let them be your teachers. So, write ten mistakes, guilts or shames and find how they have taught you something. "I'm grateful for… (a painful someone, something, or an event) because…and I feel…I wish…I learned…

For example:

- *I'm grateful for my illness, because I have dropped high expectations of myself and everyone around me. I feel sadness and joy from the hurt, yet I appreciate that I am strong. I wish I could help others to understand how to change themselves from the inside, out. It saved my life in so many ways. It has taught me acceptance and self-love. I wish people knew that self-love isn't a selfish act, but an empowered act.*

- *I'm grateful that I was fired from my piano job, because it led me to this business I'm in now and this information may be touching others, but the truth is, it saved me first. I feel so much for the deep inspiration and joy that has come into my mind, heart, body and soul. I wish everyone would allow themselves to be what they wish they could be.*

- *I'm grateful that I struggled in school and with myself physically, because I understand struggle and the beauty and wisdom that comes from it. When I see my kids, clients, family and myself struggle, I actually get excited, because I know that a struggle is the first step to a miracle and a change of life. I feel faith for those in a struggle, knowing that struggle is really a type of perception of the struggle. Are you a victim of your struggle or have you changed and grown in a new way? I wish the fear of the unknown would dissipate and be seen as an adventure.*

Now you:

I'm grateful for... (a painful someone, something, or an event)
because... I felt...
I wish...
I learned...

And I am grateful for my self-pity, because...
and I feel...
I wish...
I learned...

Gratitude
By Amy

My mother has always taught me to be thankful for what we have. I never really understood the concept until very recently. I thought my life was cursed. I've been sexually abused by my relatives, my boyfriend was murdered, in my teens my father died of cancer and our family fortune was stolen from my mother, brother and me. I have always felt sorry for myself, wanting things to be better or different, someone or something to rescue me from my miserable life. I started playing the part of a victim, wanting people to feel sorry and comfort me. I was pretty pitiful because I was always grasping for my notion of happiness (money/power). I had considered myself a failure in all of my realms because I was measuring myself against other people's success.

My mother found out, a few years after my father had died, that over $20 million in property was taken from us. Within the time my father was hospitalized (fall 1987) and died (January 1988), and with the stock market crash (aka Black Monday), we were broke. When we found out the amount of money that was taken from us on my father's deathbed, my mother was sad but thankful that we didn't get any of it. She said it would have changed us. I understand that now.

I feel really grateful the way my life has played out so far. I am able to share my experiences of my abuse, breaking the shame, giving myself a voice. By exposing myself, people around me have broken their silence and opened up. Healing is part of not passing on the abuse. I am thankful I am able to do that for myself and show others the importance of not passing on the abuse.

I am so appreciative for the love, support and lessons I've learned, opportunities, failures and the ability to be okay with who I am. Even though I find myself feeling self-pity sometimes, I realize I cannot truly see or receive gestures of graciousness from people when I am in a state of being pitiful. I love my life. Thank you for reading this.

Can you see how counting your blessings isn't about making a list of ego-gratifying possessions; it's about changing the way you look at every aspect of your life?

Now that's a miracle.

Chapter Review

I just learned…
And I feel…

Summary

Who knew how important the understanding of your sadness is? Suppressed sadness creates depression, denial, and defensiveness.

Awareness of your inner child can wipe away many of your confused thoughts and feelings in the present. The idea of being a victim or a martyr from suppressed sadness is now mind-boggling to me. No more living in pity parties! Visiting pity to find your adult and inner child's sadness and rinse through it by having a pity party on purpose is like having an un-birthday party. You can celebrate anything, anytime!

No more silencing truth for shame, no more denying imperfections for guilt, and no more trying to look strong as you deny and suppress your hurts and sadness. Look in the mirror and see yourself, all of it and wink at yourself. Turn your hurts to gratitude. Go to understanding, not condemnation!

6 Why We Lie:
Liar, Liar, Pants on Fire...
Don't Know What to Inquire!

"I have faith in you, but I do not trust you." Has anyone ever said this to you? No one wants to admit we have a liar inside us, but we all do! Therefore, knowing your liar is the first step to healing. Learning to understand your anger, fear, guilt, and shame will help your liar feel safe enough to come out of hiding. You became a liar because you were scared. So liar means...Start over! Admit it! Change!

If you hold things in, you will explode or implode later. Have you heard the phrase "Liar! Liar! Pants on fire!"? Here's how we use it in this book.

Liar! Liar! Liars are people who deny or change the truth to make it an acceptable lie that even they, themselves, can believe. A liar is scared of the shame, guilt or punishment connected to truth. A liar is confused and confuses others. As a result, the liar manipulates him or herself and other people as well so he or she can feel better, or be in control for a moment.

Pants on fire! The liar burns inside and out. This fire is passion mixed with ego and lies. This is when passion becomes intensity. This fire grows intense from the liar literally being incensed. Passion can either warm or burn the liar or others in its path, depending on how it is handled.

Don't know what to inquire! The liar has no self-questioning skill, let alone the ability to ask questions of others. The liar has no idea where to begin to research and find truth because he or she is so afraid of seeing truth. Even if the liar actually saw the truth, how could he or she even begin to understand it?

Learning Why We Lie

Your body, mind, heart, and soul are looking to be in balance. The liar feels out of balance and is actually just trying to find a way to achieve it. Because the liar doesn't have faith in the truth, he or she tries to *create* realities that might "bring about balance" while avoiding truth.

The question is: Do you know when you're "out of balance"? Can you "see" your liar coming to the rescue?

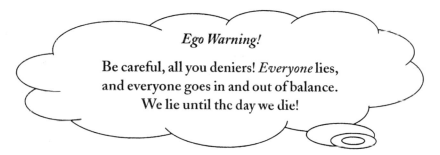

Ego Warning!

Be careful, all you deniers! *Everyone* lies, and everyone goes in and out of balance. We lie until the day we die!

I have some clients who have written stories about what causes their lies and how their liars work. Have a look!

Here Comes Grandmother!
by Alice

When I was a little girl, I lied because I was afraid of punishment.

My grandmother kept a list of all my wrong-doings in her head and frequently brought them up. In fact, I didn't have to do anything wrong. Grandmother could be angry at anything. It made no sense. So, I grew afraid of anything and everything. I couldn't look anyone in the eyes. I had a weak memory, my body was hunched over, and I said yes to everyone.

Sometimes I still lie to Carl (my husband) because I don't want to hear about what I've done time after time. My husband repeats himself like my grandmother. I am also afraid he'll speak badly of me. I feel stupid. Come to think of it, he already does call me stupid. I believe, when you "yes" people enough, you come off as stupid. I have no inner strength because I drop my truth all of the time. I lost my inner strength—along with my voice and my truth living with Grandmother.

I don't consider myself a liar, even though I lie. I know this is a type of twisted denial. Really, I try to tell the truth. Sometimes, I feel really stupid or guilty, which makes me lie again to try not to feel bad. I guess I wouldn't have to try not to feel bad if I didn't already feel bad.

I don't want to lie!

I remember my grandmother not approving of dancing. One night there was this dance at the church and I wanted to go. I lied and told her it was an evening hymn sing. But the thing I felt stupid about was the stupid lie, not the dancing.

Truth makes me scared and feel bad, I feel guilty for saying no and I feel guilty and angry if I say yes, when I wanted to say no. This gives me incredible stress. This struggle makes me fear everyone! In reality, it's the liar inside me that I'm truly afraid of.

I was never allowed to have any of my own thoughts or feelings growing up, so just saying my "truth" to a stranger is nearly impossible. I can't even say no to telemarketers! They can sell me anything! Oh, wait, sometimes the fear of my husband, Carl, getting mad at me for saying yes to telemarketers makes me upset enough to say no. Does it take one fear to scare me enough to change to another fear behavior? Looks like it.

This internal struggle may sound like no big deal, but it hurts my stomach. My hands shake and I feel crazy. I feel so ashamed of myself. I am now realizing that I hold my arms over my chest like I'm trying to hide, for no apparent reason. My whole body is stiff and uncomfortable to hug. This tightness carries into my shoulder blades. It makes me walk hunched over.

I was not hugged and my only times being touched were aggressive and painful from grandmother. I've started yoga and stretching just to be able to move my body at the age of sixty-five. So much fear and shame! Over what? Telling my truth! I'm ashamed to laugh, I'm ashamed to cry, I'm ashamed to be noticed!

1. Is it amazing that a woman, at age sixty-five, still suffers from lying habits she learned when she was little?

2. Do you still suffer from habits you learned when you were little? Which ones?

3. What does Alice mean when she says, "I don't consider myself a liar, even though I lie?" Would you say the same of yourself? Explain.

Daddy Would Never Do That!
by Lisa

Why do I lie? How could I not? I've been lying my whole life. I started when I was four. Lying to myself. My family. Everyone. I was pretending my father wasn't molesting me.

"It didn't happen, right Daddy? You didn't really touch me like that, did you?"

"No. It didn't happen, honey. Now go back to sleep."

Sleep. That's what my lies are. A fantasy world, protected and safe, like warm covers on a cold night.

I got really good at lying after a while. I even started believing the lies myself. As I got older, it became second nature. After all, everyone does it. Sometimes lies are good. "Mom, dinner was fantastic!" But most of the time the lies are a way of hiding from people. Hiding from myself and my truths. Lies can protect me from truths I'm not willing to face. But, in the end, the lies confuse and destroy my awareness.

And what happens when the lies are discovered by others? Get ready, because those warm covers that I've been hiding under are suddenly thrown back, and all of a sudden, I'm naked. Cold. Alone. And worst of all, vulnerable from having no self-awareness.

Now it's dealing time. I can try to run to the lie, but since it's not on solid foundation, it crumbles quickly. So the lie, which was once my protector, now turns into a destroyer. I have nowhere to go but to my truths, which are, "No, I don't love you anymore. Yes, I did have an affair. Yes, my father raped me as a child."

But with every truth comes growth. I don't feel it at first (I can only feel the shame of the lie) but when I'm done with the anger and the self-beat, I start to feel strength—strength from owning my own truth, and strength from understanding that the truth has set me free.

That's when I can look you and God right in the eye and smile because I know as long as I follow the truth, and love it more than I love anyone or anything else, I will become the "Light" that you want me to be! With that comes peace. A peace I have never known until now.

~

1. Why did Lisa lie? Can you understand why she lied?

2. Do you agree with Lisa that with every truth comes growth? Why do you think so?

3. What lie that you tell needs to become truth, so you too can grow?

Conflicts—Whenever Truths Are Unacceptable to Others

Typically, we lie when we are in a situation where we feel our truth is unacceptable to others, or to ourselves. We lie so that we will be liked by ourselves and others in the way we want to be liked. What's fascinating is that doing the exact opposite is what we need.

One of the solutions to lying is to stop trying to be liked. Instead, we can learn to understand and like ourselves in every interaction. Owning is the way out of hell. The need for validation from others keeps us insecure, needy and at the mercy of other judgers. Understanding ourselves and others gives us inner strength.

Stories help us "see" how others have handled lies in their lives. From their stories we can learn how to handle lies in our own lives. Don't forget to personalize by owning how you are like everyone. Put your name where even their names are and read it again. If their stories don't match yours, alter their stories to match your truth.

There are two perceptions. To block understanding, look for where you are different from someone. To be open and understanding, look for where you are like someone. Both answers are true. But, the way to grow is to see, not block seeing.

Truth Means Action
by Mike

In my life, lies have entirely taken the place of "the truth." I have been living, and still do live, in a parallel universe, where lies set me free, and the truth means pain.

Lying means everything is okay. Lies mean not facing realities. Lies come freely from my different personas: Fearful Mike, Mr. Mike Shut Down, Mr. Helpless/Hopeless and Dr. Addict. Lying is pathological with me—second nature. I'm addicted. I love lies.

Lying allows me to delay and postpone eating healthy, dealing with people promptly, cleaning my house, and getting in shape. "Just one more cookie!" "I'll work out tomorrow." "I will pay my bills next week."

All this procrastination, all these lies, allow me to avoid action. Truth means action now. This very paragraph you are reading has been delayed for weeks because of a lie.

As you can see, logic can't help me.

1. Are you at all like Mike? How?

2. Do you know anyone like Mike? Who?

3. Does that person "charm" you into believing him/her, even when he/she's lying? If that person is you, do you charm others, or do they see through you?

4. What lies are you trying to convince yourself are okay and why are they okay?

5. Have you rationalized the lies in your life?

THE TRUTH-LIAR WAR

Mike's TRUTH means......   **Pain**
                                    Hiding
                                    Not setting you free

Mike's LIES mean.........   **Everything is okay**
                                    Not living in reality, today
                                    Safe

Mike's LIAR looks and acts like... **Mr. Shut Down—Closed**
                                    Mr. Helpless/Hopeless—Victim
                                    Dr. Addict—Spinning and fixing

The Truth/Liar War comes from the Fearful Mike! Mike's fear is of the pain and shame that comes from seeing truth, which does not set him free. Everything is okay if he does not live in today's reality. He is safe in Mr. Shut Down, which causes Mr. Helpless/Hopeless to resort to acting like Dr. Addict, who is going to make him feel "good" while staying closed, stuck in a victim mode, spinning in this mess.
Mike's liar is pathological!

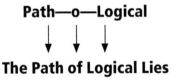

Path—o—Logical

The Path of Logical Lies

Do not make an excuse for a lie. It will block you from seeing the lie.

Many of our educational systems are set up to train us to provide answers, not to question. Many times these answers are created to please someone else. So we lose the capability to "check-in" with ourselves to "see" how we ourselves think or feel about the information we are getting. We are trained to be know-it-alls or stupid, we are people who speak in statements or do not speak at all. A wise person knows there is always more to learn. This causes confusion and conflict.

How do you deal with confusion and conflict? Do you demand to be understood and agreed with, or do you take the first step to understand?

The liar loves to create confusion and feed conflict because he or she can feed off the aggressive energy and feel powerful for a minute.

Remember, the liar in you was born because you felt powerless in the first place.

Understanding and owning can stop the need to be a liar!

Confronting vs. Approaching

There are ways to handle conflict and confusion other than lying and controlling. You can confront, or approach.

CONFRONTING: An intrusive, aggressive attack on your thoughts, feelings, judgments and behaviors stimulated by fear and anger. Statements or loaded questions that are open-ended, usually based on fear, full of righteous, egotistical opinions. Confrontation creates more anger, fear, guilt and shame.

APPROACH: A welcome invitation for information to enter in question form with an openness to understanding. Every answer invokes another question with no attempt to control the outcome. Based on peace, full of understanding, with an openness to see from as many perspectives as possible, there is openness, understanding and clarity of all.

People coming from a righteous, know-it-all, point of view will usually confront a situation. A confrontation is intimidating and controlling, swarming with blame. It creates anger, fear, guilt, and shame and conjures up lies as a defense from one or both parties.

If you want an understanding point of view of a situation, you need to ask questions with no ulterior motives, which means approaching a situation with no desire to control or manipulate.

Remember, there is no right or wrong way. There are just different ways to "see" things so we can understand more about ourselves and each other.

1. Can you remember a time that you were confronted, and a time that you were approached? Can you "see" these experiences? How did you feel? Please write:

2. *Confronting means...*
     and feels...
     and I remember when (write a confrontation memory)...
     and this made me feel...

3. *Approaching means...*
     and feels...
     and I remember when...
     and this made me feel...

People Who Confront

They have little or no sense of self-responsibility. Their goal is to vomit or unload their thoughts, feelings and judgments. They do not want to understand; they want to be right. If you want to be understood more than you want to understand, you put forth a needy and demanding energy. You are trying to control the outcome. This is not an open energy.

People Who Approach

They do not *need* to be understood. Their goal is to understand themselves and others. They are respectful, as they listen, in order to understand all sides and perceptions of a situation. They know that they cannot and they do not want to control the outcome. They understand that both the truth *and the lie* provide information that helps everyone "see" more clearly.

When we approach instead of confront, we gain deeper insight, stimulate new ideas, and have no fear of opening ourselves to truth and wisdom.

1. When you are involved in a confrontation, are you tempted to lie or be a manipulator? Why?

2. Do confrontations create a safe environment for truth? Why or why not?

3. Do you know your lies? Can you name one or two?

4. Can you see other people's lies? Name some!

5. The times you've lied—do you know why you did so?

6. When you lie, what are you afraid of?

7. What lies have you rationalized as okay?

Here's another story by another liar. Boy, they're *everywhere*, huh?

I'm Just a Good Guy
by Brett

I lie because it is easier than having to confront the truth. Facing the truth is scary.

I had never heard of the concept of approaching. I was always debated out of my point. My point never changed. I just gave up on communicating my point and shut down. Talk about losing myself! If I dealt with my truth, I was told I was being selfish or mean, especially if someone didn't like it. Since I was successful (at least I thought I was), why bother bringing the truth into my life?

I lied because when I tried to tell my truth it seemed like no one ever heard or liked it. It wasn't as if someone would have understood me anyway. I believed that lies were good because they protected me, which means they blocked me from the pain of my thoughts, judgments, truths, and feelings. If my truths were blocked, then the voices in my head were too busy and I didn't have to listen to them. Those sounds are usually voices of family and friends that I dropped a long time ago. It was their beliefs and thoughts that controlled my words and behaviors. They didn't even have to be near me, I was already subconsciously programmed with their ideas in my brain. Who knows who and where I am?! I live to please these people in my head whether they're in my life or not.

Lying is "bad" because it blocked all my truths. I had terrible stomach aches. I felt so nauseous from the spinning going on inside my head. I didn't know how to know me.

I remember when I felt my fiancé was cheating on me. My gut felt it, but I lied to myself to block the truth and not feel the pain. I kept a stale smile on my face. I hid my anger and hurt, and self-beat all day long. The self-beat made me numb so I never reacted with anger. I came off so perfect. A perfect, lying, idiot.

When my dad would get angry he would yell, attack, and hit. I remember shaking with fear, convinced it was me who caused his anger. I made everything my fault and held everything inside. That's when I started to lie and have stomach problems. When I pretended everything was okay. I had so much back-door guilt. Guilt was everywhere but I didn't know why I felt guilty. Maybe the guilt was the "bad" feeling for lying even if the lie looked like I was being a "good" person.

A lie can only hide the truth; it can't make it go away...

A lot of liars become liars because of their fear of anger, guilt, shame and punishment.

1. Do you think everyone gets angry?

2. Is it important to know how to process and deal with our anger or should we ignore it?

3. What happens if you ignore anger?

4. Is anger bad? Or is acting out in anger what's bad?

5. Because Brett didn't know how to process his anger, he imploded and developed stomach problems. Do you think the fear, guilt and anger are what "attacked" him?

6. Did the liar inside Brett become a mask to hide his anger and shame? How?

7. Did it "work?" What happened?

8. Are you helping yourself by holding in your thoughts or feelings? Why?

9. What can you create in your life from not understanding your thoughts and feelings?

10. How important is it for you to "own" your thoughts and feelings? Why?

11. Is an omission a lie? Why? What can that create?

12. Can omission hurt trust? Explain.

A little more writing!

This is why I lie...
These lies feel like...
Lies are "good" because...

Lies are "bad" because...
Lies create....
Lies can create insanity, because...

> If you are a truth seeker, lies and truths are equally valuable information. It is just as important to "see" what is not as it is to "see" what is.

Trust and Faith

Trust comes from what you choose to be. Trust comes from consistency, where words and behaviors match. When you have faith in yourself, you trust in your truth. Note that it is entirely possible for people to have faith in you, but not trust you. That's because faith is belief in your essence and spirit, and trust stems from consistent human behavior.

When you listen to people, and understand them, whether they are lying or telling the truth actually doesn't matter. Lies can help you "see" the truth as you move toward understanding, you will be understood within yourself. Then through your thoughts, feelings and behavior you will teach others how you want to be treated, because you finally understand yourself.

Stop what you are saying or doing!
Run to the mirror and look at *yourself*
before looking, judging or fixing someone else.

People will follow your lead once you understand yourself first. Let yourself go! Let people go! And stop lying to fake a sense of reality that lasts for a moment, just to relieve some pressure! Stop lying and creating images that result in living a life of fear of being found out!

Chapter Review

I just learned...
And I feel....

Summary

Liars deny or omit the truth, which makes them unaware of themselves. Memory gets lost and confused. The liar self-manipulates and manipulates others. Thoughts, feelings and memories are scrambled and lost because the passionate fire from the liars begins to burn them and others.

But if the liar finds truth, the fire can turn to passion and warmth, for the liar and for others. Everything "bad" becomes "good" when understood and change occurs. Every hurt can turn to wisdom and touch others and change our lives.

Fear of anger, guilt, shame and punishment feeds the liar. We must love the truth above all else in order to see ourselves, in order to understand any society. Balancing the body, mind, heart and soul is a constant work-in-progress.

A liar's stories clearly show his or her positive and negative perceptions. The more we understand our stories, the more we give ourselves the chance to catch our inner-liars and choose more truth. Understand why we all lie. To condemn and shame feeds this behavior and causes more pain.

Fear and shame will still pop up, and a lie will come once in a while; but we will be faster to catch ourselves and make amends.

Understanding the difference between confronting and approaching gives us the choice, in everyday life situations, to create fear and anger or depth and wisdom.

Having faith in who you are gives you strength to trust in who you choose to be. You can always go inside yourself, own your truth, and do things differently from the ways society has trained you.

"See" the truth in your lies and do not be scared! Just understand your fear and shame, and know you are not alone!

7 Fear: Prisoner of My Inner War!
P.O.W.

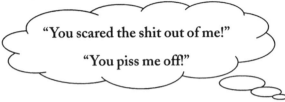

"You scared the shit out of me!"

"You piss me off!"

What is our body trying to tell us? Do you see how feelings can affect the body? Do lies scare us? Do lies affect our bodies?

Withholding, denying and blocking truth create fear that often plays out in the body. Watch how fast your body reacts to stress, anger, fear, hurt, guilt and shame. Does your stomach hurt? Does your head hurt? Is your digestion not working properly? Are you paralyzed and constipated, or running like diarrhea? Are your bladder and kidneys upset because you're pissed off?

What is scaring the shit out of you? What fear is stuck inside you, clogging you? What fear is out of control and sabotaging life outside you? What is pissing you or others off?

The Hell I Created!
by Lisa

When I first met Mona, I was a perfectly normal suburban housewife. I'd had some trouble a year prior and a friend had referred me to her. But Mona wasn't taking new clients at the time, so I gave up on her, and on growing and healing. In retrospect, I was afraid of the truth, and glad not to have anyone who might make me face reality.

One day while shopping (as suburban housewives do) I received a call on my cell. Mona had an opening. Things were going pretty well for me now and I wasn't sure I was interested. I told her I would check on childcare for my three kids, then call her. I figured, if I could get a sitter on short notice (which was usually impossible) I'd go; otherwise, I'd pass. One phone call and I was set with a sitter, damn! I had to see Mona the very next day.

Within a month of our weekly visits, my life fell apart. My husband of eleven years left me, I discovered I had cancer for the third time, and I remembered I was molested by my father (I was having flashbacks like a Vietnam vet). Hmmm. Do I ask for a full refund or continue? Having nothing to lose, I continued.

Sometimes our sessions were torture. (Okay, I'm not the best infomercial. She said to be honest). Fear is tough to face. Sometimes the session was fun. Many times, we had sessions on the phone while I rolled up in a ball in the corner of my closet. Most of the time, they were painful; not because of what she said, but because she had the ability to hold up a mirror and show me the hell I'd created.

I started listening to what I was saying. I was dead on the outside and screaming on the inside! My inner child (who I didn't know I had) was kicking my ass. I was so shut down, I didn't see it. My husband was a shut-down alcoholic who had emotionally abandoned me for years (he just didn't take his body with him). I hadn't been seeing his behavior, either. I began to see that the fantasy childhood I had created in my head was my biggest nightmare. Oh, and did I mention that I was having an affair with a neighbor (not recommended) who mirrored my issues? My life was killing me literally, and I needed to create a new one.

I started learning words such as "boundaries," "truth" and "coda" (someone who cares and worries as a form of love without truth and boundaries—a person who can be controlling and martyr-like at the same time).

I learned how to empower myself in order to grow into the person God created me to be. Freedom means freedom from fear, shame and guilt. I let myself swear (that was fun), cry, yell, and hit a pillow until the stuffing came out (great fun and very cathartic). I learned how crucial it is to breathe, and I realized how long it had been since I had last breathed freely. I learned how to look the boogieman in the face. I learned to walk into a room and read everyone's vibes—then light up a room with a warm smile and a pleasant tone in my voice. Most of all, I saw what the other side looked like. It's a lot to learn, and I blow it every day, but at least I'm on the right track.

Want to know how my life turned out? Old Lisa and her life are understood. Thank God, out of the fire (and believe me, there was plenty of fire) came new Lisa. New Lisa's not done yet (probably never will be) but she's okay with that. Her husband's sober now and takes better care of himself. He has lost over sixty-five lbs. and he likes himself too. We are still separated but working on us. My tumor seems to be shrinking miraculously as I come to terms with my childhood, and I've changed how I eat. I've also mixed holistic heath care with seeing my medical doctor. I can't wait to "see" what's in store for new Lisa next…

By the time this book was finished, Doug, Lisa and their three kids had moved back together, and are doing better then ever…just thought you would like to know. They bought a new house and are decorating their own anger room, where they can go and "rinse" anytime!

The Way We Handle Fear

Fear tells us to freeze, attack, or run—sometimes all three. Understanding what fear tells us, consciously or subconsciously, can prepare us for preventative action.

1. Do you freeze when you feel fear? If so, what happens? Do you do anything? Feel anything? Say anything? "See" anything?

2. Do you attack when you feel fear? Who do you attack? Yourself or someone else? Explain.

3. Do you run away when you feel fear? If so, in what way do you run? From your thoughts, your feelings, truth, another person? Do you procrastinate? Quit? Isolate yourself? Lie? Turn to an addiction? Explain.

THE FEAR ATTACK	THE FEAR RUN	THE FEAR FREEZE
When the fear attack happens to you, you:	**When the fear run happens to you, you:**	**When the fear freeze happens to you, you:**
• Feel guilty	• Make up excuses	• Cannot move
• Self-beat	• Create justifications for behavior you don't want or like	• Get depressed
• Get righteous		• Spin in your head
• Get aggressive	• Lie	• Become a robot
• Get physically ill	• Deny	• Shut down intuition
• Get stuck in hatred	• Make false promises	• Slow down awareness
• Self-mutilate	• Don't follow through	• Feel lost
• Blame everyone and everything for your life	• Say yes to appease others, but don't do what you said you would do	• Lock yourself up
• Starve		• Change the truth to make it an acceptable lie you can trick yourself into believing
• Overeat	• Get confused	
• Act out, repeatedly, with no love	• Are suicidal	• Get stuck in shame
• Engage in obsessive and compulsive behavior	• Fear leaving home	• Cannot think
• Turn to your addictions	• Fear taking risks	• Can't feel yourself, or others
• Create criminal acts	• Get overly busy	
• Get paranoid	• Turn to addictions	• Feel isolated
• Feed your phobias	• Go insane	• Are a helpless, hopeless victim
• Project your thoughts and feelings onto other people	• Become a victim, or a martyr	• Turn to addictions
	• Get paranoid	• Engage in rituals
	• Feed your phobias	• Get paranoid
	• Project your thoughts and feelings onto others	• Feed your phobias
		• Project your thoughts and feelings onto other people

Fear and Absolutes

Fear has its own language. It thinks and speaks in absolutes. When we are "in fear," we say:

I never...!
They always...!
This is how I think—forever!
There is no way out!
It's impossible!

These absolutes are a clear sign of fear and offer no hope. They cause us to quickly shut down, which leads to depression.

1. Never
2. Always
3. Forever
4. No Way
5. Impossible

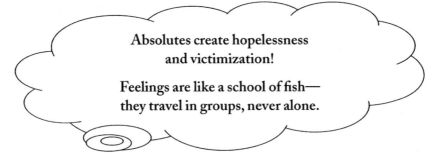

**Absolutes create hopelessness
and victimization!**

**Feelings are like a school of fish—
they travel in groups, never alone.**

Anger Is a Voice of Fear

There is an old TV episode of "Star Trek" regarding fear. Picture a bunch of dots representing a living organism that makes beeping sounds, floating through the ship. Every time this dotted organism shows up in a room, irrational, angry fights break out all over their ship. Crew members suddenly become enraged and start to attack each other. They appear to be fighting over nothing.

Fortunately, Captain Kirk—representing a balance of logic, feelings and intuition—holds his center. He could become reactive—get angry with himself or others, try to control everyone by dominating his crew. But instead, he watches and asks questions, looking to understand different perceptions before speaking or making a move.

He and the crew do a "check-in." They discover that a living, foreign organism of dots, that makes beeping sounds, is floating through the ship.

Since we know anger is fear's partner and fights are anger-based, the organism is the embodiment of fear. If someone scares you by saying "Boo!" do you notice how you jump, shut down, scream, or reach out to hit, as a reflex?

This is the power of fear. Unless we learn how to handle fear and understand it, we respond to fear in one of the three ways described above. The fear attack is all about protection, blame and anger. When the Star Trek crew finally figures out that this organism is fear, they *force* themselves to stop reacting in a protective angry blaming way when near the organism. They recognize that being "reactive" feeds the fear.

So the crew works on **understanding** their feelings. Then they **talk** about their fear until they all understand each other's angry reactions. Then, once they are "clear," the crew members **face their fear**—by facing the organism. They team up, with their arms around each other, and start laughing at it. Through their laughter, fear loses its power. Fear hates truth! It grows from blocked past or present truths. Fear is powerless in the face of truth, in the face of those who own their fears.

As the crew laughs and taunts the fear organism, they say, "Be gone with you, fear! We're onto you and we are not reacting to you! We understand you! We know what you are, and we laugh in your face!" With that, the dotted organism beep-beeps, and races off the ship.

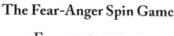

The Fear-Anger Spin Game

Fear creates anger.
Anger creates fear.
It's a never-ending cycle.
Still want to react?

Imagine...

1. How can fear, mixed with blocked truth, create anger and insanity?

2. Can you think of an example of when you saw truth or humor dispel fear? When?

3. If you feel fear, and you start to self-beat, what is the result? Can you remember a time when you felt fear and it went right into a self-beat? I remember when... And this felt... And created...

4. Has humor ever helped you stop a self-beat? If so, when?

5. Is it possible to heal when you are in a state of fear? How?

Does fear throw you "out of order"?

When you "see" the words "mental disorder" or "anxiety disorder," key into the word "disorder." Could the word "dis-order" mean that fear has entered and truth is thrown and your realms are "out of order" inside you?

How We Can Learn to Know Ourselves

Humor, storytelling or movies help us process and dissipate our fear because it's easier for us to absorb messages that aren't personal; yet stories stimulate our thoughts, feelings and memories and we can personalize and own if we choose to use a story as a reflection exercise.

Story techniques create visuals. Visuals inspire so many thoughts and feelings in our heads and hearts. Pictures transmit and drop directly into our subconscious mind. It's no accident that the Torah, the Bible, the Baghavad Gita, and much of the Koran are written as stories and parables. In the Native American culture, elders pass on information they learned from their ancestors by storytelling. The same is true of Eastern religions; much of what we know about the Buddha comes from the story of his life. Stories express picturesque points of view and sometimes tell us what we need to know more clearly, sensitively and even more intellectually than judgmental, straightforward descriptions ever could.

If you need to convey information to someone else about a sensitive matter, sometimes using a story will make a point without triggering a defensive reaction because the person who is listening could easily react by becoming frightened or self-beating. If the story is told without creating or triggering fear or shame, that person may be less likely to hide from his or her truths. Furthermore, you can tell your story and own something about your past, which instills empathy. This may prevent shame or guilt from creeping into the person who's trying to learn or hear the point.

Truth can be painful enough without including anger, fear, guilt, or shame in our thoughts or feelings as we talk. If you're using humor, keep it light and loving. Humor becomes a weapon if mixed with a vibe of anger, fear, guilt, shame or hurt. When issues are discussed with bitterness or sarcasm, they are not funny.

Being humorous and sharing stories are a couple of ways to use a little sugar to help the medicine of truth go down. Playing in truth, with no judgment, is enlightening and inspiring and shows you, effortlessly, the "light" of truth without making it a lesson. When fear faces truth—peace, clarity and love enter the picture. When fear is understood, fear turns to wisdom and transforms into "true love."

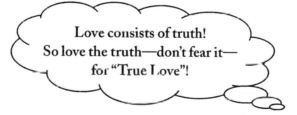

Love consists of truth!
So love the truth—don't fear it—
for "True Love"!

Absorbing Fear from Everyone
by Doug

My parents didn't like each other. My father always threatened to leave, and I was scared to death he would. What if I made him mad, and he left? So I tried to make everything better. But no matter what I did, I was convinced my parents' lives would have been so much better without me and my sister. I felt guilt and fear just for being alive.

In high school, I started drinking and using drugs to escape the fear and guilt. It was my way of running away.

My father got me my very first job. It was with one of his big-shot friends. I was so afraid of disappointing him. And thus, my career was started—on the wings of fear.

At twenty-one, I started my own business. I thought that I would please Dad, and if I succeeded, then he'd be proud and love me. And I did succeed; but still, the "fear of God" and voices of my parents in my head didn't go away. It was never enough.

The voices grew so strong that I had to drown them out. I drank. I behaved arrogantly and egotistically. Even what I called my spirituality was an exercise of my ego. I had to be "good," do good things, and be the best.

I hoped that falling in love would finally make me feel secure and safe from my fears. But how can you love if you're too scared to open up and be vulnerable? I never showed the love of my life, my wife, the real me. I was afraid she would leave me and run.

Therefore, emotionally, I ran first. I lived my life with one foot out the door, preparing for my marriage to fail and anticipating moving on. I created an environment of instability, just as my Dad had created with me.

When children came, I was afraid to even love them. If I couldn't open up alone, or with my wife, how could I open up with them? My drinking continued. My weight increased. The fears ballooned inside of me.

Finally, after eleven years of marriage and three children, I went away for the weekend. When I came back, my wife wouldn't let me back in the house. She had finally had enough of this passive/aggressive, shut-down drunk in her and her children's lives.

At the time of this letter, we have been separated nine months. Although the separation has been the most painful time in my life, it has allowed me to make some extraordinary discoveries about myself. It has allowed me to face my greatest fears and understand them.

I have found that since my childhood, I have absorbed fear from everyone. My feelings were hooked up to fear and also to the rush of ego highs. My ego had to achieve to receive love. I projected everyone's fears on myself, and this pain consumed me every day of my life. I use fear to motivate myself, my employees, and my family. Every day I created fear in order to dominate it and feel powerful.

As I have come to understand my parents' feelings and their truths, I've been better able to own my own. I'm feeling the first peace of my life. I've realized that their fears and pain are not mine. It was their journey to travel and move through, not mine.

Truth tells you what's yours and what belongs to others. I now understand the origin of others' pain and I see how it impacts their lives. I don't have to take on other people's pain in order to understand it.

I now understand why my fear is a gift. I have lived with it and have been consumed by it for forty-five years. Now I see it for what it really is.

In this quiet time of peace, I reconnect to my memories and feelings. First, I feel and own my fear, anger, and sadness. And then I gain understanding and wisdom. If I am able to "let go" of all the fears and pain that are not mine to own as I own what is mine, I can change the way I think and feel, and finally experience joy and peace without guilt. This inspires me to change.

~

Doug realized that to understand and let go of fear is to finally know peace.

Anxiety Is the Aftermath of Fear

If you have a low-grade, consistent fear, you could develop an ongoing anxiety. Anxiety comes from unprocessed fear, with care and worry in it. This is stress. Fear and stress can lead to depression, addiction and more. Addictions are attempts to self-medicate us when we feel fear and become out of balance. Addiction can feed insecurity and arrogance at the same time. More fear. The depression of addiction is the suppression of our truth and true self. Do you "see" how fear has a talent for re-creating itself? It keeps haunting us until we finally understand it—and change.

Fear has many faces. Which of the following behaviors are yours? Each of them is based on anxiety, which is based on ignored and suppressed truth.

Behaviors That Express Anxiety, From a Life in Fear

Shopping	Collecting
Biting Nails	Being pushy
Being Fidgety	Depression
Eating Disorder	Obsessive/Compulsive
Controlling behavior	Insomnia
Stuttering	Picking at one's face
Confusion	Pulling eyelashes
Nervousness	Twitching
Cutting	Isolation
Phobias	Paranoia

THE CURE

Turn: Fear into peace.
       Care into love from understanding.
       Worry into faith.

Love enters when you
begin to understand fear.

The more consciously aware of fears and self-talk within yourself, the better you can consciously make truthful decisions in the world.

The more we go out into the world, the more we risk. The more we risk, the more chances we have to screw up. If we don't know how to rinse and own, the more likely we will be to self-beat, become depressed or deflect and blame others. The more we become suppressed and depressed, the more the truth of our fears gets lost and stuck in our subconscious mind, replaced by deeper fears and anxiety.

For Doug, denied, unprocessed fears fed into an array of subconscious mind battles. The blocked fears kept trying to emerge, but the emerging fears caused him anxiety and pressure. The idea that his fears were surfacing created more fear. Doug had no techniques to process his fears and memories. To balance himself, he turned to fear's good friends, anger and addiction. That addict energy tries to make you feel better. It gives you positive feelings or feeling releases of suppressed energy, with no sense of responsibility to let truth show its head. The anger gives him a sense of strength and power because fear and shame feel powerless.

Suppressed Fears Create Addictions

Fear feeds the addict energy and suffocates the truth of the inner child. There goes your intuition. You may still have instincts, which comprise a subconscious knowingness from life experiences, but the intuition, the internal knowledge of truth, is damaged. Suffocation creates suppression; this suppression becomes depression. Don't be fooled. Even if you are successful or have a great personality, you can still experience depression. You're just a talented hider. Doesn't it make sense that if depression is suppression and you are suppressing your thoughts, feelings and memories, you get depressed in different parts of yourself? This is why depression can feel like it comes and goes.

The reason the addict parties hard is to create enough energy to block conscious awareness of upsetting truths and hurts. Notice that the truths and hurts are still there and they will be back...and so will the addict, continually followed by depression. See how and why the addict feels like a "good" guy?

The addict wants to bring you "good" feelings when you are feeling "bad." Since the addict shuts down *awareness* of feelings, fears, and truth, the addict causes insanity and chaos in the long run. The addict is built on lies and illusions that can't last. Notice that the addict is protective energy from your thought, feelings, and judgments. The addict is not who you truly are.

Marijuana, wine and other depressants shut down thoughts and feelings consciously and cause sleeping and eating issues. Often this suppresses and seems to control hysterical bursts of anger and low-grade depression. Because alcohol and drugs are chemicals, they create chemical responses in the body, giving you time to survive a triggered fear and hurt. Cocaine, ecstasy, cigarettes, and alcohol *can* give you energy, but then they pull the rug out from under you—and you crash.

Every addiction creates a chemical rush in your system. Sex, workaholism, materialism, fetishes, gambling, even compulsive lying, all rush your body with chemicals designed to balance your mind and body, which feel out of balance from upsets. Eventually, your body grows accustomed and builds a tolerance to any chemical that doesn't kill it. Addictions always require higher and higher doses in order to get to the same "high."

But again, the "addict" inside you doesn't know this. It thinks it's helping. Becoming an addict isn't a living skill—it's a survival skill. The addict seeks a way to survive and create an illusion of balance in an unbalanced situation. The key is to balance yourself in a way that works—continually.

The Super Addict

The addict says, "Don't worry. I'll give you a good feeling." And so it flies over the bad feelings, to *make* you feel good. Is it okay with you if truth is missing? What is leading your life? Is the goal to feel good no matter what? Do fear and the addict hurt loved ones? How does your body feel afterwards? Is the addict for feeling good in the long run or only for a moment? If you do not process the bad feelings, do they go away? Do the bad feelings just keep growing so the addict *has to* fly higher and higher every time? If feelings cause this much havoc, why are we not teaching a way to process right-brain feelings in our schools, religions and court systems?

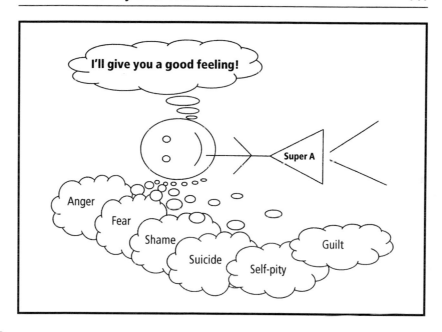

1. Do you have any addictions? If so, which ones?

2. If your answer is "no," think again. Obsessive and compulsive behavior is a sign of addiction in the mental realm. Do you date compulsively? That is addiction in the emotional realm. Do you watch TV shows obsessively? Do you need to gossip? Do you need to buy something? Do you need to nitpick? Think...

3. How does this addict energy feel?

4. If you have an addiction, what fear or hurt does it cover up for you? Is there an anxiety attached? What "bad feeling" does it help you block?

5. When did the addiction begin? Why?

6. What was happening in your life when it started?

7. What was your perception of your life at that time?

8. How did you feel?

The addict in you doesn't leave or calm down when you stop your addictive behavior. Addiction is an energy, a belief and way of thinking, not just a chemical thing. Anything that is unresolved will trigger the addiction to pop up somewhere else. Recovering addicts easily find different addictions. Dry alcoholics often start to smoke, have sex more, or become workaholics. Can you see that your inner addict has a certain kind of energy and job in your life? Can you see that the addiction is not just a behavior, it is a way of thinking? Addictive behavior is a sign that something needs understanding and changing—from the inside, out.

> **If you never learned how to process fear, your addict will process and control it for you.**

**Learning to be truly intimate and understanding
is impossible for those living in fear
and with addict energy.**

Dr. Kevin McCauley, M.D.,* a recovering addict, discovered that the frontal cortex part of the brain handles our memories, responsibilities, morals, and sensory data. Active addicts in energy or chemical addictions are not centered in their frontal cortex, but process in their midbrain. The midbrain, which takes over, "sees" no future. It craves everything now! Truth and responsibility are for later. Everything becomes a life-and-death issue, because you are not processing your truths and feelings. This blocked and suppressed energy becomes an obsessive energy, where you are led by cravings. Obsession is from suppressed, unresolved thoughts, feelings and memories. And cravings are unprocessed desires, out of control with no truth or boundaries.

The way most of us "help" an addict get rid of addiction is to make him or her feel bad about that addiction. Addiction was born out of

---

*Dr. Kevin McCauley M.D., www.addictiondoctor.com,
    800-337-7085.

feeling scared, bad and insecure in the first place. Why would more judgment, shame, and guilt help an addict out of addiction? All it creates is more fear, self-beats and judgments.

Since addiction has so much fear and pain at its root, wouldn't the addict just pull up pain and fear in those around them? We create and attract what we are. So if someone's going to help or if an addict is going to help him or herself, no judgment, self-beats are allowed unless it is in an exercise form. If the negativity and judgments keep coming, the addict is going to keep popping up to give you a different feeling to save you from yourself. And the cycle continues. Celebration and pleasure are going to be difficult as well. Pleasure has turned to the idea of a "high" or a thrill. Celebration means disconnect from your self-awareness and block true memories, thoughts and feelings and fly with little or no responsibility, causing an illusion of freedom. Freedom from what? Freedom from truth, or are addicts looking for freedom from judgment, theirs and that of others as well? Now, how are you going to link truth, with no judgments and self-beats, to simple joys, as you feel yourself? You have become numb to yourself and regular pleasures. Without the ability to process, all that's left to ease our pain…is another "high."

One of the struggles of addiction is how much the addict in you affects all of your realms. (We will talk more about realms later.) Everything is probably out of balance and just needs re-alignment.* A physical rinse of your organs and colon is crucial because of the stress and chemical residue sitting inside your mind, tissues and lining walls. If you don't cleanse your soul, mind, heart, and body the crud is still in there waiting to turn into a craving or trigger a body memory, and the subconscious is about to take over. Remember this is not an intelligence problem. It is a subconscious fear and an emotional problem, with body memories that want to take a sober addict right back to where he/she started. Once Pandora's box is open, don't play here even a little bit.

Logic is just not enough. Understand this or go to self-beat hell and spin in it. To avoid a truth, fear or an upsetting issue is to end up in a shut-down depression or seek another addict high. The only way to

---

*www.wecarespa.com

change your world is to change you. God said to love the truth, not happiness. Happiness is an outcome, not a goal.

Seeking a Bag of Solutions
by Scott

I never thought I would know Hell on such an intimate level. I had no idea how powerfully my addiction had grown until I opened the door and woke the Sleeping Giant!

On January 4, 1994, I was homeless and had to ask my mother if I could move back in with her. My probation officer was threatening to put me back in jail if I didn't start attending A.A. meetings.

That night, I attended my first meeting of Alcoholics Anonymous. Sometime during the meeting I decided that maybe it was time for me to make a change in my life and I might want to give this thing a chance.

I stayed in the program. I was learning a lot about who I was and what it was that I couldn't stand about me. I started returning to the person I had once been. I began to care enough about me by not running and hiding or smoking crack and drinking alcohol. I started being able to live one day at a time. Eventually, I began building a life of substance.

After seven years of sobriety, I was making a great income, married to an incredible woman. I had nice cars, a boat, and lived in a beautiful house on the water in Northern California. My life was filled with amazing friends and family. Any normal person would fight to keep this life.

But all the A.A. in the world wasn't going to convince me that I deserved this life. On some level, I feared happiness as much as misery.

I still remember how painfully I wanted to "use." I would be driving in my car, on my way to work, and the thought to "use" would start running through my head. The slow romantic memories started as sweet tender thoughts and worked their way into full-blown obsessions. I remember the feelings so well. They surpassed any logic or reasoning. The flood of excitement and energy raced through my body until I was like a giddy school kid on his way to Disneyland.

I clearly recall the day my pregnant wife told me it was time to have our son. As we fled to the hospital, I couldn't believe the amount of fear, not excitement, that consumed me.

My wife's labor went on for more than twenty hours, so the doctors sent me home to feed the dogs and get a couple hours of rest. Well, the addict in me decided I could no longer stand the feelings of fear, guilt and shame, coupled with an overwhelming pressure of not being worthy of this great life. So as my wife was at the hospital pushing out new life, I sat in my garage, smoking crack cocaine and watching pornography.

From this moment on, I now had proof that I was a piece of shit and was no longer deserving of my life. I would be driving in my car, sobbing out loud, saying, "I don't want to use, I don't want to use." Then I looked down to see that I was driving 90 miles an hour to go and get more.

No matter how much I would keep talking to myself to get off the freeway and go home, it was hopeless. My addiction owned my soul, thoughts, actions, and emotions. My addiction's purpose was to take away everything in my life that had a chance of making me happy. My true voice and inner child were not only weak—they were gone! I wasn't worth any life other than a dark, lonely Hell of self-hatred.

I went to countless rehabs, group therapies, and even went as far as hiking through the snow in a survival program for five weeks. I went to numerous sweat lodges and embarked on a Vision Quest (as part of a twelve-step program that focused on spirituality). I didn't stay sober long after returning home, but on this particular excursion, I did find God.

But I was still seeking God—along with all my solutions—outside of myself, just like I had with all other areas of my life. Finally, in a place of hopelessness and fear, I went to my wife and said, "I need help."

And my wife took me to Mona. Mona set regular scheduled meetings, along with groups and work assignments. I really wish I could say that I followed them, as agreed, but I can't. I continued to use on and off, and see Mona in between. The odd part about this is, even though I hardly knew her, I truly knew and felt that she was on my side, not judging me.

When I did have the courage to show up, Mona patiently taught me to process. I began to learn more about myself then I ever did before.

In six months, I acquired more solutions on how to deal with me, my self-loathing, ego grandiosity, lying and all the behaviors that I would use to fuel my addiction than I had ever known before. I also learned that God was inside me and wanted nothing but love and truth for me.

Still, my willingness to be sober wasn't there. As much as I was learning about myself, I was just too scared to apply it on an everyday basis.

It took five long years. But today, I am sober. When I feel the urge to use, I reach into what I like to call my bag of solutions that Mona taught me. I have learned to rinse what I need to rinse, be as honest as possible, and go back in time to clean up my old anger, fear, guilt, and shame.

I am learning to love all of the parts of me, good and bad, and give them a place where they can be heard. I no longer have to beat myself up every minute. I can truly say that from the things I have learned about myself, I no longer have to pray to God to remove all of my defects of character. I can simply identify, understand and accept the truth about who I really am today.

Is all of this about a perception of worth, fear of the self-beat and self-loathing with an imbalance and flipping between high and low ego?

~

We All Have a Purpose

How can blocking and twisting your thoughts, feelings and memories, painful or positive, show you who you are and why you are here? Have you forgotten that we are here for a reason? We have lost techniques for understanding, processing, and internal celebration. The more we know, feel, remember and understand our inner child's mind and heart, the clearer our understanding of our purpose for life becomes.

Unless we process our fear and learn to understand it, it thrives.

If you want to know your *purpose* on this planet, find a *struggle*, any struggle and process it. Inside the struggle is a *lesson*. And through the lesson is your *purpose*. Since there are many lessons, there are many purposes! *Look at your struggle, find the opposite of the struggle and you will see a purpose.*

1. Can you find a struggle? What's the battle going on in your head?

2. What are you afraid of regarding this struggle? Who are you afraid of? Is it you or someone else?

3. What truth can you find that you may be blocking regarding this struggle?

4. How could approaching this fear affect your life?

5. Who else will be affected by your facing this struggle and fear?

6. How is your self-beat connected to this struggle and fear?

7. What is the lesson?

8. What is the opposite of your struggle?

9. Find a purpose yet?

Let's Go, and Let Go!

When my client Kristen learned to go through her feelings of fear, past and present, she found love.

I Want to Live More Than I Want to Die
by Kristen

I spent my life feeling like I was broken. I was convinced there was something really wrong with me. I was always depressed. I had a history of alcohol abuse and I suffered severely from panic attacks. I had fooled the outside world into thinking I was okay, but on the inside, I felt I was being tortured on a daily basis.

On my first visit with Mona, she asked me if I had been molested.

I couldn't believe she brought it up. I didn't even know her. Was it that easy to see? Why had no one else ever asked? I'm sure now that it's because others were afraid of the answer. No wonder I became addicted to alcohol. I needed to bury my inner child. When I finally told the truth with my little girl's feelings, I could breathe.

During that very first session I wrote three anger letters, one to my mother, one to my father, and one to myself. I was a little surprised by the venom I held for my parents.

But the big shocker was my own self-hatred. I could, for the first time, feel it with my whole body and soul. I was embarrassed and ashamed to admit it. After I learned to walk through these horrible thoughts and feelings, I felt hope. It was raw and painful, but for the first time in my life I understood why I avoided these feelings, and furthermore, that these feelings weren't killing me—the shame and secrets were.

My work with Mona has been a slow process because I block my memories, and resist. I argue over doing the exercises and block my writing. In order to understand my relationship with the world, I have to understand my relationship with myself, then each of my family members. It's exhausting!

But still, this has been a miracle for my entire family. We've learned to understand each other much better. We've learned a format of communication that never existed for us before.

By uncovering layers of pain, anger, disappointment, and family expectations, I'm becoming more of myself. I'm no longer stuck in the past. I now feel I want to live more than I want to die. I feel like there's hope, I can actually have what I desire.

By allowing myself to grow up, I've let my dreams become realities. I've been given a raise and promotion at work. I had always wanted to go to Asia, so I've taken myself there, twice. I always wanted to buy an original piece of artwork. I bought two in October. I live with emotional and financial responsibility, but I'm learning to do what I want with boundaries. I don't wait around for something to happen. I take action. I went to Africa and lived there with women and children for three months and just opened a non-profit organization to build water wells in Africa. My life is forever different because I was capable of seeing the truth of pain beyond my imagination of abuse and trauma, and instead of withdrawing I was strong enough to show my feelings and take action. No more blocked sadness and pain.

Often when I walk through my fear, I come out on the other side with an incredible sense of relief and wisdom and yes, self-love! And this has enabled me to love all kinds of people. I am now getting ready to love a man in a relationship as one of two honest and understanding partners. I'm not scared of others or me anymore. Love of truth is spreading in me, from me and for me.

～

Once on the other side of fear,
I can hear.
It's often the idea of fear that brings
my fear's most torturous and tormenting tears.

Chapter Review

I just learned...
And I feel...

Summary

Is "hell" a state of mind called fear, where you speak in lies and create anger, as you shame both your positive and negative thoughts, feelings and memories? Does judging yours and everyone else's life create the fear of anger, guilt and shame?

Just as you cleanse your body of unwanted toxins, you need to cleanse your heart, mind, and soul. You are not alone. We all visit hell on a daily basis just by how we think, feel, and judge.

Fear is an obsession and its grip is strong. It can create depression, suicide, insanity, and hysteria. Pick your "F" word: Fear or Faith. Faith is a belief that replaces fear. But faith is in the truth, not desires.

Whatever you have experienced in the past, you are probably creating and manifesting now. You can look into your future by seeing your past and present choices. Until you understand the lesson from the past, fear will be your guide in the present and the future will consist of more of the same.

Fear is a messenger that needs to be understood and processed. When we live in fear we suffocate love and ignore truth. The inner child's truth and memories shut down when we live in fear. Then the addict energy is born to help "deal" and becomes our fear processing. The truth is blocked, as the addict lies with false promises of happiness and creates more fear and self-hatred.

Humor and stories help us "see" our fear and hurt without creating more pain, more fear, and more self-beating.

Fear, unaddressed, creates anxiety. It lives in the future as it is created from the past, repeating what it knows and believes in the present. Fear needs shame to hurt our essence, to keep truth quiet, so it can live on. The addict thinks it is a "good guy." After all, the addict is trying to block the "bad" feelings and give us some "good" ones. The trick is that the addict winds up feeding shame, creating more fear when we sober up. Fear paints *truth* as the "bad guy," which sends us back to the addict energy—and on we go.... But when fear faces the truth, it dissipates.

Turn your struggles into understandings, seek wisdom, learn your lessons, and find your purpose on this planet. Remember: Sometimes we must experience **who we are not to know who we are!**

8 Passive Aggression
Stop the War, or Love Is No More!

Love and war live inside us all. Opposites can easily trigger an internal battle that sets up bonding patterns. Bonding patterns are repetitive thoughts, feelings and behaviors that connect or enable situations to keep occurring. If these bonding patterns are connected by anger, fear, guilt, shame and pain, they become bondage.

To stop any conflict, we have to figure out how the conflict is part of our pattern (or how our pattern is part of our conflict). Then we must own it! It's not about doing anything bad or wrong or finding "fault" in a situation, it's about recognizing our patterns and how our thoughts, feelings and behaviors attract or play a part in what is happening in our relationships and life. This is how you take responsibility for your life so you can change it.

> Pattern recognition has nothing to do with determining whether you are a good or bad person. A "good" person can suppress as much truth as someone considered "bad."

Watch this! Are Love and War made of the same ingredients?

FEELINGS OF WAR	FEELINGS OF HUMAN LOVE
Fear	Fear
Anger	Anger
Guilt	Guilt
Shame	Shame
Celebration	Celebration
Victory	Victory
Camaraderie	Camaraderie
Builds Intimacy	Builds Intimacy

Human love is not spiritual or true love. Human love is full of unprocessed past memories, low- and high-ego, lying and denying of personal truths.

What Do You Fight About?

1. Is there a consistent, recurring fight that occurs in your life? If so, what is it?

2. Do you fight with yourself? In what way?

3. What issues do you most often fight about?

4. How do these fights feel?

5. Do these fights remind you of anything from your past? If you answer no, then think again. What pops into your head? *These fights remind me of...*

6. Why is human love scary?

7. *Human love reminds me of...*

8. *And I felt...*

Passive People

Anger is just a build-up of suppressed thoughts, feelings and judgments that are not owned or understood.

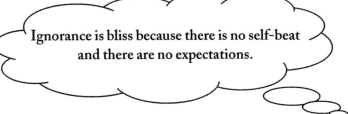

Ignorance is bliss because there is no self-beat and there are no expectations.

Do You Give Off Passive Energy?

Passive energy is a rejecting energy! If you give off passive energy, the first person you reject is yourself. This rejection comes from your own denial and suppression. You are a liar by omission, and whether you're aware of it or not, you can transmit angry, scary vibes.

If passive energy is your energy, you are an avoider! You avoid the truth of your own thoughts, feelings, and memories, as well as those of others. No wonder you avoid others and they avoid you.

If you demonstrate passive energy, you probably send out selfish or self-less, self-absorbed energy. Passive energy "sees" every situation as if it is about that person alone.

If this perception is a low-ego perception, it creates negative energy personally. If the perception is a high-ego perception, it is an arrogant, pompus energy. If you don't get your anger out, you'll continue to blame yourself and others for everything going on around you, without ever "seeing" the light of your or others' truths. This self-deprecating view makes people feel bad because they don't know you are in a low- or high-ego mode. People just personalize and assume you are judging them and they fall into a low- or high-ego mode as well. Ego mode is triggering and contagious and enhances invisible warfare.

A passive person wants to be self-ignorant, to gain happiness by bypassing truths that cause self-beat.

Passive people need to accept that they are ignorant as well as smart, drop the self-beats when not perfect, learn not to care and worry, no controlling allowed, and to let truth lead (with understanding). This is how a passive/aggressive person becomes patient and assertive!

Passive people, if and when they speak, often speak in **reasons or excuses** for what they or others think, feel or do. No self-awareness or owning here. These excuses are defenses for uncomfortable truths because these people are fighting judgment and a self-beat.

Sometimes, when we are passive, we think that we are being nice, even good. But as long as we are suppressing what we truly see and feel, the energy we live in is negative and uncomfortable for us as well as others.

BONDING PATTERNS BECOME BONDAGE.

Here's My Pattern!
Think of a pattern you repeat, over and over again. Write it down! How is it based on a thought? A feeling? A visual? A behavior? A habit?

1. *One pattern I repeat is…*
2. *The thought I have that repeats is…*
3. *The feeling I have that repeats is…*
4. *My visual is…*
5. *The behavior is…*
6. *The habit is…*
7. *This pattern makes me feel I'm in bondage, because…*
8. *I would like to break this pattern, because…*

Here's How My Pattern Developed
In my past I…
1. *Had a **thought***
2. *Then a **feeling***
3. *That became a **visual***
4. *Which developed a **behavior***
5. *The **behavior** repeated*
6. *And became a **habit***

To Break a Pattern
> *In present time...*
> 1. *Find the **habit***
> 2. *Identify the **behavior***
> 3. *See the Picture or **visual***
> 4. *Understand the **feelings***
> 5. *Go to the past to find the **thought***

Then...
> 1. *Change the **thought***
> 2. *Celebrate and understand the **feelings***
> 3. *Create a new **thought** from a "wish" of what could happen*
> 4. *Make a new **picture** or **visual***
> 5. *Decide on a new **behavior**/break the Pattern*
> 6. *Repeat the new **behavior** until it becomes subconscious*
> 7. *Now you have a new "**habit**"*

Why Do We Become Passive?

Humiliation and fear can cause your energy to shut down. When we shut down our thoughts, feelings and memories, we suppress our inner child and soul causing a disconnection with ourselves and with others. Why are we disconnecting from ourselves when our power or life source is still "on"? After all, we are not dead yet. So why unplug from life's realities?

Why wouldn't we want to be connected to ourselves? Don't we want to "be there" if something happens that affects us? We need to understand why we self-disconnect. Why would we want to turn off self-awareness?

When you disconnect, are you feeling others and then feeling yourself or are you feeling yourself, denying it and then projecting your feelings onto others and pretending it's how they feel?

The only reason to shut down is to survive jail, being abused, or getting through a trauma. Being shut down in these situations helps you survive. When your trauma is over, rinse and own to let go of these survival skills, so you can live again. If you live your life disconnected from yourself out in the world, your energy creates internal and external wars and you are the one who loses.

Why Do We Live Through Others?

If you are shut down, your disconnected subconscious mind experiences your thoughts and feelings through the actions or reactions of others. It's others reactions that awaken you mentally and emotionally. Feeling through others' lives and reactions is sometimes the only way a shut-down person can allow him- or herself to feel at all.

This roundabout way of feeling through others can cause emotional suffocation or hysteria, in others as well as in oneself. Since there is no truth as to whose feelings belong to whom, feelings end up all over the place. This is why you need to check in with yourself!

Take Me Out (of Me) at the Ball Game

Did you ever notice how someone who is normally composed can lose all composure, scream, yell or even fly into a rage at a ball game?

The composed person is shut down and passive in everyday life. Passive people love feeling through others. For example a person feeling *through* a ballplayer can lose it at a ball game. All he or she is doing is regurgitating feelings that are no way about this ballplayer. There is no true relationship with this ballplayer. Instead of being open and feeling *with* the ballplayer, that ballplayer is all about what the passive/aggressive person believes and feels. So, the fan becomes a fanatic, who takes personal disowned beliefs and feelings and projects them onto this poor ballplayer. Hope that ballplayer doesn't trigger a past issue with this fan. Whatever feelings the fan has suppressed are now on the ballplayer. Even though the energetic release of pressure can feel good at the time, no honest release has occurred. The true issues and feelings remain active and will return, and so will the fan, unless the ballplayer lets the fan down too much, then comes the aggressive attack...

All My (Inner) Children

How can some people become hysterical, addicted, enraged, depressed, nervous, and gossipy over a celebrity or a story line in a TV show and sustain such feelings for hours, days, weeks, or even years?

People who do this are living *through* a person or story that has everything and nothing to do with them. There is something in that character or story line that mirrors parts of these people. There is something they are not consciously "seeing" in their own lives. They are disconnected, shut down, and not owning this "thing" in the story that is a reflection of them.

Let's say that I put ten people in front of you.
They all really seem like "jerks."
As "jerky" as they may behave, not all of them are going to get under your skin.
Only the jerks that act like you, your family, or loved ones will bother you.
That's why you need to take a look at everyone who bothers you.
The reason? The jerks who bother you are about you.
There's something in that person you need to "see" and own.

1. Who are you "triggered" by? Who really bugs you?

2. What does this person do that bugs you, if anything?

3. How does this person make you feel?

4. Does this person remind you of anyone from your past? Who? If not, does this person remind you of you? How?

Now, write a letter to this person:

Dear _____,
When I look at you I see...
When I look at you I feel...
You remind me of...

Now, turn the "You's" to "I's" and "me's"! Take the very words that you've just written and change them so that what you originally said about the jerk, you now say about you.

Example:
  I am
  ~~*You are*~~ *an obnoxious showoff.*

If you own that these "jerks" bugging you are a part of you that you have disconnected from, you've just become wiser! Don't self-beat! When you find an imperfection in yourself, do you accept it, or fight it? Do you want war or love? Pick one—they are very similar.

The War Inside You

War! We love it and hate it. We watch love and war on TV. We go to "see" them at the movies. We'll do anything to hear, talk about, or "see" humans in war and love. Why?

In a shut-down family or society, war exists because it becomes a catalyst to release suppressed, big feelings, without owning those feelings or telling our truths. It's like blame or projection. We put our issues onto someone else or onto another issue. Watching a war is so much more fun than acknowledging the one being waged inside us!

Homework!

A visual or a picture can show you things in a thousand ways that will stimulate your conscious and subconscious mind. That's why I'd like you to rent a movie. A movie may feel time-consuming, but it's time well spent, because it can help you "see." There's an old saying: "A picture is worth a thousand words."

The movie to rent is *Mystic River*. Then answer these questions:

Note About the Movie

Please note that there are some painful scenes in this movie. If these scenes are too painful, fast forward. You'll get the point without the play-by-play blows.

Thoughts and Questions About *Mystic River*

1. Dave told stories to his son of a brave, lonely "boy." Dave never explained he was "the boy." Dave died inside after the molestation and he began to call himself "the boy" as a way to disconnect and shut down from the trauma. Talking about

"the boy" helped him deal and talk in a roundabout, "safe" way ("safe" meaning without owning the pain all the way). **Why did Dave tell his son stories about "the boy"?**

2. Dave felt violated and alone. Unless he spoke to someone with similar experiences who had processed their trauma and recovered, he "saw" no way out. He took on shame, dirtiness, humiliation, fear, guilt, and anger from the experience. Clearly his experience wasn't his fault but nonetheless he felt like an alien, broken forever. When he came back to his regular life, everyone felt "bad" and uncomfortable. The pain created from his trauma affected his present life. Everyone who loved him went into a survival mode so they just ignored it or him. No one was trying to be insensitive or cruel, there was no processing skill for anyone. This is why he was called "damaged goods." How could he ever feel truly "good" again? The "good" was damaged. **Why is Dave disconnected and shut down?**

3. When Dave ran through the woods, as a child, he felt like a trapped animal. He heard his own voice as an animal cry. The animal cries were outside him and inside him. (When the inner child experiences pain, it is guttural and animalistic.) He called the molesters werewolves, because they felt like animals to him. Soon he felt like an animal himself. **What were the animal sounds from inside like? How did they feel? The animal sounds from the abusers were like...and felt...**

4. A vampire is a metaphorical picture of "the living dead" and existing in the dark or night. This is a metaphor that the psyche is using to communicate and show Dave how he looks and feels, due to his inner trauma. His subconscious is trying to show how he truly feels and talks from his subconscious mind by creating an attraction to vampire movies. **What am I attracted to or obsessed about?** The obsession is a picture of how he is living. The psyche wants him to "see" himself more clearly. The subconscious mind and our dream states often try to communicate who, what and where we are to help us see

ourselves. If metaphorically, "the Light" is a spiritual light, representing the truth and vampires are people who have been hurt and want to avoid the truth, because it is too painful so they isolate in darkness after having the blood (representing the flow and beauty of life) sucked out of them. Vampires prefer isolation as do hurt people, because if they can remain in the "dark," all alone, their pain has less of a chance of being triggered—or being processed. Dave Boyle felt like a vampire because on many levels he was the living dead. **Why is Dave obsessing over vampire and werewolf movies?**

5. This trauma and his bonding patterns were killing Dave's capabilities for self-love and relationship love. He was in bondage. He had created a great wall around him. You cannot connect with yourself or someone else if you cannot own and speak about your truths, mentally and emotionally. The wall was meant to block past and future hurt. No one could get into his mind, heart or soul. **How does this affect his ability to love?**

6. Dave killed a man because he saw a boy in a car with an older man and the boy looked frightened. Dave was instantly "triggered." His subconscious took over. His mind went into the past and mixed it with the present. He felt and judged the little boy from his inner child's memories. He knew the boy needed him! He wanted to "save" the little boy because he "wished" someone would have saved him. The "wish" was stronger than logical thinking. He was not an evil man. This is how the brain works. This is what "losing it" means. It is time-traveling to the past and compounding it with a present-time situation. **Why did he kill someone?**

7. The murder could have been avoided if he had only had an honest outlet where he could rinse his pain with no fear of being called crazy and develop a sense of boundaries—spiritually, mentally, emotionally, physically, and sexually. He needed to be able to process. He simply suffered from Post Traumatic Syndrome (PTS). This syndrome is a *survival pat-*

tern that people who have suffered upsets and traumas develop as a technique to feel okay. PTS is full of protective behaviors that try to control or block memories and feelings; it is a survival mechanism, not a way to live. If we don't process our PTS, our memories and pain can be "triggered" and stay in our subconscious for the rest of our lives. "Crazy" is a judgment word for someone "stuck" or "lost" in pain. If Dave Boyle had understood himself he could have helped the boy, stopped the abuser, and taught the community what this is all about. **Could wisdom have happened here instead of violence? Could this killing have been avoided, or handled differently, if his pain had been processed? If so, how?**

8. The war and love of this neighborhood stemmed from fears, hurts, and lack of truth. When people "loved" someone, they "protected" that person even if it meant hurting or killing someone else they loved. Their power struggles were out of control. Their suppression and lies made everyone a "time bomb." Love easily turned to war, and war to love. This love and war pattern contained blocked, big feelings that easily became obsessions! The war, love, and obsession dynamic played out as a type of camaraderie. The camaraderie developed through a sharing of everyone's secret pain with no processing skill. Their secret pain bonded everyone in bondage, creating a type of intimacy. Through this war and love exchange, they celebrated and felt victorious using protective strength to celebrate the domination of each other's anger, fear, guilt and shame, calling it care, and worry. They all felt and lived in fear. **In this neighborhood, could you feel the war feelings and the human love feelings? Can you explain this in your own words? What did they create and why? How did they feel?**

9. Even the "good guy," Sean the cop, was disconnected and shut down. Unable to process his past thoughts, feelings, and memories, he was closed to intimacy, too. He had severe survival guilt. **Why was Dave taken and molested and not him? Why didn't he help him? Survival guilt kills self-love. Does**

he deserve joy or love? **What is your survival guilt and how does it affect your life today?**

10. The cop's wife left him while she was pregnant. It wasn't because she didn't love him, it was because she couldn't feel and connect to him. Being pregnant magnifies awareness and feelings of these issues. Hormones, negative thoughts, and misunderstood feelings from the past come forward and this is not a pretty mix if you can't own or process. She became aware that she couldn't be "seen" or "felt" by her husband because he couldn't "see" and "feel" himself. Notice, love without the truth wasn't enough. **Did the "cop," Sean, have his own war and love battles? What are they? Why couldn't he love his wife fully?**

Remember, all visuals are teachers, because visuals trigger and create memories and are the language of your psyche or subconscious mind and worth a thousand words.

One way to better understand a movie is to write a letter to the movie, or to a character from the movie.
    For example:

Pick a movie or character and write:

Dear _____ *, (movie or character)*
When I look at you I see...
And I feel...
And you remind me of...

When finished change the you's to "I's," "me's" and "my's" wherever possible to make this information about you. If the stories aren't exact matches, alter them just enough to fit your truths. Do this to *Mystic River* or any other movie or character.

All of this creates a picture to better "see" and understand yourself and others through someone or something outside yourself that mirrors you in some way.

We need to feel in order to feel alive. If we can't release feelings through truth, we'll release feelings through a "high" or shut them all down! Do not think you have no anger. There is no such thing on this planet. It is just a matter of time before someone or something loves you and then angers and scares you.

How Do Negative and Positive Energies Mix?

A positive number mixed with a negative number usually equals a negative or neutral. This mixture takes away our instinct to trust positive energy as we fear negative energy following. This mix can make us feel out of control, develop anxiety, hysteria and addictions, or shut down in depression and experience different levels of insanity.

A negative energy mixed or multiplied by another negative energy equals a positive. What is that about? Well, let's see. If a negative action is processed with its true negative feelings and is understood and owned, it creates change. The truth of negative thoughts, feelings or behaviors with negative events and feelings equals a positive outcome because they evolve into truth and clarity. This negative pile of energy flips to a positive result called wisdom. Sounds positive to me.

A positive energy does not make a negative go away or visa versa. Each has its own energy and message.

War is a high! It's full of positive and negative mixed energies: The goal of "good" and rescuing, having rights and compassion mixed with murder, prisoners, trauma and disconnection, creates insanity. Most of us are not skilled or patient enough to take anyone through this kind of pain because we will get triggered ourselves. So to protect ourselves, we judge people scared and traumatized as broken, and then drug them with little or no hope of a way out. Is it because there is no hope or because we would have to work very hard on ourselves to take anyone through the trauma of their pain and dark side?

The Vietnam War—A Passive/Aggressive War

Many who served in the Vietnam War experienced tremendous mental and emotional torment. For example, a soldier could be walking through gorgeous lands, feeling calm and peaceful, while up above him, the beautiful trees camouflaged a sniper. The very atmosphere set soldiers up to be caught off guard. They felt sucker-punched and nervous, at all times. Could this positive and negative energy mix be so twisted that it could take a perfectly balanced person and flip that person, subconsciously, into PTS (post traumatic syndrome)? Could that person become so frightened and untrusting of positive images that he or she lives triggered by simple pleasures only to see them as bad as horror pictures? Could this create paranioas, phobias and superstitions? Is this the insanity we so-called regular people hear about? This is an anxiety disorder that can last years after the war is over if there is no psychic deprogramming. This is not a logical process, so keep logic out of it.

The horrible experiences of Vietnam veterans could easily take their psyches to an insane place fast. Just imagine, for a moment, that there is a sniper in your vicinity, right now, about to end your life. Now try to imagine that this is always the case, day and night. Can you see how that might affect your psyche? It is the same kind of trauma that many victims of domestic violence or child abuse experience, never knowing when the next explosion is going to happen. It's the way that prisoners feel in jail, the way that street cops feel on the street.

Some people who've been traumatized like this live waiting and waiting for that bullet for the rest of their lives. Do you "see" the anxiety and insanity that can result? And since anxiety releases chemicals (adrenaline, peptides), can you see how prolonged exposure to such stressors can lead to an overload or to being out of balance, in all realms? This creates mental, emotional and often even physical symptoms such as stomachaches, headaches and heart palpitations.

The Vietnam War was full of hiding, waiting, and surprise attacks. Does that sound like your life, sometimes? We may not all be veterans, but we all have to "see" the warfare in our own lives.

The American Civil War—An Aggressive/Passive War

Using the American Civil War as our next metaphor, America's Northern and Southern states lined up a bunch of cannons and guns, formed a frontline, and blew each other up. Do you think that the soldiers in the frontline knew that they were probably going to die? Each and every one of them was, in some sense, a kamikaze. Every soldier knew he had to be willing to die.

Civil War soldiers were trained to think: "If I run away, everyone behind me will know it. I will be humiliated, and my family will be humiliated, and shunned, and perhaps even killed. The only way to have honor is to prepare myself to die." This is a type of survival skill based on brainwashing. If you create a thought and mix it with strong feelings that sink in, you have a belief.

Honor. Do you think Japanese Kamikaze pilots used that word in WWII? Do you think that suicide bombers in Iraq use it? Notice the power of the mix of fear, which is negative, with honor and bravery as a positive and suicide, which feels negative to me.

What kind of mentality was used to train you to be aggressive in order to survive? In the aggressive/passive mix, your passive self holds your vulnerabilities, feelings of love, peace, anger, fear, guilt, shame, hurt, and sadness. These feelings are not allowed to be activated, because if they were, you couldn't complete your "mission." Soldiers are programmed to shut down on the inside, to focus on outward strength. It's a purposeful numbing. These are tools for survival, but do you want to live this way?

When we dominate our fear in order to survive, we attempt to dominate all of our thoughts, feelings and behaviors. This creates aggressive/passive energy. We live among barriers and rigid rules, not boundaries and self-awareness. We are unable to own our thoughts, feelings, or truths, because we are living in a suppressed emotional lie. We are not our true selves. We are stubborn and bossy or a zombie follower. Because we are not truly living, we are often living dead inside. Death feels like a relief to some people existing in these situations. Suicide is about killing the pain, not the person.

People in an aggressive/passive situation are often operating in a state of high ego, flying far above their true thoughts, feelings and memories. In a passive/aggressive situation, where everything beautiful creates a fear of disaster, people lie low, "under" their thoughts and feelings. Hiding and omitting information, they are suffocated and suppressed, and not truly alive.

Unhealthy Passive/Aggressive Person	Healthy Patient/Assertive Person
1. Holds and hides feelings inside; fear-based, self-beating.	1. Understands and processes thoughts, feelings, and memories.
2. Judges self as stupid and shut down.	2. Is self-loving with understanding and boundaries.
3. Insecure in self-doubt.	3. Appreciates that mistakes are an opportunity for wisdom.
4. Acts in surprise attacks. Is overly concerned with image.	4. Asks a question before going directly to an answer or statement. Approaches; does not confront.
5. Has nice guy/girl syndrome (image).	5. Doesn't think for others.
6. Needs attention and validation, but denies it.	6. Questions own thoughts and feelings to reach a deeper self-understanding.
7. Disguises emotions, both to self and others. Passiveness turns into a judgmental and punishing energy causing a type of lying/denying, creating anger internally and externally.	7. Makes no judgments. Moves immediately toward understanding.
8. Says what he/she "thinks" people want to hear.	8. Processes to understand all perceptions of self and others—and "owns."
9. Hates self; never good enough.	9. By owning, feels loving and peaceful about being unique.
10. Is untrustworthy—often nicknamed "the Snake." Uses words and behaviors that don't match.	10. Without an attitude, asks permission to enter another's physical or emotional space. Allows others their own space.
11. Denies anger. People love this behavioral type until they get too close. People find out this "nice person" will never be open and honest.	11. Listens without anger, fear or judgment.
12. Is powerless. Has no trust in personal instincts or intuition.	12. Owns and understands self and others. Is honest and intuitive.
13. Overly controlled and suppressed. Selfless.	13. Respects others; doesn't need to control.
14. Liar, people-pleaser. Someone is always "better than" or "less than."	14. Does not self-beat. Has no need to be "better than" or "less than."
15. A codependent, who creates anxiety due to fear of self-beating and judgment from self and others. Loves in a care and worry way with no truth.	15. Shows no care or worry. Only wisdom.

Unhealthy
Aggressive/ Passive

Healthy
Assertive/ Patient

1. Holds and hides feelings inside that are anger-based; attacks others.

1. Understands and processes thoughts, feelings and memories.

2. Overly strong/pushy.

2. Is self-loving with understanding and boundaries.

3. Arrogant/righteous.

3. Appreciates that mistakes are an opportunity for wisdom.

4. Intimidating/confrontational

4. Asks a question before going direct-ly to an answer or statement. Approaches; does not confront.

5. Controlling and bossy. The aggres-sive person first denies his truth, which causes him to become con-trolling, inward toward self and out-ward toward others. Speaks in state-ments.

5. Doesn't think for others.

6. Needs to be the center of attention.

6. Questions own thoughts and feel-ings to reach a deeper self-under-standing.

7. Very judgmental. Aggressiveness turns into a judgmental and punish-ing energy, creating fear.

7. Makes no judgments. Moves imme-diately toward understanding.

8. Blames everyone for everything. Denies personal truths and creates more fear by attempting to domi-nate everyone's thoughts, feelings and ideas.

8. Processes to understand all percep-tions of self and others—and "owns."

9. Denies hurt and vulnerability. Is always right.

9. By owning feels loving and peaceful about being unique.

10. Is a denied victim with a chip on his/her shoulder.

10. Without an attitude, asks permis-sion to enter another's physical or emotional space. Allows others their own space.

11. Denies fear. People fear and some-times hate and avoid this behavioral type. People often blatantly lie to this behavioral type—definitely by omission.

11. Listens without anger, fear or judg-ment.

12. Is power hungry—lives in fear of personal aggressiveness.

12. Owns and understands self and others. Is honest and intuitive.

13. No self control. Selfish.

13. Respects others, doesn't need to control.

14. Egotistical.

14. Does not self-beat. Has no need to be "better than" or "less than."

15. Is a "know-it-all" who rarely knows the whole truth, including his or her own self truth. Love must be proven.

15. Shows no care or worry. Only wisdom.

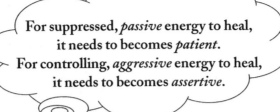

For suppressed, *passive* energy to heal,
it needs to becomes *patient*.
For controlling, *aggressive* energy to heal,
it needs to becomes *assertive*.

It's time to write!

1. In what ways can you be passive?

2. Why do you think you are passive?

3. When you were growing up, who in your life was passive?

4. What do you remember about that person's behavior?

5. How did that person's behavior make you feel?

Greediness is Neediness

Opposites have the same base again, they attract and repel. For healing, link them together and flip-flop back and forth. Needy is low ego and greedy is high ego. Where is the balance?

> **Needy = Greedy**

People can become needy simply because their unique personality is not understood by themselves, their family, friends, or educators. A lack of understanding creates a needy feeling. If understanding is what love is, then not being understood can cause an emptiness and a void inside from not feeling loved. This emptiness turns into needy energy, shutting down self-awareness, and is not processed to be understood by itself. This person can become passive/aggressive.

Needy's energy can easily turn into a greedy energy. This is an inner child craving. Unfortunately anyone playing a parent role while you are actually an adult is too late and it will come off as controlling. Adults have to self-parent themselves or be controlled. We can never get enough if we are waiting for someone else to fill our void. If I come to you as an adult for understanding, no amount of your understanding will ever satiate me. I will just be greedy for more. Only by understanding myself will I satisfy my neediness and cease to be greedy.

If you are passive, you can come off as needy, greedy.

If I am aggressive/passive, then I start off in greedy energy. I want something from you and I fully intend to dominate and get it. The greedy energy is still based on needy energy. So while it might look like I'm greedy for what you have—love, money, understanding, power, sex—what I really am is needy inside for my inner child to be understood by my parents or caretakers. I am lost without you because I'm lost within me. The only way I'm getting out of this aggressive/passive, greedy/needy cycle is to start giving myself what I really need, which is self-understanding and self-boundaries.

If you are aggressive, you can come off as greedy, needy.

Whatever we hate, resist, or disown still has its own energy, existence and vibe. Whatever we resist—persists! The stronger we resist the truth, the more hurt and confusion grow energetically. Resisted thoughts, feelings, and beliefs become manipulative, and controlling! Just because we don't like our thoughts, feelings and memories doesn't mean they will go away.

1. Is being mentally and emotionally passive a form of abuse to yourself or other people in your life? Why?

2. How can passive energy create aggressiveness?

3. In what way are you aggressive?

4. Why do you think you are aggressive?

5. When you were growing up, who in your life was aggressive?

6. What do you remember about that person's behavior?

7. How did that person's behavior make you feel?

8. How does self-beating create passive energy?

9. How does self-beating create aggressive energy?

10. How are you needy? Why are you needy?

11. How are you greedy? Why are you greedy?

12. Why is "no" such a difficult word for nice, passive/aggressive people to say?

13. How does saying the word "no" make *you* feel?

14. Why is "no" such an immediate word for aggressive/passive people?

Fear of "No"

The fear of saying "no" begins with feeling scared or guilty about how people will react to it. "No" is a part of truth. "No" can create struggles. You better see struggle as a step towards our journey to wisdom and peace.

Why are struggles "bad?" A struggle can often stimulate and inspire people. Why should we miss the opportunity to be inspired? Inspiration is a creative energy that comes from your subconscious. A struggle is the first step to new thoughts, feelings and behaviors. These truth struggles are a crucial step toward owning who you are and developing wisdom. "No" is a map that shows you and others where you and they can and cannot go. That's all. "No" is not a rejection if "no" is the truth. No is a limit.

> **No struggle,
> no growth!**

Remember when we talked about opposites having the same base issues? The same is true about passive energy and aggressive energy!

> Trust that something new will happen once you understand a struggle.
>
> Aggressive attacks are filled with anger—they create guilt and spread more fear inside and out!
>
> Passive shutdowns are filled with fear—they create shame and spread more anger inside and out!

Point/Counterpoint

Passive and aggressive warfare feeds the judger and makes owning impossible. Passive energy usually acts as if it lives in the wrong and aggressive energy acts as if it lives in the right. People who need to be "right" argue and debate. They behave greedily, but inside still feel needy. If they don't understand that their issues stem from the past, everyone is going to spin.

People who need to be right don't learn from others easily. Rather than listen and understand, they are more concerned about making points. They personalize everything and react. This kind of negative communication goes on every day, all over the world. It's a major reason why people don't get along, and why wars are fought.

Take a look at the bonding patterns below, where Shannon and Keith are point/counterpointing. Does this look familiar to you?

POINT/COUNTERPOINT!

Shannon makes a point!

"I was pissed that you left me alone at the party."

Without addressing or hearing Shannon's point, Keith makes a different point. There has been no understanding or closure to the first point.

"It was a great party and I deserve to have a good time."

Shannon casts aside her original point, and makes a new one related or unrelated to Keith's point!

"My parents used to take me to adult parties and leave me with strangers while they had a good time."

Keith, not to be outdone, makes another counter-point before there has been an understanding or closure to any of the three previous points.

"I saw lots of people I knew at the party and wanted to talk to everyone."

1. Do Keith and Shannon sound needy and then greedy to be understood from each other with no responsibility?

2. Are they in adult energy or inner child hurts?

3. Do they know they are in inner child issues?

4. Are Shannon and Keith getting anywhere? Are they moving any closer toward understanding each other?

5. Could they be needy?

7. What was the situation? Why? About what?

6. Have you ever done this? Why do you think you acted the way you did?

Love and war are what we know. We've learned it from our families, our coaches, our teachers, the news, and from TV and movies. Battling and warring may not feel good, but they feel comfortable, because they represent what we know.

On the other hand, few of us have been taught how to love ourselves or to be loveable. We may be miserable, but we're comfortable with our war-like behavior, which invariably wins out over unknown thoughts and feelings like love, owning and understanding.

> Hey! You argue just like my parents used to!
> This is awful!
>
> But...strangely comfortable!
>
> Let's get married!

Open Communication
Here are some tips on how to enhance open communication:

Listen and Make Notes
- When someone makes a point, listen and understand that point before making your point. Wait a few beats. If you are truly listening to understand, take a breath of air and let that person finish talking.

- Write down your points. If you are afraid or feel rushed, you may forget them. Jot them down so you feel less pressure about getting back to them.

- Take turns making and understanding a point, without interrupting each other.

- When someone brings up a point, take the time to own and understand that point before moving on to your point. Understand first!

- There is no need to personalize a point or react to it if your goal is to understand and grow.

- Where possible, ask questions instead of making statements. Questions will help you "see" another's points more clearly, and even your own.

Use Humor
- It's great to be funny and "light." Free up this part of yourself. Humor can break the tension and allow many thoughts and feelings to surface.

- Humor stimulates creativity.

- Humor breaks down the hierarchy, so no one views others as "above" or "below" them. Hierarchy sets up competition, which sets up insecurity and jealousy.

- Don't mistake sarcasm for humor! Sarcasm is unprocessed anger, fear, guilt, shame, and hurt mixed with humor. This can be a weapon.

Create a Feeling
- **Feeling and memory go together**. For memory to work, feelings and visuals are vital. By drawing pictures, telling or writing stories, your memory subconsciously activates and awakens your wisdom and awareness. You can create new behaviors as you own and understand yourself through feelings and visualizations.

- **A picture is a sensory skill that stimulates memory and creativity**. Stories create pictures within your mind. A picture, whether metaphorical or literal, can activate other, subliminal pictures. If you're open to learning (without judgment), your memories and creativity will start to flow.

- **Share yourself.** Being open means understanding that there is no right and no wrong. Without a sense of right and wrong, fear and judgments do not enter your energy. Share and own your thoughts, feelings and memories with awareness. Go with the flow.

- **Help yourself not become defensive**. When you become defensive, you are personalizing. Either you or someone else has triggered your unprocessed thoughts, feelings and memories. Both defensiveness, sales pitching and proving are reactive behaviors. These reactions and projections sabotage efforts for understanding and clarity.

- **Think of yourself as part of a team** with everyone else. There are no enemies! Even scary, angry people aren't enemies; they are just people whose actions have been triggered by upsetting messages of their own. Everyone is a messenger. The message may not be delivered honestly or lovingly, but if you can listen for the message and not the delivery, much is to be learned.

- **Welcome and understand different ideas and opinions**, whether you agree with them or not. Be an example of who you want to be and how you want others to be. Others will soon come to understand you by watching you. Be patient. Understanding may not happen right away. Breathe, write and own.

- **We are all facilitators and guides for each other**, as well as for ourselves.

- **Talk, listen and behave the way you want others to talk, listen and behave.**

The Frustration of Point/Counterpoint
by Mona

I want to scream at the top of my lungs!

My girlfriend and I just had a five-minute **point/counterpoint**. Luckily, we became aware of what we were doing in time to stop it from getting out of hand, but still, I'm so frustrated! She is highly intelligent with a typical Brooklyn-Italian edge. Her career has trained her to be powerful and authoritarian. Help me!

Don't cross people like her—tough, smart, and trained to attack. This is fun if you want to:

Yell	Get locked up and go "crazy"
Throw things	Shut down and submit
Become hysterical	

She's a 5' 5" pitbull. I call her Mighty Mouse. From this book, thus far, you can probably sense what I'm like when I'm "off center." If we have a difference in perception, we two egotistical, stubborn "know it alls" will fight to the very end.

So here's the dispute. We were planning to book a hotel for friends and ourselves for her birthday. She called the hotel and they offered her a room for $139 a night. I found a room in the same hotel on the Internet for $124 per night. I called to tell her the good news.

Let the games begin:

Her: I booked the hotel!

Me: No, I booked the hotel!

Her: I got a deal for $139.00 a night.

Me: I got a deal of $124.00 a night.

Her: (She will now defend her point). That's impossible; I got the last room. (She's ignored my point about getting a better deal, and made a counterpoint. She is ready to defend this point. Her tone is getting stronger and her back is stiffening).

TRUTH is saying: Who cares? Drop it?

BUT—

Me: (I shall now prove my point). Listen. I've traveled around the world and there happen to be different prices under different packages for the same places if you go under different programs. (I've ignored her point about getting the last room and stayed on my original point about different deals for different rooms. Oh, and I'm smug. She hasn't done her research; I have, she's wrong, I'm right.)

Her: (She will now sell her point). That is not true! A hotel could not do that legally! (A new counterpoint! The law! She's moving to familiar territory for her).

TRUTH is pleading with us: Who cares? Drop it!

Me: My head hurts.

Her: That's because you're being stubborn.

Me: Oh, like you're so easy to talk with. (Great. Now I'm being sarcastic. I'm not addressing her point on whether I'm stubborn or not; I'm just attacking her back.)

Her: (Nothing) Uh, oh. (Now she's going passive/aggressive. When two people are being passive/aggressive, the conversation doesn't have much of a future. Note that being silent is a counterpoint, because the previous point is still being ignored. Silence is an energy and therefore a statement.)

Me: Let's just drop it. I'm sure your reservation is just fine. (I've now ignored the many counterpoints and returned to some original point from way back when, while tossing in some more guilt and minimizing her feelings. Think this is going to help?)

Her: Oh, no. I'm always "wrong." Remember? (Sigh. New counterpoint. Fights from the past. Plus sarcasm, more passive/aggression, guilt talk...)

Me: This is so stupid! What a dumb fight! I'm just judging us and taking us on our, what, fifth path in one argument? Agh. We're spinning and I'm about ready to shut down.

Do you see why I want to scream? Passive staring, heavy breathing, laser eyes, aggressive/passive jabs.... After being worn down, we "know it alls" realized that I booked a regular room for $124.00. She booked a suite for $139.00. Who knew? Did we have to point/counterpoint?

Do you recognize this pattern? If you keep repeating yourself, you'll just create **hysterical deafness**, meaning…the repeating of information with the lack of owning and understanding creates hysteria for people making righteous, stubborn points that shut down hearing, ending in mental and emotional deafness. Ever experienced it yourself?

There is a gift of wisdom on the other side of every struggle.

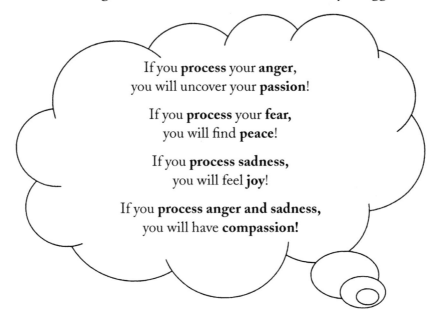

If you **process** your **anger,**
you will uncover your **passion!**

If you **process** your **fear,**
you will find **peace!**

If you **process sadness,**
you will feel **joy!**

If you **process anger and sadness,**
you will have **compassion!**

Chapter Review

I just learned…
I feel…

Summary

Aggressive: Aggressive people hold on to anger. If they don't process *anger*, the best they can be is…*intense*. (Intensity is passion mixed with anger, fear, guilt and shame.)

Passive: Passive people hold on to fear. If they don't process *fear*, the best they can be is…**content**. (Contentment is a false sense of peace. It is a shutdown mixed with fear, stuck in a depression, yet functioning!)

Aggressive and Passive: Aggressive and passive people hold on to sadness. If they don't process *sad*, the best they can be is…*codependent*. (Codependent is victim energy, helpless, stuck in blocked sadness with no action. They will end up in self-pity, feeling alone or living for others.)

Let the games begin!

9 True Love:
What's Love Got to Do with Care?

To answer the question "What is love?"—first, we need to talk about what love is not.

Love Is Not Care and Worry

When is caring love? When caring is in the form of supporting someone incapable of being responsible for themselves, mentally, emotionally, physically, sexually or financially.

To care otherwise can cause havoc, accidentally. Feel free to look up the word care in your dictionary. Care often felt upsetting to me and I couldn't figure out why. When someone cared for me I felt suffocated, guilty or often controlled. Look at what I found. And yes, I was shocked, yet it felt true.

Do you want to fully understand this? The next box gives you an example of how to take any vocabulary word and personalize it. Take the definition and put "I," "me" or "my" wherever possible throughout the definition so you can see yourself in the word and put the words into sentences. Go ahead and try it for yourself.

Understanding care as an anxiety disorder will alter your perception of love and show you why we fear it. I have taken two of the main ingredients for care and worry and personalized the definitions by inserting "I" throughout. You will see how being caring and worrying changes the intention of love to fear, anxiety and control.

Anxiety Disorder = Care and Worry

Webster's New World Definition:

> **CARE:** Anxiety, pain, heed, charge, oversight, has regard or liking.

Using "I," "me" or "my" with Webster's Definition:

When I **care** I have *anxiety* and *pain* towards anything I care about. I take *heed* and *charge* which causes *oversights* over anything I have *regard* or a *liking* for.

Webster's New World Definition:

> **WORRY:** Seize or trouble, harass, utterly concerned, with useless care or anxiety.

Using "I," "me" or "my" with Webster's Definition:

When I **worry** I go to *seize* someone or something which creates *trouble*. I *harass* others and myself when I am worried by being *utterly concerned with useless care*, creating *anxiety*.

When I care about people, I take them over and try to control them. Why? Because I love them. So loving them becomes about how I feel and how they are affecting me. I can't tell you how many times I've heard statements like, "I'm yelling at you because I care about you. I can't sleep because I'm worried about you. How could you not call me back, don't you care about me? I'm spanking you because I care about you. I could be like those other parents and not care how you turn out."

Whenever someone cared or worried about me, I wanted to scream.... *Don't care and worry about me, please!* How can I possibly think care is love when all I feel is anger, fear, guilt and shame when someone cares or worries about me? Care feels fine when it is caretaking such as emergency assistance. Other than that, care feels controlling and makes me hysterical or shut down.

When people care about me, I don't feel understood. I feel I have to understand them. If people worry about me, I feel they have no faith in me. I do not feel empowered; I feel weak and powerless. If I make a mistake or need help, I like questions and ideas for support. I do not want anyone to tell me what to think, feel or do. Life is full of lessons. Can you have faith in me to figure things out? If you ask me questions, I can be stimulated to think differently. Let me learn my lessons and find my purpose without you personalizing my life.

If you are worried about me, you are really worried about you. If you are caring for me, you are saving yourself from upsetting or uncomfortable thoughts or feelings.

I Should've Had Some Damn Coffee and She Wouldn't Have Been Mad at Me!

When I was about twenty years old, I saw a young woman on the streets of New York City, in the winter, on the ground, hurt, in a fur coat with shorts and a halter top underneath the coat. This seemed strange to me. Why was she wearing such an outfit at night, in the dead of winter? It was about 3:15 A.M. I was coming home from a late shift at work, when I saw her there, lying on the sidewalk. I told the driver of the cab to stop. He said, "Don't put that whore into my cab." I was shocked he said such words. I said, "Please don't make me leave her here." He reluctantly said, "Okay." So we loaded her into the cab and dragged her up to my apartment. I washed her wounds and stayed by her side all night until she awoke in the morning.

When she woke up, I smiled and said, "Are you alright?" The young woman said, "Who the hell are you?" I was taken aback at her tone. She seemed so angry. Of course, I know now, anger represents blocked fear, and who wouldn't be scared waking up in a stranger's apartment? She then said, "What are you, some god damn, good Samaritan? You know, no one asked you for any help, so know you did this for yourself. You didn't help me. Do you have any coffee?" I replied, "No, I'm sorry, I don't." Then she really flew off the handle. "Well, fuck you! And the next time you want to help someone, have some damn coffee!" She then slammed my front door and left. Well, as you can imagine, I was dumbfounded. What just happened? All I did was simply "care" and "worry" about someone. I was being a "good" person.

I later learned how the streets worked. You should not mess with things you don't understand. You see, she was a prostitute, which explained the clothes. The reason she was so pissed was because in my "caring," I knew nothing of what I was doing. If a prostitute leaves the eyesight of a pimp, she better come back with some cash or else...cigarette burns on her arms or legs, a beating, a rape or worse. I was lucky I wasn't robbed. She could have hurt me and didn't. She took a big chance leaving me empty-handed. I can do more now because I have learned when to step in and when not to. Helping when not asked to help is about you and your feelings. Helping when asked is supportive.

If you see a parent be abusive to a child and this upsets you, do you correct this parent, grab the child or lovingly ask the parent if he or she is okay? If you upset the parent, that child will pay for it later, because the parent will blame that child for your intervention. So did you help or were you reactive in a way that was about you and your feelings?

So, when you find yourself caring, ask yourself, "What am I caring about, and why? What am I worried about? What do I see in this person that teaches me something about myself? Why am I worried about me? Is it my issue that's triggering me?"

1. What happens when you "care" about yourself or others?

2. Can you think of an example of when "caring" for others hurt them, or held them back? Or when someone else's "care" about you hurt you or held you back?

3. How does it feel when someone cares about you without faith? How about when you care about someone else, without faith?

4. If someone cares about you, or you care about someone else, do you find yourself lying or withholding truth to not upset someone? Does caring hurt truth? Explain.

5. How does it feel when someone loves you without care? How does it feel when you love someone without care?

6. Can you think of examples of how you were helped (or touched) by someone loving you without care or worry? Or how you helped (or touched) someone by loving them without care or worry?

Love Is Not Fear

Real Love Scares Me
by Kelly

Dear Mona,

I have to quit working with you because if I keep on this path, changes might actually happen. I know that I'm close to something different. But I'm afraid of what different is like.

This path I'm on looks great...I can picture it. I will fall in love, get married, and have children. I'll be able to travel and provide my children with a life better than the one I have. My work will make the world a better place and I will laugh so much it hurts. I will have people who support me and love me for who I am.

But honestly, Mona, this "real love" that I see in my future scares me to death! I truly believe that real love hurts, more than I can stand. And the risk is too great.

Don't you get it? I know loss. Real loss, it's called death. My biological father died when I was very young. He was the only true love I'd ever felt. I never want to endure such loss again.

I've made a lot of progress, haven't I? Can't I just say, "That's it, I'm done"? Can't I just say, "This is good enough"? Mediocre is enough. You piss me off every week, Mona! Why do you want more from me? I've done a lot of growing and changing! If I grow more I'll kill everyone in my family! Literally!

Why? My family can't handle the truth. They can't own what they've done to themselves, or to me, or to each other. If I get too honest and too loving, they will "see" the truth in me, and in them, and they'll die!

So what if I'm a coda? Who cares! Shut up! I never thought I would get this happy. I've stopped drugs, gambling, drinking, and lying. Let's just celebrate that. Who needs wisdom? It's too much!

Let me explain this in terms of weight. Say, I've lost thirty-five pounds, and there are fifteen more to go before I'm no longer "overweight." But if I lose the last fifteen pounds, that last weight is tied most tightly to guilt, my family will be able to see the real me. If they realize their mistakes they'll get hurt. Then they'll feel so "bad" they might start to hurt themselves. If they hurt themselves, I will feel guilty, and go back to the way I was.

I'd rather just keep the fifteen pounds, Mona—literally and metaphorically. Let them wear sunglasses so the "light" won't hurt their eyes. They can understand enough to get by, but not too much. They don't have the skill or openness to not self-beat themselves to death! They'll crumble. They act tough, but they're really not tough!

Mona, leave me alone!

～

Here's what I wrote back to Kelly.

Dear Kelly:

When I was thirty years old, my parents and I were going through a rough patch. We were barely speaking to each other. But in one of our brief conversations, my mother announced that there was a group of our relatives, whom I had never known anything about, living right near me in California. When we got off the phone, I was so upset.

It took a while before I looked them up, and called. I was afraid of what they would be like. I made so many excuses not to come and see them that finally they just came to see me.

They were wonderful. One of my cousins spoke with so much understanding I shook inside. I didn't know what to do. Part of me wanted to run out the door and cry hysterically. The other part of me wanted to grab her and never let go. What was this?

They barely even knew me, yet they invited my son and me over for Christmas. They spoiled us with presents and so much love. They didn't drink. There were no freak-outs. No fights. No trauma. It actually made me scared way inside. I kept waiting for that surprise fight, but none came. There were only gifts, gifts, and more gifts. And they didn't even know us! Why were they doing this?

I grew more and more uncomfortable. They had no judgment or "care" about who we were. Their attitude was: just come on in!

At the end of the night, as I was thanking them, one of my cousins hugged me with such warmth, I simply lost it. I sobbed in her arms in front of everyone for an hour and a half. I felt traumatized by the unconditional love from these strangers. Yes, love made me scared and hysterical.

Kelly, when love first enters your life, it feels like it hurts. It can feel scary in a way! Love gets a bad rap. It's not love hurting you. It's love triggering the hurts so you can understand them and heal the pain.

Love doesn't cause the pain. Only by understanding pain can we grow and move on. Love entered me that day, Kelly! Love triggered my mental, emotional, physical, and sexual pain and memories for what seemed like forever. But it wasn't forever.

You're not crazy, Kelly. You're healing your hurts through love's understanding of the hurt! It gets easier. You may have to "let go" of your family for a while, and that might make you *feel* like you're losing them. But you're not. Remember, feelings aren't necessarily facts. Separation is often necessary for patterns to be broken. Just focus on you, keep changing and growing, and let them (and you) be afraid or angry. As you grow wiser and stronger, your family's fear will calm down and they'll probably come back. No promises, but it worked for me! The love I feel for myself has healed many hurts with my family and old friends. We're better than ever. We get to really love each other, rather than just spend time together harboring silent resentments.

It's a chance worth taking.

1. Have you loved and been twisted with anger, fear, guilt, shame and hurt? Can you explain?

2. *Love with fear is like...*
   And it feels...
   And it creates...

3. *Love with guilt is like...*
   And it feels...
   And it creates...

4. *Love with shame is like...*
   And it feels...
   And it creates...

5. *Love with hurt is like...*
   And it feels...
   And it creates...

6. *Love with anger is like...*
   And it feels...
   And it creates...

7. What happens if you separate love and truth?
   a. *Love without truth is like...*
      And it feels...
      And it creates...
   b. *Truth without love is like...*
      And it feels...
      And it creates...

Love is Not Scary

Love is Not Shame

Love is Not Guilt

Love is Not Anger

Love Does Not Hurt

If your experience of love has left you with a memory of hurt, there's a good chance that you are not going to let yourself get near "true love," even if you want it. You will create codependency, guilt, martyrdom, fear, shame, master/slave relationships or victimization. If you mix positive and negative energy you're going to get pain.

No wonder we mix love and fear. Is love scary because we drop truth? Is that what losing yourself means, dropping your truth? Do I coda you or do I love you? Big difference. Have you ever heard, "I'm so scared, I think I could fall in love with you"? Well, *there's* a formula for failure! A negative, I'm so scared, and a positive, I could love you. Is anyone listening to what anyone is saying?

How do you get over the hurt, pain, and fear of childhood twists and old relationships? How crucial is it for you to love you before you even think of loving someone else? This is incredibly hard for many of us. Schools don't have classes on "self-love." But if they did, the "rules" would probably look something like this:

The Rules of Self-Love

1. Want to love someone? Love yourself first.
2. No blaming your thoughts and feelings on others.
3. Take responsibility for yourself. Nobody owes you anything, including a living.
4. You can't have clarity without sobriety.
5. Your goal is not to be right, it's to understand.
6. Your goal is not to fight over points that are not the point. Do not engage in point/counterpoint.
7. Do not choose an "air-head" routine. Face the truth.
8. Own your role in any situation.
9. Know your weaknesses and embrace them. Only by loving them through understanding will you be able to even see them.
10. Don't expect anyone to understand or accept your weaknesses before you do.
11. Learn to let go of control battles.
12. Don't fight over "stupid" stuff.
13. Avoid telling others how and what to do.
14. Accept people for who and how they are.
15. Develop your sense of humor.
16. Learn not to shut down.
17. Share thoughts, feelings, and beliefs; they lead to intimacy.
18. Don't save or protect others. Relationships should not be about rescuing and saving.
19. Don't go down with the ship. Preserve yourself rather than a relationship.
20. Nobody is better or worse than anyone else.
21. Gossip does nobody any good.
22. Understand and set boundaries for yourself.
23. Understand the good, bad, and ugly truths of your loved one, with no attitude.
24. Love your truths first. Love yourself second. Love others third.

Love Is Not Stubborn

If you refuse to emotionally process your experiences by going back in time to understand how and why you feel hurt and scared, then stubbornness will build a wall around your heart and soul. Stubbornness is the center of fear. It is a false sense of self and power that will put you in your ego mode and shut down your intuition.

You've heard the song "Feelings"? It's called "Feelings," not "Feeling!" That's because we have so many feelings, all at once.

However, when we get caught in stubbornness, we stay stuck in one feeling. (For example, fear, anger, or disappointment.) Stubbornness is like a spider web. Once its sticky fibers grab you, it's very difficult to get out. When we are able to "let go" of being stubborn and allow the rest of our feelings to come out, the first feelings out of the gate are usually anger and fear. Don't forget that anger and fear are attached to guilt and shame.

Underneath, there is sadness and hurt. All of these feelings are hidden by our stubbornness. Only if we lift stubbornness can we "see" what's under its hood.

All our feelings want is attention and understanding. Every feeling has something to tell us. Every feeling has an energy. If this energy is not understood, we end up suppressed. If we are suppressed, then we become depressed.

Find your stubborn voice!

To move through your "stuck" emotion, you need to find your stubborn voice. Stubborn energy is attached to fears and self-beats. So find all three to pull the root out of this weed.

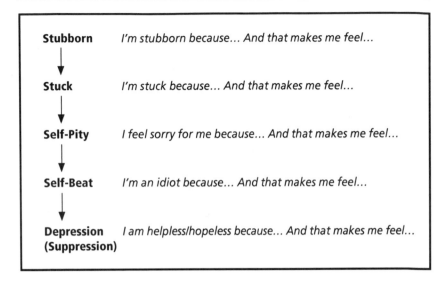

Stubbornness thinks it's a "good guy" giving you strength and power. But the truth is:

1. Being stubborn keeps fear alive.
2. Being stubborn allows no love or truth in.
3. Being stubborn keeps you self-beating and blaming.
4. Being stubborn means you have to be right, and creates pressure.
5. People who are stubborn have no understanding of different truths.
6. Being stubborn keeps you acting in egotistical ways.
7. Your egotistical ways will manifest in insecurity or arrogance.
8. When you're stubborn, you block your inner child's voice, memories and feelings, as well as your spirit's intuition and ability "to know."
9. A stubborn person doesn't take the time to "check-in" with true thoughts and feelings.
10. Being stubborn is a survival skill! Processing is a living skill! Do you want to just survive, or live?

If you are living in fear, then stubbornness is here. Do whatever you can to force yourself to take an action that will push through fear and stubbornness. A stubborn person is an emotional person, stuck in one feeling.

An Emotional Person   versus   A Feeling Person

An Emotional Person

1. **Emotional** is *one* feeling, stuck and spinning.

2. **Uncomfortable.** When we keep circling in anger, fear, guilt, shame, sadness, or self-pity with no understanding, we make ourselves and other people uncomfortable. Often, others don't know why they are uncomfortable around us, but they know they can't help us, and it *seems* we can't help ourselves.

3. **Self-pity** is an *emotional state*, not a *feeling* one. Self-pity *circles* in sadness because the self-pity is not processing and understanding the sadness. Self-pity is victim energy and it will not change any behavior or become its own rescuer.

4. **No recovery or changes** are possible when we are emotional, so we can't move *through* a struggle. We are spinning inside on a feeling, while our conscious focus is on someone or something outside us.

5. **We're waiting** for someone to come and get us and tell us what's going on. We have no self-understanding, ability to process, or change. "Waiting" is an anger word.

6. **We're "stuck"** in an emotional state, and that creates frustration from stubbornness. Having no processing makes it worse. Either we do not speak at all or we speak in statements of arrogant knowingness with no openness.

7. **We have no question-and-answer technique** for our feelings. We just repeat or shut down our thoughts, feelings, and memories.

8. **We have no understanding of self.** We judge instead of feeling ourselves and/or others.

9. **We're out of control and personalize.** We are narcissists. Everything is about us, in a negative and helpless way.

10. **We blame others** for our victim life, for our feelings and situations.

11. **We punish and are vindictive.** We gossip and spin in our stories, going nowhere fast. Fighting inside and/or outside.

12. **We are depressed and shutdown.**

A Feeling Person

1. **Feelings** are energy and vibrations. Feelings move through each other.

2. **Feelings travel like a school of fish,** in groups, affecting each other delivering messages that can change our thoughts and feelings. Feelings can stimulate our senses and show us pictures to help us find actions.

3. **Sadness is a feeling we know we can use to rescue ourselves.** We process to release and understand our sadness. Then we change our own thoughts and behaviors. We don't need someone else to fix or change us. Support us, yes; save us, no.

4. **We are understanding and able to change our beliefs and behaviors,** because we are processing our different feelings. We are taking responsibility and growing.

5. **We "own" and process** for self-understanding, which helps change our thoughts and feelings, beliefs and behaviors.

6. **We flow by a process of asking questions** of each thought and feeling, taking the time to answer each question.

7. **We understand personal memories.** We understand that by questioning and answering family routines, secrets, and beliefs, judgment dissipates.

8. **We let the thoughts and feelings go through each other,** without judgment.

9. **We do not personalize** or react to others' thoughts, feelings and beliefs. We hold our center and take action.

10. **We flow through life with wisdom from owning.** We "see" hope and choices. "Fair" is not a word we use in processing.

11. **We own with forgiveness and understanding** with no self-beat or punisher.

12. **We are free, understanding, creative, and empowered.**

Love Is Not Emotional,
Yet Love Is Full of Feelings

If we are emotional, we don't love others, we hold them *emotionally hostage*. That means we "care" about them, we "worry," we personalize, and we make ourselves into victims with them. We energetically force others to walk on eggshells.

When we hold others emotionally hostage, we hold ourselves emotionally hostage, too. We have no sense of self. Don't disagree with us or we'll get sick or throw a fit and make you miserable. We will then find a way to blame you for these feelings and act-outs, creating backdoor guilt for you. Do these emotional states scare you from having feelings? When we are emotional, we are not in a state of balanced feelings. In the same way care gives love a bad rap, being emotional gives feelings a bad rap!

1. Do you have a quick temper? Are you easily upset? Are you moody? Are you unpredictable?
     a. If you answered yes to any of these, then answer the questions below.
     b. If you answered no, then think of someone you know who does have these traits, and answer the questions as if you were that person.

2. Do you use your emotions to hold others in fear of your emotional time bomb, therefore making them your emotional hostages?
     a. If so, how and why?
     b. Where did you learn this?
     c. How did that make you feel?
     d. And what can you do to change this dynamic? (Remember, don't blame someone else for making you that way unless you want to stay a victim.)

3. Do you hold yourself emotionally hostage?
     a. If so, how and why?
     b. How does that make you feel?
     c. And what can you do to change this dynamic?

4. Has anyone ever attacked you—spiritually, mentally, emotionally, physically, sexually or financially?
   a. Has this person threatened to leave or hurt you?
   b. Can you write, I remember when...

5. Were you held emotionally hostage?
   a. What was it like?
   b. How did it feel?

Love Is Not Selfless

Those of us who think unconditional love means "selfless" love may not understand the meaning of the phrase. Loving unconditionally means listening, self-owning and providing empathy and understanding with no judgment. Love means understanding all truths with patience. So, unconditional love is not selfless, because you must be full of self-awareness to offer such understanding.

If you are selfless, you are in a state of low ego. If you are selfish, you are in a state of high ego. If you are self-loving, you are centered in a state of essence or spirit. These three states of mind—high-ego, low-ego, and spirit—create totally different life experiences.

If you are **selfish,** you are in a state of high ego. You are powerful and narcissistic and need to dominate others and yourself. You need to be in control. Ironically, it may *look* as though you are focused on yourself, but you're not. You're more concerned with other people and how they feel about your image rather than being your true self! When we are selfish/powerful/high ego, we need to be adored, intimidating, and controlling. That means we seek success, power, and adoration outside ourselves. This means we aren't confident within ourselves; instead, we are arrogant with little or no self-love. Which means we have no true love to give to ourselves or others.

When we are **selfless,** we're in a state of low ego. We feel powerless. Our peace and happiness are contingent on the beliefs and happiness of others. Therefore, we are just as focused on others as we are when we are selfish! In both states, we have given control and our centers to someone else although seemingly for different reasons! When we are selfish, we obtain our sense of self-worth by dominating the powerless. Being selfless means living to please and satisfy the powerful or over-caring for those weaker than us. A selfless person can have incredible skill in saving people in a trauma situation. The question is, how does this dynamic play out in regular life? In neither state do we gain power from within ourselves. In neither state do we experience peace and joy on our own. And because we do not experience self-love, we have no true love to give.

Most of us flip between low- and high-ego states often, perhaps constantly. We start off powerful, but then we are challenged, and feel powerless. We try to be selfless with one love, but feel taken for granted, and start behaving selfishly to balance the selfless behavior from the past. If we flip back and forth fast enough, just like a hummingbird's body, we may look as if we are confident and centered. In actuality, we are moving at a fast, furious pace, going back and forth at incredible speeds, providing the illusion that we are not moving at all. Nice try. More fun with opposites that attract and then repel, looking different yet the same, needing balance.

We need to check-in with what, why and how we do things. Otherwise, we may stay in these power struggles forever. Who are we really fooling? Many people can tell what we're doing. We are triggered by our past and not even aware of it. That explains why some powerful people who don't get their way turn into children. Our childhood is where these battles begin.

Can you "see" why selfless or selfish people cannot experience true love? What matters to them will be beyond their control, and their behaviors will get more and more erratic, they will flip from high ego to low, faster and faster, in the pursuit of a balance they will never find this way.

So:

Love is not selfless
Love is not selfish
Love is not powerful
Love is not powerless

Check-In
1. What are you doing?
2. Why are you doing "it?"
3. How are you doing and how are you doing "it?"

Love Is Being Empowered

Empowered means "*in* power," power from within. Empowered people are "in" their own power because they aren't trying to control themselves or anyone else. They recognize that the problem and the solution are not outside themselves—they are within. Empowered people seek understanding of ourselves and others. More love of themselves and others comes from owning the fact that we are like everyone. An empowered person is immune to the powerful/powerless dynamic and cannot be controlled internally.

We have to own our inner "powerful/powerless dynamic" and rinse it.

Love Out of Balance Creates
Selfish (Narcissistic) and Selfless (Coda) Behavior

Selfish/Narcissistic	Selfless/Coda
1. Barriers/walls with no owning, no way in or out	1. No self-boundaries, no self-love, no faith
2. Suffocation of thoughts, feelings and memories, with control bursts	2. "Care" and "worry" (anxiety disorder)
3. Rules! Rules! Rules!	3. Confusion and lack of clarity
4. Self-absorbed! It's all about *me*, and don't forget *me*!	4. Overly giving in self-pity. No me, and please forget me
5. Egomania	5. False humility
6. Blamer/Attacker, a processor of "right" and "wrong."	6. Shamer/Self-Beater. A processor of shame "in" and guilt "out."
7. Narcissistic (Trust me, be for me, live for me)	7. Martyr (It's okay, I don't matter, how are you?)
8. Tunnel vision	8. No vision

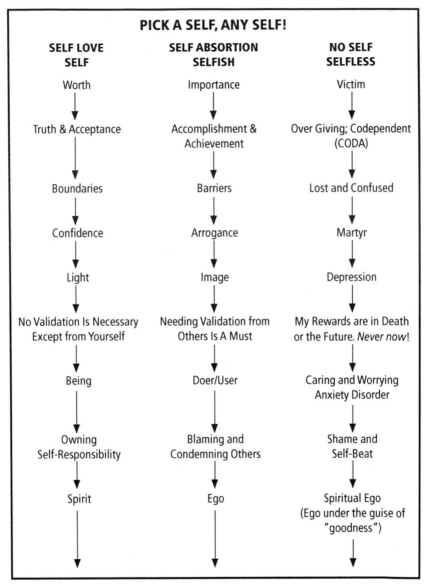

PICK A SELF, ANY SELF!

SELF LOVE SELF	SELF ABSORTION SELFISH	NO SELF SELFLESS
Worth	Importance	Victim
Truth & Acceptance	Accomplishment & Achievement	Over Giving; Codependent (CODA)
Boundaries	Barriers	Lost and Confused
Confidence	Arrogance	Martyr
Light	Image	Depression
No Validation Is Necessary Except from Yourself	Needing Validation from Others Is A Must	My Rewards are in Death or the Future. *Never now*!
Being	Doer/User	Caring and Worrying Anxiety Disorder
Owning Self-Responsibility	Blaming and Condemning Others	Shame and Self-Beat
Spirit	Ego	Spiritual Ego (Ego under the guise of "goodness")

1. Do you know where your "self" is? Where?
2. Are you selfish? What part of you is selfish?
3. How does it make you feel to be selfish?
4. Are you selfless? Where are you selfless?
5. How does it make you feel to be selfless?
6. Are you self-loving? When?
7. How does it feel to be self-loving?

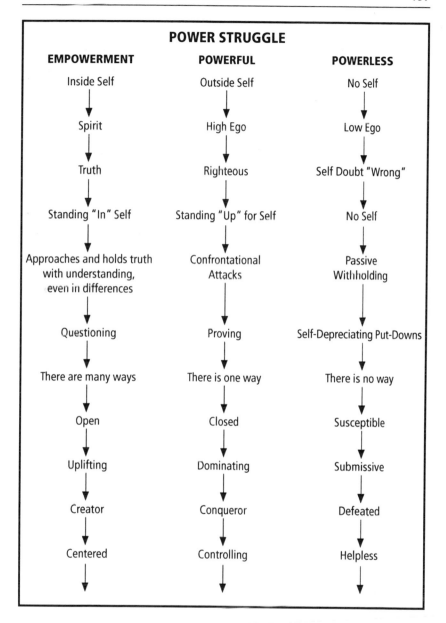

POWER STRUGGLE

EMPOWERMENT	POWERFUL	POWERLESS
Inside Self	Outside Self	No Self
↓	↓	↓
Spirit	High Ego	Low Ego
↓	↓	↓
Truth	Righteous	Self Doubt "Wrong"
↓	↓	↓
Standing "In" Self	Standing "Up" for Self	No Self
↓	↓	↓
Approaches and holds truth with understanding, even in differences	Confrontational Attacks	Passive Withholding
↓	↓	↓
Questioning	Proving	Self-Depreciating Put-Downs
↓	↓	↓
There are many ways	There is one way	There is no way
↓	↓	↓
Open	Closed	Susceptible
↓	↓	↓
Uplifting	Dominating	Submissive
↓	↓	↓
Creator	Conqueror	Defeated
↓	↓	↓
Centered	Controlling	Helpless
↓	↓	↓

1. How are you powerful? How does being powerful feel?
2. How are you powerless? How does being powerless feel?
3. How are you, or can you be, empowered? How would being empowered make you feel?

In marriage it is often said that two become one. How do two people become one? Who dies? Do two drop half of who they are, so two halves become a whole? Does one drop out totally to live for the other? Is this why marriage is an institution? Is this why we have so much fear of marriage? Do I have to lose me to love someone else? Can't two remain two, so the two aren't through?

Live For You, and Let Go of Others

Living as a codependent, I would take care of you without any regard for myself. I used to think that made me a "good" person. I later found out that this caused me to resent others later because I felt ignored and forgotten. Back to self-pity again. Then I would yell at myself for feeling this way, making myself feel guilt. I would also keep getting sick because I would not take care of myself. Codependency (coda, for short) is love with no truth. As a codependent, my goal is to please you, whoever you are. How you treat me or think about me is how I will think and feel about myself. It would kill me if you had a bad day, because I would blame myself. After all, I love you so I can be about you, not me. Do you even like it when I lose myself in you? Why do the flight attendants tell us to put our own oxygen masks on before trying to help someone else, even children? Because helping anyone else can't happen until we're okay first. If we are not solid, how can we possibly be of service to anyone else?

The Coda Release!
I Can No Longer Die For You, I'm Sorry!

1. *I live for my mother by…*
   And so I act like…
   And I feel…

2. *I live for my father by…*
   I act like…
   I feel…

3. *I live for _____ by…*
   I act like…
   I feel…

> 4. *I live for* _____ *by...*
> *I act like...*
> *I feel...*

The "Let Go" Letter

Once we are aware of how we suppress ourselves for "love" and create codependency and martyrdom, we are able to release ourselves, and others, from this kind of relationship and from mental, emotional and sometimes physical bondage. If you are not living in truth and love together, check the road you're on and be sure it's where you want to be!

How do we let go? A "Let Go" letter can be helpful when we are breaking up with someone or when someone is dying, but it also works to help end codependency and control with people in our everyday lives.

If the person you are writing about is someone who will remain in your everyday life, don't be thrown off by the "finality" feeling of the "let go" letter's language. What you are letting go of is the codependency and control, not the person.

Dear _____,

I need to say good-bye and "let go" of you because...
I love you because...
I hate you because...
I'm scared of you because...
I'm scared of me because...
I love me with you because...
I hate me with you because...
I hate me because...
You taught me...
I learned...
I feel...
Thank you for being in my life because...
Letting go of you (and others) is like...
And it feels...
My new boundaries for me to love myself and someone else are...

    Goodbye.
    Love, _____ *(your name)*

When you say good-bye and let go, you're not saying, "I'm leaving." What you are saying is, "I will keep my issues, desires, beliefs and expectations of control and neediness off you and I cannot take yours on. It is then that I can begin to truly love you. So good-bye. I let go of you, I can now love you."

Setting Boundaries

You need to know yourself well before entering into a commitment with someone else or having children. Your words and behaviors will communicate to others how to see and treat you. You can show them how to love you, criticize you, judge you, hurt you, ignore you, respect you, listen to you or trust you. Watch what you are thinking, feeling, saying and how you are behaving. Someone is listening and watching you. You are showing them who and how you are. Are you powerful/powerless, selfish/selfless or empowered with self-love?

A way to show others who you are and what you want is to express your truths and limits. Be in touch with yourself first, then someone else. Setting boundaries is a way to communicate your limits. Boundaries are not mean. They are mean only if your energy is rough, bossy or sarcastic. Setting boundaries for others can be controlling. In truth, without causing physical harm or the threat of punishment, you can't make people listen, so create boundaries for yourself in every situation. Now you can develop self-confidence and self-love.

What To Do When Someone Sets You Off

1. Give yourself a time-out—time to leave the room or area.

2. If you can't leave the room, practice holding on to your truth while that person is angry, hurt, or scared. Do not react or personalize their action. It is not your turn.

3. Do *not* engage in point/counterpoint.

4. Do *not* be stubborn. Drop your point until you understand the other person. This does not mean you need to drop your truth.

5. Do *not* try to be understood. Just *understand* the situation and go to your place of wisdom.

6. If that person gets violent, get out of there immediately—period. A person who resorts to violence when not threatened with violence needs a solid program to process emotionally, so stay away, and give that person the space to seek help. And if that person is you—reach out for help. Now!

People who are emotional, sick, or good at making others feel shame or guilt, often use mental, emotional and physical tricks to make those who are selfless behave the way they want. A creative mind can be amazingly manipulative! If you are unable to feel self-love, you can easily become an emotional hostage, or make someone else your emotional hostage. Don't do this! In the long run, resentment, rebellion and punishment are the outcomes.

When you let someone who is "off" dominate you into losing your truth in a confrontation, you lose any form of empowerment. But when you are in self-love, you hold on to truth with understanding of all sides, you maintain a sense of self-boundary in all circumstances.

REMEMBER: Don't fight, and don't crack! Hold on! A lot of our actions are nothing more than habits. They are reflexes and reactions caused by not understanding the meaning of truth or love! They do not understand their minds can be remembering the past and be in the present at the same time. Do not seek understanding from those who judge or are out of center! Do not celebrate with someone depressed or jealous. You are in charge of your vulnerability. Don't kill it! Teach people who you are and how you want to be treated. Don't wait (anger word) for people to read your mind, to prove (needy and egotistical) they love and understand you, for you to feel better.

No matter how hard the truth is...

if you find your truths, you find yourself.

Fear is your lesson, love is your purpose,
lies are your teacher and truth is your guide!

Love Is Understanding Truth

To find love, you have to process and understand all true thoughts, feelings and memories. This includes anger truths, sad truths, fear truths, and happy truths. You don't have to agree to understand. You do not have to make yourself "right" to have worth.

Only understanding leads to truth, and only truth leads to love.

1. Whether you've experienced love without care or worry or not, can you create a visual image of what love looks like/ without anger, fear, guilt or shame?

2. *Love without anger, fear, guilt, shame, care or worry is like...*
   Feels like...
   And creates...

3. Find an actor, friend or movie that shows traits of what you would like to be as a mother, father, lover, business person or a child. These can be aspects of someone—maybe one person represents a gentle tone you would love to have as a part of yourself, and another person may be a picture of great strength. Mix as many parts of different people to better see aspects of who you would like to be. These are pictures for you to use as a way to create a new self. It doesn't matter if these pictures are literally true for the actor or not.

   Then write:

   Dear _____,
   When I look at you I see...
   When I look at you I feel...
   I wish I could be...

   When you are finished, replace their name with yours and re-read what you wrote again. Begin integrating these aspects to yourself. Re-read this daily to let your mind take it in and manifest. This is creation.

4. *"True love" is...*
   Feels like...
   And creates...

5. *True love needs truth because...*

Chapter Review

I just learned...
I feel...

Summary

Even before I read the real definition of "care," I knew that when someone said they cared about me, it didn't feel "good." And I knew that if I "cared" about others I felt controlling, stressed, and pushy. "Caring" made someone else's life about me; and their choices, about my opinions.

People often pray for their "true love" without knowing or telling the truth. How can we create something we are not practicing? Love with no truth creates selflessness and codependency; and truth without love creates selfishness and dominating control. These two power sources are hurtful, and sometimes dangerous, if separated. They are meant to be connected.

If having a self means knowing truth and having understanding means creating love, then understanding truth creates a self with love. If I have no self or love for me how can I give of myself, lovingly, to you? Notice I said give of myself, not give myself away or to you.

Pick the self you want to be! Selfish is of "high" ego, selfless is of "low" ego, and self-love is our balance in spirit. Your spirit versus your ego—*pick!*

An emotional person is not a feeling person. The emotional person is stuck in a feeling with no processing or understanding of his or her feelings. If you want to stay "stuck" using stubbornness as a way of having a strong self based on fear, war is your outcome, not love. Fear of judgment and self-beat will make anyone an emotional hostage.

Truth shows you your boundaries, while love understands all perceptions so that you won't judge or take on and personalize issues and feelings that do not represent your truth. This is crucial to holding a center in upsetting situations and de-personalizing them.

If we were born to experience love we must experience its opposites—hurt, fear, anger, shame, guilt, lies, judgment, victimization, confusion, insanity, depression, obsessions, and addiction. To know cold, you must know heat! Life is all about understanding who you are by understanding who you are not!

10 To Rinse or Not to Rinse:
Cleansing the Wounds of Your Thoughts, Feelings and Memories

One day, my thirteen-year-old son came home from school very angry and lashed out at me. Here is what happened between us in three steps: The Rinse, Writing and Talking, and The Result, which is the new behavior.

The Rinse

I said to my son, "Hey, why don't you go upstairs and *rinse* this before it turns into something creepy?" You see, we have a walk-in closet that I set up for physical rinsing. Rinsing means to work through your anger and related feelings in a safe environment, where no one, including you, can be hurt.

My son learned how to do this kind of physical rinsing years ago, but he resists it just like everyone else. Still, he stomped upstairs and went for it. While he was in the walk-in closet, he called me every name in the book. I concentrated on breathing and not reacting. After all, it is his rinse and I either get killed in the rinse process or we go to war in life. These are just feelings and energy that need to be released to find the truth and issue underneath. He is being emotional. He needs the feelings to move through each other for wisdom to arise. In a rinse exercise, he's allowed, in fact, encouraged, to say whatever comes to his mind. As long as he is not in my face, he can say whatever he wants and have no fear of hurting my feelings. I am depersonalizing because it is his turn, not mine.

He was upstairs for a long while. I didn't know what I'd done to upset him, if I'd done anything at all. If the anger was really related to me, I had faith that the rinsing process would allow him to bring it up with a calmer and more aware energy. If it wasn't about me, the rinsing would allow him to talk about it with me more easily, if he wanted to. Either way, my job wasn't to "worry" about him or control him, but to just let it go and allow him to process.

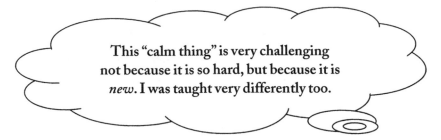

This "calm thing" is very challenging
not because it is so hard, but because it is
new. I was taught very differently too.

Writing and Talking

When my son finished his physical rinse, he took his pen and paper
and wrote, "I learned... and I feel..." to understand as much as he
could from the rinsing exercise. Finally, he came to me and began to
cry. It turned out he was actually upset with the kids at school, not me
(this time).

The kids had teased him about going through puberty. So we
talked about what was going on with his body, mind, and hormones
(which I call "horror-mones"). After the rinsing, understanding, and
talking, J.J. appeared very soft and sweet. His "vibe" was totally different from when he had first come home. His thoughts and feelings had
shifted. All I had to do was listen, ask questions, understand him and
own my embarrassments when I was his age. Thankfully, I didn't react
to his energy, I didn't personalize his behavior and make it all about
me. His issues were about him, and they stayed that way.

Which would you prefer: a thirty-minute rinse, or two weeks of
invisible warfare without any understanding? Suppose I had reacted to
him. It would have been easy to point/counterpoint him. We would
have ended up stuck in the blame/shame game. He was in a state of
shame about his development and he didn't know what to do with it,
so he turned it into blame and put it on me to get it off him. This is
how projection works. If I had reacted, he would have felt guilt on top
of the shame he was already feeling. This is how people can drown in
shame and guilt and never get to the truth.

Instead, he had a way to process his feelings, understand them,
and own what he was thinking and feeling.

Logically, I know I can't and shouldn't protect him, because this is
life and he needs these experiences to grow. If I try to take "care" of
him or "worry" about him, I won't exercise "love" and "faith." But feel-

ings have little or no logic: therefore, as the mom, I should have seen this coming and protected him better! Here comes the self-beat/back-door guilt for the mom.

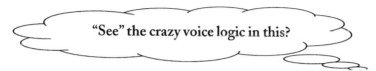

"See" the crazy voice logic in this?

So, off I went to the rinse room to clean myself up, to set him free. I needed to clean my own energy. Children will copy and practice what we do. If we don't do our emotional work, neither will they. This is how I can be understanding and clear for my son.

The Result

About an hour after his rinse, my son started to burst out in laughter. I asked him, "What's so funny?" He said, "I was thinking about my anger work/rinsing and what I was saying during it. I sounded so silly. How could I have been so serious about everything? So next time I'm going to write or talk faster about things that feel stupid to me."

Logical thinking is back and active and so is clarity. I told him, "Sometimes anger and crazy voices are pretty funny later, huh?" He said, "Yeah! I wish I could remember how funny I am when I'm in it."

I said, "Me too."

It's okay to think and feel *anything* as long as you rinse. But it's harmful to pass rinses and crazy voices onto others unless they understand what you're doing. Otherwise, you risk creating defense mechanisms, attacks, or shut-down warfare between you and other people.

I'm giving you a blank "anger rinse" form. It's a couple of pages ahead. This information saves my life daily. It is one of the most used pages of this entire book. Type it into your computer, photocopy it and get comfortable with it. Hopefully, you'll be using it a lot.

The idea behind the feeling rinse sheet is to fill in all the blanks as well as you can. Often, you are already aware of something that angers, scares, or upsets you and you can jump right into the exercise. Other times it feels like you aren't feeling anything, and getting started can be challenging.

If you aren't aware of feeling angry, scared, hurt, or embarrassed, then purposely think of something that angers or scares you—silly things like traffic, long lines, or mean people. Other examples are people from your distant past, a friend who upset you, or something your mother said that really got under your skin. It's even okay, for the purposes of this exercise, to manufacture anger. Anger towards a movie or fictional situation works great to ignite feelings that lie dormant. Even fake anger will lead you to the roots of the real anger inside.

The truth is we're all angry, scared, hurt, or embarrassed somewhere inside us. And we have to dig those feelings out. If we let them be, they affect our decisions and then our life. If we unearth them, they teach us—and what they teach us is always valuable.

So dig those feelings up! Fill in all the blanks, on a separate piece of paper, so you have more room. Let's "see" where the information leads you.

A Note on the Word "Fuck"

On the next few pages, I'm going to use the word "fuck" a few times. I hope it doesn't offend you. I do not recommend the use of this word in your daily life. But feel free to use it when it comes to feeling rinses.

Why? Because "fuck" is a strong word that triggers a lot of anger. It represents an old anger that has been festering. It can help us channel our energy in a constructive way and let go of control.

In fact, many people who are truly stuck, and can't find their anger, need first and foremost to find the "fuck you" they are withholding. They need to get to that deeply imbedded "fuck you" in order to push themselves through their energetic walls. Some of my clients can't even start rinsing at all until they've learned to shout "fuck you" at the top of their lungs. Now, you may not have this issue. But if you do, try a big, loud "fuck you" on for size. It can't hurt you or anyone if you say it in private, right?

Feeling Rinse Paper

Feel free to rip this out and make copies for yourself.

Dig for Feelings

I am angry because…
And that makes me feel…
You (the object of my anger) ruined my life because…
I hate you because…
I hate me because…
I am scared because…
I am afraid because…
I feel bad because…
Fuck you because…
I am guilty because…
I am ashamed because…
I am embarrassed because…
I am disappointed because…
I feel sad because…
I am hurt because…
I feel sorry for myself because…
I feel sorry for you because…
I love you because…
I like you because…
I love me because…
I like me because…
I'm happy because…
This makes me feel…

Time Travel

This reminds me of the time when…
and I remember when…
and remembering this now makes me feel…

Create and Visualize Something New

I wish…
If I could do this over again, I would…

Realizations

Doing this exercise, I learned….
And I feel….

When you have completed the rinse, go back through, as your inner child.

Congratulations! You've just finished your first feeling rinse.

Rinsing is one of the most essential elements of processing in this book. But truly understanding ourselves—our histories, our traumas and victories—is not a process that can be done with only our intellect. It must be done sensorially as well. Human beings are part spirit and part animal. We need to let our feelings out on a purely animal level to "see" them for what they are without logic, fear or judgment. And the more you can "see" and feel your own thoughts, feelings, and memories with understanding, the more you will "see" and understand others.

Processing life-long habits is not a sign of weakness. There is a stigma to admitting shortcomings and the feelings that emerge from our memories and present-time mistakes that cause so much shame. How do you live on this planet and not screw up? Deep-seated thoughts and feelings and old resentments are often buried under years of denial and repression because of this stigma. But they will never go away unless they are allowed to be seen, felt and understood. And to get them out, you have to pull them up even if you are full of fear and shame. Do not let fear and shame win!

So. Are you up to it?

What you'll need is an anger package, or a tennis racket or mallet, gloves, and some old pillows, your bed, a mattress, a punching bag, anything that can take a beating.

Got the ingredients? It's time for...

The Physical Rinse

1. First, take your "feeling rinse" paper from above, with your answers already written out, and put it on the floor.

2. Now put your pillows on the floor next to the "rinse paper."

3. Get on your knees or sit on one of the pillows.

4. Put on gloves. Seriously, when feelings hit, you're going to be strong. No jewelry.

5. Grab your tennis racket or mallet.

6. Now whack that pillow. A few times, just for practice. Whack, whack, whack. Go for it. I mean it. Hit the pillow hard. Stay on your knees or in a sitting position. Make sure you have a solid swing but that you don't bring your elbows up over your shoulder and don't hit yourself in the head. (No joke, people do). The racket should come up and down like it's a hammer and the pillow is a nail. Don't swing the racquet like a bat. You could accidentally hit an inanimate object or become out of control. Don't stand up. Keep the body humble at the same time unless you are kick boxing or punching a punching bag.

7. Now start reading off the "feeling rinse" paper, while you whack the pillow. Talk, whack. Talk, whack.

8. Now start to yell or intensely talk. I'm not kidding. Yelling and talking from the diaphragm, not the throat, or you can get hoarse.

9. Create some visuals as you scream and whack. Picture some-one's face or a situation on the pillow, someone you are angry with at the present or in a memory. Perhaps yourself. That's okay. Everything's okay. This is an uninhibited exercise. You can't say anything wrong. It usually starts sounding like this (with the capitalized words the words you hit the pillow on): *"Fuck YOU, you SUCK, I hate YOU because..., how could YOU do this to ME you son of a BITCH! You fucking SUCK, you LIED to me when..., you HURT me like.... You made a MESS of me when..., you FUCKED ME UP. You don't deserve to LIVE because...*

10. Turn the words and the hitting into a fluid movement, so that it all develops a life and rhythm of its own. Don't stick to what's on the sheet. Free associate. Ad lib. Let your thoughts and feelings take over. Don't just hit the pillow. Verbalize your thoughts and feelings in order to learn from them. Ex-periencing a physical movement while talking intensely and feeling stimulates all of your senses and can actually affect your biological chemistry.

11. Now here's the trick. While you're whacking that pillow, you'll eventually begin "getting it." This sensation is like being in a car, hitting the turbo. All of a sudden, you'll just take off. Please go for it! Yell louder, hitting twice, three times as fast, breathing heavier. You'll get into the zone, and some of the most amazing information will come out of your mouth. You're cleansing yourself, letting it all out. Letting out all the crap you've been holding back.

12. When you are more experienced with this, you'll leave behind the "feeling rinse" paper altogether and just use that template to free-associate all the way. But *do not forget*: when you are finished, always write, *"I learned... And I feel..."* in order to get a deeper clarity from the rinse.

The goal is to release thoughts, feelings and energy from your mind and body in a constructive way, not a destructive way.

No hurting yourself, others or inanimate objects.

Even though breaking things can feel good momentarily, doing so puts you "out of control!" This will scare you inside because you will lose the constructive environment and lose self-confidence.

That's not our goal!

Trouble-Shooting

Are you getting stuck? You don't have the energy to hit the pillow? You don't feel angry? Do you just start to cry, or shut down? You're afraid that someone will hear you?

Here are some tips:

1. Are you limited physically or do you feel like doing the rinse without being so aggressive? Okay, try squeezing your legs, buttocks, stomach, and arms together. Hold tightly and yell into a pillow to muffle the sound if you need to. Tighten as many of your body parts as possible. Hold this position for five to ten seconds, and then let go. While doing this, say your feeling words and/or yell your life situations out loud. Don't forget to listen to yourself! This is an isometric way of moving your chemistry too.

2. If you feel uncomfortable or stuck, stop and try again in a few minutes (but no longer). Some people need to work up to this. Don't give up. Getting sad is a helpful rinse too. Some of us deny we have anger or sadness at all because we think that having anger makes us a "bad" person and sadness makes us a weak person. But anger is a healthy messenger that needs releasing and understanding. For example, without processing anger, we can't be passionate; we can only be intensely, passionately angry. Work yourself! Remember: anger unexpressed becomes rage. Suppressed anger eats away at us inside. Let it out!

3. Judgment and shame may try to block your thoughts and feelings. Don't let them! When a physical rinse connects with your logic, you gain clarity. When the pictures in your mind connect with your feelings, you bypass all embarrassment and judgment, and start to learn. Feel fee to let the judger voice out, just don't let it lead or make your decisions.

4. You aren't angry with anyone? No way. Go back in time. Find someone in your past. Start with that person. If you feel flat or depressed, you are angry. Go to fear or guilt to kick in the anger. Just find something. It's all connected.

The Goal of the Rinse

The goal of isometric and physical rinsing is to connect your thoughts, feelings, and memories with your body and alter your chemistry. Once you allow the chemicals in your brain and your blood to flow through you, you will begin to touch long-suppressed issues.

Over time, suppressed thoughts, feelings, and memories can affect your overall body chemistry. You can end up moving slowly, feeling weighed down; or becoming hyper, and flighty. The heaviness can chemically affect your metabolism and cause weight gain, weight loss, stomach problems or headaches.

TRIGGER: A trigger is a psychological mechanism causing a thought, feeling and memory to awaken from your subconscious mind that affects and influences your thinking, feeling or behavior in present time. When a trigger is activated, it can cause an irrational response, an over-reaction, or a reverting to past behavior, even that of a child. Don't be surprised if an instantaneous shutdown can turn into a crazy feeling or a freeze from all movement, ending with you feeling depressed. Having a reaction totally unrelated to the circumstances at hand is very common when you are triggered into a memory that was upsetting. This is why the addict is so prevalent in our world. Addictions help to block feelings and awarenesses from triggers.

A few years ago, I taught physical rinsing to a group of second-grade students. I told them how thoughts and feelings become "vibes" and work like electricity. I showed them how electricity is invisible, yet very strong and powerful. I demonstrated how a switch turns a light on and off, and how a switch is a metaphor for a "*trigger*." A trigger sends you into the past or future, where you time-travel to thoughts, feelings and memories that have been stored in your subconscious mind. You may feel that you are reliving that experience, or responding to it as if it were happening today. Please know that this idea can be very scary. You are not reliving it. It's over. You are okay. You are psychically "seeing" it, because you need to understand the experience and recover from it by using new information you learned today. You can recover energetically by rinsing, time-traveling, changing your ideas and behaviors. A way of re-dealing with the situation is to physically and visually re-enact, like a play, and handling it the way you wished you could have handled it in the past. By using the information of today to understand the old experience, we can process anything. Any upset or trauma you have that has altered your psyche can be healed if you process it. Remember that when a trigger happens, you are no longer psychically living in only the present.

Triggers act like switches that can turn our internal and external energy on or off. If our spiritual energy or "light" is on, we are alive and receptive psychically. If our "light" is off, we feel dead inside and blocked. It is said that through a child's eyes, you can "see" what is true. It is through your inner child's eyes that you will find your soul and purpose. Without rinsing ourselves, we are in a type of darkness and cannot "see" what is right in front of us.

Darkness can be frightening, yet the light can be too bright and hurt our eyes if we don't understand them both. Rinsing helps us welcome the light by seeing through lies, confusions and hurts that have left us blind to our truths, creating a type of unawareness and darkness in our life. Turning the switch on deliberately is the trick, but how? When the light becomes comfortable and darkness becomes understandable, darkness is no longer frightening or unknown. Then even if we visit darkness in the future or in our rinses, we will know how to use the light to help us see through the dark. Once we rinse, we clean our energy, we can move from darkness to light and light to darkness easily. If we deny the dark and live in a shut-down state, unaware of our truths logically or emotionally, we become heavy, confused, angry, and depressed.

After we finished talking, the second-graders drew me pictures of their perceptions of anger work. Here are some samples.

Perception: Releasing hate with no punishment, shame or guilt.

Perception: The little girl is angry with her mom, but she rinses her anger. Her mom shows understanding of her rinsing her anger. This makes anger feel safe, so it doesn't have to grow.

What is your perception of this one?

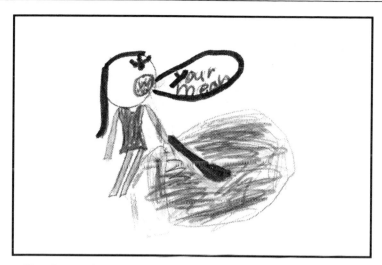

Your Perception:

Your perception:

Your perception:

Draw a picture of how *your* inner child "sees" you.

Have fun with this. Imagine you are your inner child, and take a look at yourself. You don't have to draw well, but draw! When's the last time you drew?

Your perception of your picture:

The Crash of Mental Stress and Emotional Trash

When you rinse memories, thoughts and feelings that create "toxic trash" in your life, you feel renewed energy. This energy helps you "see" clearly so that you can create from your "wishes" rather than from the stuck place where you've been repeating what you've always done.

When toxic energy is stored inside you, your awareness is blocked, which can cause stress and depression. If this energy stays suppressed, it becomes more and more mentally, emotionally, and behaviorally lethal and can lead to addiction and insanity. Stress is not about how busy you are; it is a state of mind, based on judgment and pressures from your low or high ego.

Many people exercise, work out, and participate in sports to *control* this energy and attempt to release it. If they don't get to their true thoughts, feelings and memories, exercise is just a short-lived adrenal release. Exercise is a crucial ingredient for health. It is not, however, a replacement for rinsing.

Let's Philosophize!

What will it take for the world to improve?
I will see differently when...
Until someone else realizes...
It's not about me because...

Memories and issues will never go away! Imagine that your computer stored all of your life data and experiences within its memory and didn't process or file it away in any organized and productive fashion. Wouldn't your computer start to slow down, or even shut down? Don't you think the same is true of you and your brain?

Rinsing will relieve you of stress, and provide you with an understanding of your traumas and insanities so you'll be prepared to take steps toward creating your wishes. If you don't rinse your thoughts, feelings, and memories, this energy will back up, become toxic and turn against you, causing invisible and visible warfare. Memories, thoughts and feelings control your subconscious mind whether you like it or not. Think about it. Do you want all this energy rolling around your subconscious mind, controlling how you think, feel and act? Don't you want to be aware and be able to make choices about these things?

Releasing Your Toxins

When your digestive system has used the nutrients it needs, it gets rid of the rest. This is called elimination. If you get constipated, you're inclined to get sick because the excess waste, which is not needed, becomes toxic and begins to back up into your system. This affects your metabolism, blood, immune system, digestive system, and colon, creating headaches, allergies, and other illnesses. Some people take enemas or use cleansers to clean their colon, especially if they have a fever or infection. This cleansing process works as a release of toxins which frees the digestive and circulatory systems to move and flow again. This boosts the immune system and supports the body's chance for recovery by eliminating excess waste and re-feeding your body with proper nutrients after the detox. If the digestive system is not clean, the best of supplements won't help you. Nothing can be assimilated and carried to other areas of the body for repair and strength.

Feeling rinses work the same way. A rinsing detox builds up your belief system. If the belief system has to fight and control extra mental and emotional waste, it grows weak and vulnerable. The mind, in weakness, tends to travel to the past and future, subconsciously. If we fight and try to control toxic thoughts, feelings and memories, our clarity, confidence and self-love become weak and confused as well, creating mental illness and addiction. Imagine how your heart, mind, body, and soul will work after a few mental, emotional, and physical rinses. These rinses release your toxins and make room for new awareness!

YOU HAVE TWO CHOICES

EITHER: You go after the thoughts,
feelings and memories,

OR: The thoughts, feelings and
memories will come after you.

Which will it be?

Circle the ones that relate to you or add your own...

Things I Think, Do or Say That I Don't Like

1. I hit my siblings or children.
2. I curse and get out of control.
3. I lie or exaggerate.
4. I argue.
5. I don't speak up for myself.
6. I have a bad temper.
7. I'm too nice.
8. I say what I think people want to hear so that I won't upset anyone.
9. I cheat.
10. I overeat.
11. I hurt myself.
12. I steal.
13. I drink or do drugs.
14. I am a pedophile.
15. I am a criminal.
16. I am compulsive/obsessive.
17. I am insane.
18. _____
19. _____
20. _____

If you are sitting in your room alone eating, drinking, sleeping, crying and spinning, do you feel stupid, silly, or ridiculous?

When you're yelling at people, hitting and losing control, do you feel stupid or embarrassed?

Why is it okay for us to do mean, hurtful, angry, act-outs and not feel stupid?

That's why rinsing makes sense. We can let out thoughts and feelings with no harm, no anger bursts, no violence, no shame. So let's rinse!

If you simply will not do anger work, at least do some kind of cardio exercise. For instance, go jogging, kick boxing and running or bike riding. When you're out there, yelling or intense talking about your thoughts and feelings, out loud, would be a start. Don't forget about the rinse paper as a guide. The goal is to affect as many levels of your brain and body at one time as possible. The more you rinse your memories, thoughts, and feelings, the more you affect and create a physical, mental and emotional chemical shift. Most people say that their rinsing/anger work, although physically tiring, in the end, makes them feel energized.

There are some who think this physical rinse technique brings up old wounds and think, by pulling up their memories and pain, things will get worse. That *can* be true if you *stay* in your pain as a victim and don't change your thinking, feelings and behavior. Rinsing must be followed by "I learned... And I feel..." so that you can *own* your pain and change. Once you own, you can move forward and not be a victim!

The rinse is designed to bring as much as possible from the unconscious mind to the conscious mind, where we can begin to see it and understand it.

That means understanding your and others' perceptions and then taking actions to *change*.

You cannot stay the same and change your life!

The goal, in the end, is to understand yourself (spiritually, mentally, emotionally, physically, sexually, financially and psychically), and then learn to understand others. That means understanding the people who have hurt you as well. I know this may be difficult to think about, but it is the only way out of victim hell. If you don't *understand* yourself and the abuser or "bad" guy, that person still occupies and invades your mind, heart, and body. As long as you still carry the pain and the shame, you are in "survival mode," unfortunately, a place where your life decisions will come from pain and shame. Rinsing and then understanding the "bad" guy changes you. It allows you to heal, and move forward.

There is no such thing as something being gone or over with forever. Your brain is a computer with computer files. These files can be triggered by something as simple as a smell, color or sound. Each time you rinse your triggers, and therefore own and change yourself, you will become empowered. The true goal is to be triggered less and to process faster!

Trigger less, process faster!
Grow with understanding, and take action.
That's as good as it gets!

Once you are able to bypass judgment, you can get to blocked issues, memories, thoughts and feelings faster. The judger inside us all can really slow us down. Can you imagine choosing how you want to be rather than being a reactive or shut-down person?

Do We Solve Problems by Creating More Problems?

Let's say your family forgets your birthday. Depending on how you feel about birthdays, there's a chance your feelings will be hurt. If you don't care about birthdays, pretend you do for a minute, so you can understand this point. To deal or cope with the hurt feelings, your judger may rear its little head and tell you something like, "Get over it and grow up." This opinion will now sit on top of your hurt feelings (because your feeling brain isn't about logic unless you pull logic up), causing you to become suppressed and depressed. Something so small (compared to major crises in the world) creates toxic thoughts, feelings, and vibes in your life. Your depressive thoughts and feelings are stuck, because you judged yourself instead of rinsing those thoughts and feelings!

Do We Shut Down, Or Do We Rinse?

1. **A lot of diseases are stress related.** Stress is not necessarily about being busy. Stress can be caused by anger, fear, guilt or shame on top of unprocessed thoughts, feelings, and behaviors derived from life on this planet. How about adding a judgmental stupid, bad or ridiculous thought too?

2. **We all go through periods of hurt, fear or rage.** Rage is the combination of past fear, hurt and anger, mixed with present feelings. Anger is present-time pain. Rage is toxic, old, blocked anger from the past. The question is, how do you process it? (Should we do anger/releasing rinse exercises, shut down or act out?).

An **issue** is a struggle that you do not understand, yet.

---

1. *One of my issues is...*
   And it makes me feel...
   And I act like...

2. *Another one of my issues is...*
   And it makes me feel...
   And I act like...

3. Do you think rinsing a judgment will help prevent that judgment from coming back into your life? Why do or don't you think so?

Can you do a physical rinse on these issues? Go for it !

Life Took My Breath Away Because
I Didn't Know What to Say!

All of us have these strong thoughts and feelings. Some of them appear to be overpowering as others lie dormant inside us. How we deal or not deal with them literally determines how we live our lives. We have three choices when it comes to handling realities and truths of life:

Skip over them—an aggressive/dominant form of suppression
Duck under them—a passive/submissive form of suppression
Walk through them—an assertive/patient form of rinsing and owning

Do We Suppress or Do We Own?

People who skip over "big" thoughts or feelings tend to:

1. Talk without listening
2. Change subjects rather than address issues
3. Act funny or sarcastic at inappropriate times
4. Overachieve or underachieve and lack balance
5. Become very loud and aggressive
6. Lie or exaggerate
7. Have high levels of energy and fear, causing "hyper-disconnection"
8. Become hysterical
9. Behave self-righteously
10. Seek to control or demand
11. Become obsessive/compulsive
12. Develop addictions
13. Attack themselves and others

People who duck under "big" thoughts or feelings tend to:

1. Oversleep
2. Want to be alone
3. Get quiet and withdrawn
4. Speak little, or not at all
5. Be very passive
6. Get sick
7. Avoid confrontation
8. Deny/lie
9. Space out/behave in air-headed ways
10. Pretend to listen
11. Succumb to depression
12. Nit-pick and complain

People who walk through "big" thoughts or feelings tend to:

1. Allow themselves to "see" and feel all thoughts and feelings, whether or not those thoughts or feelings make sense
2. Appropriately share with others and speak up assertively but respectfully
3. Understand memories, thoughts and feelings
4. Own their feelings
5. Own their thoughts
6. Own their behavior
7. Not see people or themselves as victims
8. Own memories so history doesn't repeat itself
9. Rinse the memories, thoughts and feelings attached to a self-beat
10. Change their behavior with self-awareness
11. Take risks

> **Time doesn't heal everything,**
> **but it can suppress everything.**

1. If your memories, thoughts, and feelings represent part of your energy, what happens if you ignore them?

2. Would you ignore and do nothing about your environment while in the middle of a tornado, hurricane or earthquake? Why? Are some of your memories, thoughts, and feelings "internal" tornadoes, hurricanes and earthquakes?

> Suppressed energy is like a volcano.
>
> Negative and positive energy mixed together create a tornado!

3. Is suppression a lie? Why or why not?

4. How does suppression make you feel and behave?

5. How do suppressed thoughts and feelings turn into behaviors that affect you and others?

Often when I say something that people aren't aware of consciously, and it's true, that person says, "Oh, yeah. You're right!" After the shock turns into a realization, that person often follows up with, "You know, deep down, I knew that all along."

We all *know* our truths inside.
That's why we need to tap into our subconscious mind and soul.

Any experience that has happened to you—whether it's beautiful, exciting, uncomfortable, or abusive—is about you, because it's *inside* you.

If I have the flu and I give it to you, who's responsible for taking care of your flu?

It's in your body. Even if I help, I can't force you to see and deal with your flu. It's not your fault that you have the flu, but it's your responsibility to deal with it.

Every memory, thought, and feeling inside your body is your responsibility to understand, rinse, and own.

We've all been victimized at times in our lives because we've all been hurt. So-called abusers are nothing more than hurt victims acting out their hurt as well. We've all been attacked spiritually, mentally, emotionally, physically, sexually, financially or psychically in our lives. We can remain a victim, continue to be an abuser or learn how to achieve wisdom.

Chapter Review

I just learned...
I feel...

Summary

If rinsing means to clean, wash and spin, and cycle means a rotation of events or to move in a pattern, then a rinse cycle means to clean your movements that are spinning and rotating in a pattern. If we can "see" ourselves as people who get stuck in cycles and patterns from our life experiences, interpretations, judgments, thoughts, and feelings, **we can grow beyond what we know.**

Many of us are enmeshed inside ourselves and lack the self-processing to detangle our thoughts, feelings and memories. Once we can understand ourselves spiritually, mentally, emotionally, physically, sexually and financially, our psyche moves forward, and change follows! Our thoughts, feelings, and memories are subliminal pictures and subconscious voices, all hoping to be "seen," "heard" and understood just like children. Once seen and understood, free choice can enter our lives and we can evolve.

Since we are intuitive and feeling beings, we can easily pick up mental and emotional energy and make it our own without ever consciously realizing that we're doing this. Our life experiences add to this energy and continue to build. This way of living can energetically and behaviorally be passed from one generation to the next until someone starts to process, own, and understand the family and culture's subconscious and conscious beliefs.

All of us need a spiritual, mental, emotional, physical and family-line detox. We either go after the feelings or the feelings go after us. The only way to truly forget our thoughts, feelings, and memories is to get a lobotomy, which some of us obtain metaphorically, through alcohol, drug abuse or letting ourselves mentally slip into insanity.

Don't create new problems on top of existing problems. Release them by understanding your thoughts, feelings, memories—and change instead.

11 Time-Travel:
The Past Unravels, the Future Reveals

Time-traveling is a way of subliminally re-experiencing past events using hindsight vision and, when clear, seeing from the psyche the future flashing through our minds. Utilizing these exercises and visualizations, you can change your perception of any experience, which can change your thoughts, feelings and behaviors in the present, changing your patterns and altering your future.

Time-travel happens in two ways. The first kind of **time-travel** is **subconscious**. This means, while in the present, visuals, scents or words trigger us and send us to the past or to fear of the future. If we are subconsciously experiencing a subliminal memory that is upsetting, we may not activate enough present-time wisdom to help us handle the current situation with present-time awareness. So, if we are remembering something from early childhood, let's say at age twelve, we are probably operating from that twelve-year-old's information. Present-time awareness is temporarily non-existent. This is the reason for immaturity and childish behavior versus age-appropriate awareness and child-like behavior at times like these.

If we were to time-travel to a beautiful memory, we would probably exhibit child-like behavior. If we time-traveled to an upsetting memory, with conscious awareness or on purpose, we would be able to see with present-time information and wisdom. See? Everything is understandable, if we step out of the familiar and see with no fear, judgments or opinions concerning a traditional thought or idea. Supporting new concepts means asking questions and finding new ways to perceive old ideas as well as new concepts.

Consciously choosing to **time-travel and rinse** is a way to re-visit the past as a way to study your personal and cultural history. Everything is a choice, including awareness. We are going to time-travel whether we admit it or not. If you time-travel rinse, you are purposely choosing to see history with hindsight wisdom. You can see and re-experience life through subliminal memories. Wouldn't it be eye opening to see our life shown to us in a movie to better understand it? Well, we can. Our subliminal pictures fly through our mind at incredible speeds. Let's pull these subliminal visuals forward to the conscious mind and change our perceptions and decisions that will affect our future. To forgive and *forget* is impossible without major disconnection through chemicals, insanity or a lobotomy. To forgive and understand is evolving!

So your two choices for time-traveling are...to time-travel subconsciously with no awareness, or to time-travel on purpose and consciously to understand.

Understanding Your Present by Exploring Your Past

Your present-time life is constantly affected by subliminal memories. An unaware time-travel can cause insanity. A time-travel rinse may create a miracle.

If the past is confusing, hurtful, denied, or blocked, we can be subconsciously controlled by these denied pictures. Subliminals flash through our minds, triggering thoughts and feelings with no conscious awareness. These subliminals are fast enough to create an internal movie that we will play out with little or no understanding. This is what can cause a subconscious earthly trance.

My question is, should our history be taught with only facts, such as names and dates, with no visuals or *feelings*? Don't we need visuals or feelings to create an **emotional** movement so history won't repeat itself? If our history is felt, rinsed, and understood from as many angles as possible, then perceptions are changed and miracles start to happen. After you achieve wisdom about someone who's different from you— try judging that person!

Studying our own histories gives us the feeling of being "the wise man in the village." If you can't get to a village, let me bring the wisdom of the village to you.

1. Why would you resist "seeing" your own personal, inner child, family and cultural history?

2. Who in your past judged you and yelled at you for going near a family truth? How did this make you feel?

3. If you study your family history, are you afraid you might be disowned, or feel guilty?

4. Would seeing and understanding your history, not judging your history, affect your life? Explain.

Everyone in your family line is human. That means everyone is imperfect. Everyone is struggling with their own truths. Everyone has, or had, something to learn. You'll go further in understanding your past if you refuse to judge yourself or anyone from your past except in a rinse exercise.

To understand yourself, go back *through* yourself, your parents, your grandparents, and everyone's culture and religion. Whether or not you live by your family's cultural and religious beliefs, these beliefs are ingrained in your family's thoughts, feelings, behaviors, and what you've been taught.

1. *My culture is...*
2. *My culture feels...*
3. *Mom's culture is...*
4. *Mom's culture feels...*
5. *Dad's culture is...*
6. *Dad's culture feels...*
7. *Mom's religion is...*
8. *Mom's religion feels...*
9. *Dad's religion is...*
10. *Dad's religion feels...*
11. *I just learned and feel...*

Ready? Time-travel!

1. Think of a present-time situation that bothers you and write... *I am bothered by...*

2. *This makes me feel....*

3. *This reminds me of... Back then, I felt...*

4. *This past memory affects me today like...*

5. *Take this memory through the Rinse Paper.*

You can do this anytime on anyone or anything. How can you connect your present-time adult with your inner child?

Rinse Your Inner Child

To feel and hear your inner child, change the position of your body, or go to a different area of your house or room to write. This will help change your energy from adult to inner child. Remember that the adult self and the inner child express themselves differently, because your adult self and your inner child see the world from different angles and perspectives.

Now write a letter from your inner child:

> *Dear Big* _____ *(your name)*
> *When I look at you I see...*
> *When I look at you I feel...*
> *Do you remember when...*
> *And I felt...*
> *I wish...*
> > *From,*
> > *Little* _____ *(your name)*

Now let's go a step deeper.

Picture the Memory

Find a picture of yourself when you were around the age of the memory from the previous exercise (if you have no physical picture, picture yourself in your mind.) "See" yourself as your inner child. Think of the situation that happened to you and begin to write to your inner child:

Dear Little _____ (your name)
When I look at you I see...
I remember when...
And I feel...
 From,
 Big _____ (your name)

Ask your inner child some questions.

Dear Little _____ (your name)
How do you feel about (Mom? Dad? Other family members? Friends?)
How old are you?
Where are you?
How do you feel?
What do you remember?
How did that make you feel?
Do you feel angry, scared, bad, hurt or sad?
What do you wish?
 From,
 Big _____ (your name)

Big to Little, Little to Big

Now, in your notebook or on your computer, let your adult self and inner child use the Feeling Rinse Paper as a guide. Let your inner child ask you why you are angry, embarrassed, or guilty. Then ask any question that comes to mind. (Little to big: Why are you married? Big to Little: What are your dreams?)

Ask questions back and forth from your inner child to your adult, and the adult to the inner child.

The more you do this, the faster and more connected you will be to your inner child, and, therefore, to your inner self.

The Time-Travel Rinse

We've all had experiences or traumas that affected our thoughts, feelings, beliefs and decisions. And those experiences and traumas affect us to this day. To reduce the influence these experiences have over our lives, we have already discussed how to relive traumas and "rewrite them." Now we'll learn how to relive traumas and "rinse them" using the feeling rinse.

Pull out your rinse sheet, your pillows and old rackets. Start with an upsetting memory from the past, the one above or a different one. Here are some examples to get you started.

A. Past Memory

I remember when _____(Joe)_____ would yell and yell and yell at me or hit and shame me, or ignore me and I would just take it. I would die inside! I had no rights! I was eight years old. I thought I blocked it, but I didn't!

B. Present-Time Result

I actually got used to being shamed and yelled at. I blocked out most of the experience with _____(Joe)_____, but I developed a pattern of being attracted to people like _____(Joe)_____ .

For years, I'd go to these similar-acting people and just sit and take it!
I'd play out this trance! I actually beat myself up internally just like
_____*(Joe)*_____ *did.*

C. Now Rinse the Past!
I remember when...
And that made me feel...
You ruined my life because...
I hate you because...
I hate me because...

Now do the rinse! Use your copy of the rinse sheet and do a physical rinse on how you feel right now! This will feel better and get easier.

Breathing and Letter Writing
Breathing is a great way to relax if you are hyperventilating, having a panic attack or would like to slow the conscious mind down to allow the subconscious to come forward with visuals and messages. Through this physical movement, your mind, heart, and pulse calm down. When you are in bed at night and start to fall asleep, take note of how your body breathes, naturally. See how your chest barely moves if it moves at all?

When we breathe deeply, we can be open. We allow our deepest thoughts and feelings to surface. Even if you don't like the thoughts, feelings or memories that come forward, be willing to look, rinse and write. Thoughts become conscious for a reason. Don't run or hide from them. Suppressing them again will not help you. They will not just go away. If you do try to control or ignore them, the panic will return. If your breath isn't suppressed, your thoughts and feelings may not be as well. Check how much you hold your breath. Are you breathing now?

Writing a letter is one of my favorite exercises for ending confusion and suppression, especially a letter of absurdity. I write or talk out loud, absurdly, whenever I feel a lot of thoughts and feelings that are big, confused, ridiculous, or twisted. What I do, in this exercise, is make my confusion real, (not necessarily true!) and then I exaggerate my confusion as much as I can, to make it absurd. The exaggeration is similar to the concept of a magnifying glass. The bigger it is, the more clearly I can see.

The idea is to take the confusion, lie, or truth, and put it under a magnifying glass. Seeing in this way keeps me sane. Lies and confusion are messages that are just as important as truth; they, too, provide information. If you think of confusion, lies, and truth as messages, you will see the wisdom in the ridiculousness, and clarity will shine right through. You'll be able to wash away lies, guilt, hurt and confusion in just moments.

Absurdity Letter—Example
1. Blame First

First, find the blame. Be nasty on purpose. Write what happened, and how that makes you feel…(don't forget to be mean to release as much negative energy as possible).

> *Dear Stanley,*
> *You lied to me and tricked me. I risked my job, my life, my heart, and my family to be with you. You made promises and broke every single one. I stayed supportive and understanding throughout. You took my money, you didn't pay it back, and then you lied about everything. There was nothing I could do to stop you!*
> *(And I feel…) Now, I'm crying. My heart hurts, and so does love. I am crushed. I will never love anyone again.*

2. Absurdity/Exaggeration

Feel free to exaggerate the story to make the other person sound good and make yourself look bad if you choose. No guilt allowed. You're just energetically eliminating—and getting toxins out. Go ahead! We'll own it all in the end.

> *Dear Stanley,*
> *Oh, you were so loving and honest with me! I twisted it all. I was such a jerk! Being with me was torture. I lied and forced you to take my money. You said "no." You spoiled me rotten and I spit upon you!! I feel so horrible for the way I treated you. I couldn't be loving if my life depended on it.*

3. Self Beat

Next, turn the story into an angry self-beat attack. You are the "idiot," you are awful and the other person was completely innocent. The goal is to magnify the ridiculousness of your shame for someone hurting you. Write the opposite of the truth to wake yourself up. Start with what happened, and then how it made you feel.

> *Dear Stanley,*
> *I'm so stupid. I deserve to be tortured because I don't care about me at all when I am with a man. I am trained to worship them so I wind up hating you. I am a loser!*

4. Read Your Letters

Now, grab the tennis racket or mallet and the pillows and read your letters out loud, pounding away. Get the anger and hurt out. Feel it. Grab the feeling release paper and let it rip. Don't forget the time traveling!

Now own. Tell the story with true ownership. This includes how you've treated yourself and others as a result of this situation.

> The truth of my end of this situation is…

5. The Ending, As Usual

"I learned… and I feel…"

If a "bad" feeling from the past attaches to your present-time conscience, self talk and belief system, you could:	If a "bad" feeling from the past has a self-beat and it attaches to your "drive" because you are a driven person, "bad" creates:
1. Fail and/or have a sense of failure	1. Over-achievement
2. Quit	2. Egocentricism
3. Be an addict	3. Narcissism
4. Hate yourself	4. Obsessive/compulsive behavior
5. Develop anorexia	5. Exaggeration
6. Develop bulimia	6. Overeating
7. Use drugs	7. Alcoholism/addiction
8. Feed your insecurity	8. Control battles
9. Be needy	9. Righteous behavior
10. Become controlling	10. Arrogant behavior
11. Feel insane	11. A need to dominate
12. Have criminal tendencies	12. A need to control
13. Self-mutilate	13. Blocking and attacking
14. Become delusional	14. A need to be a conqueror
15. Experience depression	15. Evil thoughts and actions

What Punishment Teaches Us

What causes the "bad" feeling? Time-traveling to times we've been punished will show us where we learned how to treat ourselves. Most of us are pretty tough on ourselves. Many times people remember a punishment with no recall of why they were punished. What did punishment teach us? Is that where fear and the judgmental piranha come from?

1. Who punished you in the past?

2. What were you punished for?

3. How were you punished?

4. How did the punishment make you feel?

5. How did you react to punishment? Did you rebel, shut down or avoid it by lying? Explain.

6. How do you play out punishment with yourself or others in present time?

7. Now, do a physical rinse on one of your punishers/punishments. Be mean and upset on purpose.

8. What does inner child time-traveling look like? Look ahead.

Homework
Rent this movie if you want a visual!

   My favorite "time travel" movie is *A Christmas Carol*. Please watch this movie, even if you have seen it before! It has so much wisdom in it.

   Starting with:

The Ghost of Christmas Past
1. "See" where Scrooge was happy, then hurt and sad as a small child? You are watching Scrooge's inner child!

2. Notice that Scrooge needed to "see" and "feel" his past in order to change his behavior in present time, which then altered his future.

3. One of Scrooge's biggest love sources was his sister. Did her dying in childbirth affect his capability to love? Explain.

4. Could this have caused him to hurt so much he shut down? Explain.

5. Could he have emotionally blamed the baby (his nephew) for killing his sister and resent him? Explain.

6. Could the death of his sister cause him to feel so out of control that he shut down with his fiancé and begin to hoard money as a way of control? Is this a needy/greedy example? Explain.

7. How aware was Scrooge of his inner child? Were you shocked that he was shocked and in such denial? Explain.

Now fill in the blanks:

The Ghost of Christmas Past

1. *Dear little Scrooge, when I look at you I see... And I feel...*

2. *When you were young, you were like...*

3. *Which reminds me of my...*

The Ghost of Christmas Present

1. How did Scrooge's past set up his present behavior?

2. How aware was Scrooge concerning his present-time behavior?

3. *Dear Present-Time Scrooge, when I look at you I see... And I feel....*

4. *You are like...*

5. *Which reminds me of my...*

The Ghost of Christmas Future

1. Did you notice that the ghost of Christmas future does not speak? Why doesn't this ghost speak?

2. If Scrooge learns to understand his past, could those revelations change his behavior, present time and then future? Why?

3. If he refuses to understand his past, do you think his future will change or stay the same as predicted?

4. How about you? If you learn to understand your past, how will your present change? How will your future change?

Find the Fear, and You're Halfway Home

A life full of patterns of fear and anger creates a self-fulfilling prophecy!

Although fear is of the unknown in the present, fear is often created from the past.

Fear is a messenger telling you what you are doing today that will reveal itself in the future. Wake up and rinse to find the patterns you are living now that are continuing to hurt.

What you fear for the future, you are creating now!

Find the fear!

Wake Up Your Intuition!

Until you understand your parents or guardians, get ready to turn into them!

"See" if you are integrating their thoughts, feelings, beliefs and behaviors or attracting people similar to your parents or guardians into your current life.

Rinse and wake up your inner self's intuition to show you what you can be instead! If you are truly open and feeling, you can create so much from just a wish. This is a way to go beyond your intelligence and personal life experience!

My Own Christmas Carol
by Mona

I decided I was on my own path. I used my intelligence and will to decide I was not going to play out my parents' issues. I did not "own" or "rinse" my past. I logically and intellectually decided what I was going to do and not do. I am strong-willed. By the way, my strong will, in actuality, means that I'm stubborn, insecure, needy, angry, fearful, guilt-ridden and shame-based, which is attached to my drive to succeed and conquer!

So, in my strong-willed behavior and stubbornness, I began, subconsciously, to play out my parents' relationship, which was completely unknown to my conscious awareness!

Think I'll create what I *think* I'm creating?
Doubt it!

My father is a charming, wanna-be professional ballplayer. He was a minor league baseball player who became a realtor. Missing his sports life, he felt that he never "went for it" all the way. My father, although a talented and sensitive man, is emotionally unaware and lives as a people-pleaser. Tuning out became his defense mechanism so he wouldn't get hurt or feel too much from his past, in his present or for his future. He has no feeling-processing capabilities to handle big feelings and past traumas or future fears. If someone triggers him into a time-travel, he blocks it.

Even in a crowd, he feels alone. With all "good" intentions, he didn't understand that dropping his logical and emotional truth caused a lack of intimacy and connection in his and our lives. Don't misunderstand me or get me wrong; I love my father, he's a funny and well-meaning man. He is successful and took very good care of me and created magic energetically.

So my subconscious mind, against my "will," was immediately attracted to a man who actually became my husband, who was very much like my father. I said, "Aha! I'm not attracting my father because

I'm so logically aware. This man is a musician, not a realtor or an athlete! Did I "see" my father and remember his past? *No!*

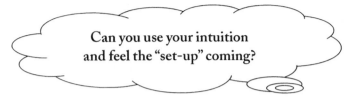

Can you use your intuition and feel the "set-up" coming?

My husband was a wanna-be professional musician. He was a guitarist and singer with a pre-law degree and honors, but he just never "went for it" all the way. He was emotionally unaware and a people pleaser. Tuning out became his defensive mechanism so he wouldn't get hurt or feel too much. You won't believe this, but he became a realtor (after we were married). Didn't I just say, I will not marry an athlete or realtor? He just wants everyone to get along. He had all "good" intentions. An intention is upsetting because it feels like a covert excuse for pretending something didn't happen because he didn't mean for it to happen. Then I get to feel guilty for having upset feelings over "whatever happened" which didn't matter because he didn't intend it so it didn't count.

There goes truth right out the window! If there had just been some kind of an own, I'd be okay, but no such luck because it didn't happen. To admit it happened would take away the intention. So, it didn't happen. Oh my God, I feel nuts! So, I wait for it to happen again. Now I start lying and pretending that I'm okay, to block being upset too.

I loved my husband; he is a funny, well-meaning man. He has been successful and took care of me when I was physically very sick. He led the way to my healing through alternative care, which he, fortunately for me, had a passion for. But the question is: Did I marry my father? Did I play out my past?

Here's the hard part: If I attracted someone like my father, who did I become? I certainly did not become my mother. My mother is a bossy, strong and talented woman who hides her sensitivities. She is also very intuitive. She uses humor and sarcasm to mask her vulnerability. My mother is a controlling, brilliant woman.

No, this can't be true. I'm sweet, quiet, and innocent. I would never control or ridicule my husband. Damn it! I love my mom and have a blast with her, but she can get so out of control and blames everyone for everything. "Owning" is very difficult for her. My mom time-traveled constantly and had no conscious awareness of her time-traveling. She lived in the past, present and future at the same time. But not me!

My ex-husband had a blast with me, but I would get so out of control and blame him for everything. I was time-traveling constantly with no conscious awareness. I was in the past, present and future at the same time. How did this happen? I "willed" myself not to do this!

I remember one day, early in the relationship, wanting to fight with my ex-husband. Do you believe that I had to teach him how to fight, too? I said, "When I say blah, blah, blah, you're supposed to say blah, blah, blah."

Who wrote these rules on how to fight? My parents, that's who!

There's a red flag. My husband hated fighting; my dad hates fighting. My dad is emotionally shut down. My mom energetically feels him shut down, as he denies his feelings and truths. It's about to be her turn, yep, she's going to do it. She will now play out my dad's denied feelings and go berserk.

My ex-husband was emotionally shut down. I energetically felt him, as he denied his feelings and truths. And, yessireeee, you bet I'll play out his denied feelings and go berserk for him. That way, he won't have to and I get to be the crazy one. I didn't rinse or own. Can you "see" what happened?

Hugs & kisses!
Mona Scrooge

~

The sins of the forefathers shall be passed down from generation to generation, unless you "see" and tell your truth, then rinse and own it

Don't try to process the voices in your head, in your head! Write the voices out! If you keep the voices in your head, your rational mind, full of excuses and reasons, will ignite, waking up your judgmental voice, which will attack everyone and everything and send you into a spin. The subliminal mind begins igniting subconscious memories and future premonitions and fears, sending you into a time-travel. Be careful!

That's all it takes to shut down, get depressed, or wake up the addict. So, write, Write, *Write*!! rinse! Rinse! *Rinse*! Go into your parents' cultural or religious beliefs! Go into your own! Do crazy voices! Time-travel and physical rinses!

Post-Traumatic Syndrome

We all suffer from Post Traumatic Syndrome (PTS). Obviously, some of us have more extreme cases than others. But we've all experienced this type of trauma that has thrown us off our true intuitive path, causing many types of disorders, which makes us at least a bit "out of order."

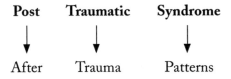

After a **trauma** you develop **patterns.**

In fact, each of us has a *bunch* of PTSs! Our subconscious mind remembers all of our traumas. Any such "little" or "big" experience alters our self-development, and changes the behaviors or beliefs of who we are. Can you "see" how important it is to understand our past traumas?

It's a myth that a trauma has to be horrible. Many traumas are violent; but some can be as "simple" as a parent being sick or depressed, or a "difficult" pregnancy, or a threat that was never carried out. All of these experiences can traumatize the mind's belief system and create a survivor pattern.

Don't minimize any such experience you've had. If you live with an upset and you minimize it, you will miss its significance and the opportunity to heal it. Pay attention to yourself! And watch your vocabulary. If you are using words such as those in the next chart, you are minimizing and blocking.

Emotional, Manipulative Words	
Kind of	I'm *kind of* happy.
Sort of	I'm *sort of* good.
A little	I'm *a little* sad.
Maybe	*Maybe* I can go.
Perhaps	*Perhaps* tomorrow.
Probably	I *probably* did it.
At least	*At least*, I showed up.

Right-brain dominant and left-brain dominant people handle traumas differently. Left-brainers usually shut down and get depressed, become addicted or obsessive/compulsive. Right-brainers often get hysterical, addictive, depressed or go insane.

Intelligence can prevent understanding by awakening the judger inside you unless emotional processing is allowed.

The pain created after a trauma can have a domino effect, bringing all kinds of realities, one after another, to the surface. What is real and what is true?

Real is a *belief* based on how we think, feel, remember, and perceive things. True is what *is*.

For example, when a ninety-pound girl looks in the mirror and "sees" an obese woman, she is "seeing" this in her mind's eye because of the weight she energetically feels in her life from heavy burdens. The anorexic perception is based on an energy or feeling. Energy and feelings are so strong, the subconscious will sometimes make them real. This perception is a real situation causing real thoughts, feelings and behaviors, but is it true? Is something that's *real* something necessarily *true*?

Our thoughts, feelings, memories, and perceptions are very real to each of us...but they are not necessarily true.

To find out what is *true*, rinse what feels *real*.

For example, a molestee can sense a "rapist" energy in a complete stranger because the molestee will sense a familiar, comfortable, energy in the rapist. The molestee may even feel he or she has known this person his or her whole life. Energetically, this is real, but not literally true.

A molestee who blocks past traumatic experiences from his or her conscious mind may still fall prey to the thoughts, feelings, and behaviors manifesting in the subconscious mind. The molestee may be consciously unaware of these patterns, but personal decisions and behaviors will still keep coming from these memories. This person may actually attract a rapist and let that energy into his or her life, or become the rapist. If our subconscious is triggered by a subliminal picture from such a trauma, and we time-travel, we may play this out as if the past were happening today and have no recall of this memory. If the conscious mind is disassociated, which is a bigger disconnect, a time-travel will take us to the age we were during our trauma, without the older self's awareness. We may even be able to pass a lie detector test if the older self is taking the test. You see, the older self didn't do it. There is no "vibe" of guilt. Any PTS person with a sense of compassion will feel mortified and horrified at being accused of such upsetting behavior. The disassociation means an abused part of that person is triggered and is playing out what it remembers without conscious awareness. This part can be played out in either role, as the abusee or as the abuser, depending on the trigger.

To accomplish anything, we would have to take this person through a time-travel to when the trauma happened. If this person fears punishment, there is no way for recovery unless we can make this person feel safe. The trauma would need to be rinsed and the person would need to be taught a processing skill for self-forgiveness, and understanding would need to be learned. If this person feels fear, guilt or shame when consciously realizing that he or she has played out the trauma as an abusee or an abuser, the person may become hysterical and suicidal. You don't want to make a PTS person too conscious without solid processing skill.

1. What is a trauma, upset or confusion you have experienced?

2. What are the patterns that you have created from this trauma?

3. How does this pattern throw you out of order(check your realms), creating a type of "disorder"?

4. How does this make you feel?

5. What can you do to change this pattern?

6. What is another trauma you have experienced?

7. What are the patterns you have created from this trauma?

8. How does this pattern throw you out of order, creating "disorder"?

9. How does this make you feel?

10. What can you do to change this pattern?

(Keep repeating these questions as many times as you can...)

To Grow More I Need a Screen Door

A screen door is a metaphor for the filtering processing that you train yourself to develop so that you can choose what vibes and energy to absorb and take in and what energy to leave with others, based on your intuition and wisdom, rather than based on your will and the will of others. To interrupt your trauma trances from re-occurring you need a screen door. We are all energy-based molecular patterns that are reacting and interacting with others. With this in mind, answer the following questions:

1. What is the purpose of a glass sliding door?

2. When a glass sliding door is left wide open, what is allowed to happen?

3. What happens when the glass sliding door is closed?

4. What is the purpose of a screen door?

A closed glass door keeps the environment and other people out and you locked in.

This is a barrier. No one gets in and you don't get out!

If the door is wide open, everything and anything can come in or out no matter what you think or feel!

A screen door filters what comes in and out.

This is a way to depersonalize spiritually, mentally, emotionally, sexually, financially and psychically!

Check In

1. Are you a closed door when you are isolated and blocking everything and everyone from coming in or out of your life? When? Why or why not?

   Or

2. Are you an open door when everything and everyone's energy affects you against your will? Why or why not?

If the answer to either of these questions is "yes," then you need a screen door!

3. My screen door is like or would be like…feel like… and create…

4. When you go back and read #1, #2 and #3 take out the word "door" and personalize the information by adding "I" and "me" to your writings wherever necessary.

Story Time

Marti is someone who has to rinse and own all of the pain from herself and her family. She has to own all the pain because she feels it in her body, mind and heart. Some of this pain is not her fault, and some of it is the result of her act-outs from not processing these hurts. Unprocessed hurt does what it knows; it creates more hurt. Finding fault or blaming herself never stopped her pain or stopped her from passing on the pain to others. Finding a way to take responsibility worked. Marti has learned to own her behaviors, her reactions, rebellions, addictions and even her fights. No more pain!

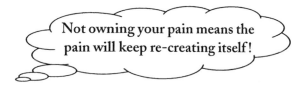

Not owning your pain means the pain will keep re-creating itself!

A Hamster in a Wheel
by Marti

It is so difficult to "see" myself or remember how my life was back in 1996.

I was so shut down; my vision of the world was as a little girl, a carrier of darkness as a depressed addict. By 1996 I had survived molestation and the death of three brothers—one to cancer, one to a heroin overdose, and one to a slow deterioration that lasted over eight years.

My family was filled with grief and my family's grief became mine. I was so heavy (depressed). My parents and remaining siblings lived in shame, anger, and sadness. There were so many unspoken thoughts and feelings buried inside all of us.

I was bisexual, unclear of my desires, my dreams, and my heart. I was thirty-three and had no sense of self, nor could I come close to my pain because I didn't think I could get to the other side…(at the time, I couldn't even imagine I might someday live the way I do now).

To compound the congestion of my heart and soul, my best friend was hit by a drunk driver in 1989. She lived in a coma for a year. Three years of hospitals and rehab, and she still suffers from brain injuries. She will never again live an independent life.

I repressed my heart and my feelings. I pushed them all into a tiny box and then I hid that box deep inside me. I was so afraid to tell anyone who I was. I had no idea who that was anyway. I was constantly on a roll, using humor to keep people laughing so they would not see me crying. My days were either full of highs, or hiding on my couch in the dark.

My spirit is what saved me…although I wasn't connected consciously to it. My heart may have been broken, but I always knew, down deep, that something good was around the corner. My spirit gave me strength to believe I could do anger work. It was the hardest work I've ever done. I resisted every step of the way. There was so much suppression in me that I felt if I let out the tiniest bit, I would explode.

That's why I had to do it, piece by piece...body part by body part...

Body Memories and Body Rinse

Like your mind, your body has a memory. The body stores everything. This is why some people flinch, twitch or shake when there is nothing physically wrong. The body is remembering being hurt and anticipating that same hurt over and over again. This reflex is from a subconscious signal that is way too fast for the conscious mind to catch. This is why we do a physical rinse. It's a way to release the body from reflexes that were developed from memories that we do not want to play out in present time. Rinsing your body parts is a way to listen to your body's memories. Finding the truths of your body releases traumas and shame that can engulf you energetically. This is invisible warfare with yourself. Who and what are you fighting when you criticize your body?

 ### Body Rinse

Dear Head:
When I look at you I see... And I feel... And I remember when...

Dear Eyes:
When I look at you I see... And I feel... And I remember when...

Dear Nose:
When I look at you I see... And I feel... And I remember when...

Dear Mouth:
When I look at you I see... And I feel... And I remember when...

Dear Hair:
When I look at you I see... And I feel... And I remember when...

Dear _____,

(Fill in the blank. Keep talking to your body parts until you are finished).

Please continue with the following list:

Ears, skin, breasts/chest, buttocks, hips, penis/vagina, hands, feet, arms, fat, stomach, legs, ankles, and any other body part.

Take Your Body Back

Recalling your memories is the first step. The second step is to take back the experience and end it differently! Through the subconscious mind, you can visualize and create new behaviors for that situation from the past, as if it were now, using new information from today. Pull out your acting skills and start recreating your wishes. The past is remembered and re-enacted in the present, changing the programmed information that was planted in your mind and body, against your will. Repeat your words and/or actions over and over until they become a habit. This can help you create a new, empowered, subliminal picture that says, "My body belongs to me!"

For example, if I was attacked from behind, while lying on my stomach, my body's memory might cause me to freeze or have panic attacks when lying on my stomach. This can happen even if no one's around. I can feel crazy if I judge myself and don't understand that I'm remembering via a time-travel. Having a body memory from just lying in this position feels frightening. To get my body back, I can lie on my stomach and remember what happened to me. Then, rather than do what I did in the attack, I can make up a new "saving myself" movement. I can strongly turn my body to the side, see the person who scares me in my mind and kick the person, even though an actual person is not there. I can scream, "Get the hell off of me!" I can run. I can do anything I want. I can come up with a new ending to my story. Don't worry. The mind and body will get it. They don't need it to be actually true. It will be accepted as real if visualized, felt and physical movements made and repeated.

Now, let's say that my parents used to slap me across the face. I can relive that experience; and this time, instead of just standing there, I can turn the other cheek, or grab their arm and yell, "*Stop!*" My memory has power over me only if I allow it to be perceived in the old way.

Whatever "new" movement you choose,
do it many times, to subconsciously
change the subliminal picture in
your mind and create a new habit.

You do not have to ignore or succumb to the past.

 Give yourself a choice!

1. *My painful memory is...*
   And made me feel...

2. *But my new "ending" is...*
   Now play it out physically.
   And I just learned...
   And I feel....

My Meditation

My mind carries everything in my life—good and bad. I am okay, because I am here. Memories are not going to hurt me, but I will "see" and feel them. I will become aware. I have gone through the memories. Therefore I have already achieved success.

I have to feel and understand the negative to feel and understand the positive. "Seeing" and rinsing clear the way for me to create my life consciously. Sometimes, I feel the hurt and it scares me; but then I remember how to process the anger, hurt, and fear and I feel empowered. I am stronger than my memories.

I will be wiser and live with inner confidence, not insecurity, false humility or arrogance. I will know my adult self, my inner child, and my spirit by understanding my past fears and my present-time denials.

Once I know and can reach myself—I am centered and can affect others on the planet in a much different way.

Congratulations on your strength to keep going!

Chapter Review

I just learned…
And I feel…

Summary

The mind time-travels every day. Being aware and conscious of this fact opens the door for many new discoveries. You will be less reactive and more understanding as you begin to understand which of your thoughts, feelings, and memories are "real" and which are "true."

Our early exposure to others' perceptions of our culture, religion, and family affects our thoughts, beliefs and behaviors in the future. That's why understanding our entire history is crucial.

We all have many voices in our heads, and many of them are simply recordings of ourselves and other people's opinions and ideas or our own perceptions of how we have seen the world. These voices are "real" and they affect our thoughts, beliefs, and behaviors, but what they are saying may not be true. If they are not necessarily our inner truths, why let them dominate our lives?

Most of us have been trained to want the world to change. We haven't been trained to want to change ourselves, first. Let me ask you this: Is it even possible to change the world if you haven't had the experience of changing yourself?

12 Our Realms:
Could Disorder Mean They Are Out of Order?

In an old video called "Himself," Bill Cosby talks about how intelligent he and his wife seemed to be *before* they had children. The moment children arrived in their lives, the couple suffered brain damage, and lost their intelligence altogether. The video is hysterical. Being a parent myself, I agree with Mr. Cosby.

My son is only thirteen years old and I already feel guilty about all of my visible and invisible mistakes. Believe me, I know my day in the hot seat is coming too. But that's just the way it is. He has to deal with his history too.

Many people have watched me make mistakes in my business, personal relationships, and in the raising of my son. (That's the scary part about being an open book, everyone can "see" everything!) Sometimes, I feel spiritually, mentally, emotionally, physically, sexually, and financially naked. It's hard to be that open.

We're all doing our own live reality TV shows. It's difficult to be watched and judged. I pray that whoever judges me learns to *not* judge themselves. Perfection is an illusion and an impossibility.

The Six Realms and Their Alignment

If I had to summarize my thoughts, I would say: Take this information in, discern it by checking-in with the realms defined on the following page. See what rings true, with no care or worry attached, and go! Do your own check-ins. When we blame others for influence they have had on us, we are victims, with no self. Learn to feel and sense your self and be self-responsible. Unless there is a gun, no one is making you do anything. A realm is the order and cycle of your mind, heart, body and soul. The life-long goal for me is to align my own realms and be able to keep them in alignment for at least a couple of minutes. I do not have time to gossip, be depressed or sabotage my life. The focus required for these realms is a 24-hour-a-day job just to achieve partial alignment.

Here are the six realms. They were put in the following order for balance, which we will discuss further.

1. **Spiritual:** Truth, Love, Creation, Empowerment
2. **Mental:** Thoughts, Logic and Rationale
3. **Emotional:** Feelings (past, present, and future)
4. **Physical:** Body and Animal Energy
5. **Sexual:** Gender, Sexuality
6. **Financial:** Powerful and Powerless Struggles

Your turn! List the order in which you value your realms:

1. _____
2. _____
3. _____
4. _____
5. _____
6. _____

Are your realms "in sync" with the previous order?

Whatever you resist persists!

When **Spiritual** is your first realm, truth and love are your first check-ins. If you want to lose the feeling of insanity, create from truth and love! Your sense of self comes from within you, not from outside you. This means your power is operating from the place of empowerment. Your ability to "check-in" with your soul and inner child creates a centered confidence, and a life that is not thrown off by anything or anyone outside you.

If **Financial** is your first realm, your power and low- and high-ego are your first check-ins. Your life consists of domination, and the fear of being dominated. This is both a powerful and powerless struggle. If your ego is holding your center, your focus is on your and others' perceptions of being important. Everything becomes about what you have, what you have accomplished, and what you own. If you are focused on finances or success and you're on the powerless side of the struggle because you haven't "made it" yet, your self-talk is a strong self-beat topped with self-pity and defensive behavior. Are you fighting a helpless/hopeless state of mind? Ego, either powerful or powerless, is full of insecure and/or arrogant self-talk that has been programmed into your subconscious mind from the past. These voices are the gods or guides controlling the decisions you make to steer your life.

It is said, "It is easier to drive a camel through the eye of a needle than for a rich man to enter heaven." That may have meant that some-one in ego, focused on money and power, cannot find inner peace. In-ner peace comes from the power of self-empowerment. Isn't inner peace what heaven represents? Could it be this power struggle is our teacher on what *not* to do, so we know what *to* do? If power becomes our foundation of importance, then feeding our ego is a must. If you are experiencing this power struggle, how does your stomach feel? Can you sleep at night? Do you get headaches? Do you experience anxiety disorder?

So the difference between choosing the spiritual and the financial as your first realm is the difference between living on a powerful/pow-erless see-saw and living on an internally and externally balanced form of empowerment. You can create an entirely different life, just by re-arranging these two realms!

Here is an example of a person whose realms are scrambled and, therefore, out of balance. Is this you, or someone you know?

An Out-of-Balance But Possibly Outwardly Successful Person

1. **Financial** If you put your financial realm first, you can obsess about having or not having money and possessions. The goal is being important. Being powerful is getting respect. Domi-nating and controlling others means protection and safety. If money and power is all-important, truth and love will be sac-rificed.

2. **Mental** Mental, then, means being sharp and righteous, in-timidating, dominating and manipulative. You debate, argue or threaten, overtly or covertly, to succeed.

3. **Physical** You become either an addict with work, food, drugs, exercise, surgeries/makeovers, or you become lonely, shut-down and isolated.

4. **Sexual** Two choices: The conqueror and seducer "loves 'em and leaves 'em," or possesses them. There are sex addictions or the opposite—sexually shut-down sexless energy. This can turn to sexual abuse, an act-out from disowned sexual pain!

5. **Spiritual** God can be part of this, or not. If God is in this scenario, it's not God's perception of truth and love that you see. Truth from this angle comes from an opinionated judger and punisher who may forgive after the punishment, or you interpret love to mean giving up your truth to offer your life in self-sacrificing ways—giving up yourself rather than giving of yourself.

6. **Emotional** Emotions are to be controlled and shut down; anger, fear, guilt and shame are hidden inside. Emotions are not to be understood; they are to be denied and truth bows to judgment. If this doesn't fit you, how about emotional craziness or hysteria? Feelings, out of balance, can throw your psyche directly into hell.

Can you "see" how realms, out of order, can become toxic? Let's look at all the realms and get to know them better.

The Spiritual Realm

When you are centered in your spiritual realm, you feel *inner strength*. This strength comes from knowing and understanding your truths. Truths come from your intuition. This intuitive voice speaks from an inspired place, replacing the egotistical pusher energy from the "drive." The drive can be exhausting and controlling. Inspiration is a spiritual energy that frees your essence and soul to subconsciously create **beyond what you know**. However, hearing this voice isn't always easy. If it were, everyone would hear it and there would be no judgment or personalization.

To hear your intuition's voice, you need to clear negative self-talk and rinse! Cleaning the voices from your life experiences empties irrational and dishonest thoughts, feelings and judgments from your mind. This clears the way for an opening to "see" and "hear" from within.

So, the spiritual realm is a state of *being*. This realm embraces the understanding of all other realms.

The Mental Realm

A computer computes. It is a high-speed machine that performs mathematical or logical processes and retrieves and stores programmed information. Does this sounds like the left part of the brain? Every now and then, a computer drops or loses its information and memory, right? If it tries to do too many tasks at once, or it's dropped or treated improperly, it will not function. If it gets too full of data, it runs slowly, freezes, shuts itself down, even crashes. How much energy, time and skill do you need to reboot your computer?

Your brain has information, reactors and memories, too. These components are stored, consciously or subconsciously, and filed away when not in use.

If your computer encounters a glitch in one area of its process or memory, other stored information may also be affected. So imagine, if you lose a sense of your truth, memories, thoughts, or feelings, you may freeze, shut down and scramble other thoughts, feelings, memories and truths. When these are distorted, your entire perception of the truth can become confused, and lost.

The good news is, with appropriate knowledge and perseverance, you can retrieve what's been lost.

A processing or memory locked in the subconscious mind is filed away and stored, but is still energetically active. This information stays in the subconscious file until you have the capability to process and deal with it. If these stored thoughts, feelings or memories are not processed, rinsed, and understood properly, they can lead to lost and/or scrambled information. When programming inside the human brain is lost, distorted or twisted, you can become depressed and shut down; short circuited, scrambled and insane; maniacal/criminal and/or addictive.

Many times we use depression, insanity, drugs and alcohol to lose, suppress, or control truth, thoughts, feelings and memories. Will this affect the functioning of our brain? Absolutely! The pre-frontal cortex will engage or disengage concentration, focus or empathy regarding every thought, feeling and memory. It will discern, judge or shut down altogether. These mental gymnastics don't delete your memories. They simply exist in a subconscious file. Your mind and behavior are still affected by this information without your awareness. Your life experiences and perceptions can't really go away, can they?

If your thoughts, feelings and memories are not dealt with, how can you claim that you are aware of yourself, or that you truly understand yourself, let alone others? If your life experience is stuck in your subconscious files, then so are you!

Understanding our mental realm requires a deep knowledge of our thoughts and memories. Even if we accept, understand, and comprehend everything we can dig up, is it possible to ever know it all? The mental realm is the I.Q. (the intelligent quotient/answer). To truly achieve higher intelligence, don't we need an E.Q. (emotional quotient/intuitive knowledge), as well?

1. What do you think of the idea that thoughts, feelings, and memories can affect your life and you can consciously know nothing about them?

2. Can you think of ways that your stored, unprocessed thoughts, feelings and memories are slowing down your brain? How?

3. Has this slowing down ever turned into depression or bursts of anger? How?

4. Has this speed ever turned into obsessions, neurosis or hyperness?

How the Brain Responds to Stimuli

1. An experience happens.

2. Thoughts and feelings enter the brain.

3. The left brain identifies logic or truth, consciously or subconsciously.

4. The judger inside you expresses an opinion about the experience.

5. Perception evolves from your thoughts, feelings, truth, judgment, and opinion.

6. The right brain feels, reacts, or shuts down to this perception.

7. A visual is created and becomes a subliminal.

8. The prefrontal cortex concentrates, focuses, and empathizes, or shuts down, disconnects, and interferes with your left and right brain processes.

9. The consciousness then responds to the experience—either in an enlightened, feeling and open way, or with an act-out or reactive behavior designed to block or twist the experience of the truth.

When we feel the need to "protect," we are attempting to block, fight or begin an internal or external war against the upsetting truth!

But truth, understanding, and boundaries are all the protection we truly need for clarity, wisdom and sanity!

The Emotional Realm

Remember the difference between your left and right brains?

The right brain is the feeling message center. It's the part that makes your computer brain come alive. It's animated, and has sounds and a personality. It communicates and relates in pictures.

The right brain can easily tap into your psyche. That means your right brain affects your subconscious mind and your dream state a great deal. Dreams are often the subconscious mind trying to send a message to the conscious mind via thoughts, colors, pictures, metaphors or subliminals. These pictures and messages, which aren't necessarily literal, attempt to bypass the fearful and judgmental voices that live closer to our left brain's intelligence and logic.

The left brain is logical and intellectual. While the right brain relies on experiential learning, the left-brain depends on logic and reason. It's the part of your brain that wants to make order out of chaos.

While the best way to find balance is for both sides of your brain to work diligently together, most of us lean more to one side than another. Feelings, creativity, and imagination come naturally to a right-brain dominant person, but are difficult and challenging for a left-brain dominant person. A right brainer might throw a temper tantrum at the very idea of being organized. And the left brainer can easily go to judge the expressions and talents of a right brainer. By the way, both of these parts are inside you, so the war isn't just on the outside. This fight is one of the biggest internal, invisible warfares we know.

We need both sides of the brain to feel balanced, complete and centered. Since the sides of the brain are so different, they rarely understand each other. So it falls to you, your conscious mind, to understand how your logical and feeling brains process differently, so that you can connect them and get them to work together as a team. If you do not, your two halves can engage in an internal battle just by having two innocent, conflicting points of view. If neither brain has an understanding of itself or the other, it will be thrown out of balance, and the rest of you will be, too.

For example, most of us are taught to use our left brains in order to think, and our right brains in order to feel. Our logic and intelligence live right next door to the Judger, and our right brain lives right next door to the Creator.

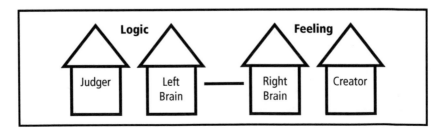

If the left brain doesn't connect to its opposite, which is feelings, the Judger will step in where feelings belong and throw it out of balance. This judgmental interruption causes us to self-beat and blame ourselves and others. This process can make us hardened, insensitive, and cold. If a right-brain person doesn't connect to logic and truth, the Creator will cause destruction, and sabotage as a way of creation.

Without logic and feeling operating in harmony, there is no ability to understand the entirety of your mind, heart, body and soul.

Although opposites attract, they soon repel. Are balance and peace achieved when all opposites can meet without friction? How do we connect opposites?

Where's the middle guy who connects the left and right brain? The Prefrontal Cortex is a triangular portion of the brain that assimilates the capabilities of the right and left brain.

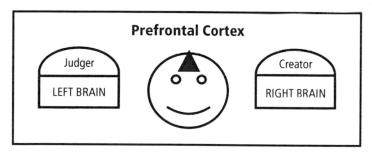

The prefrontal cortex is in charge of you. It houses the conscious mind and the subconscious mind. It's the headquarters of the brain as well as the brain's storage center. Your memories, deepest feelings, and judgments are handled here. Love, sensory perceptions, metaphors, literal facts, spiritual views and discernments are all processed through the prefrontal cortex.

If there is a shutdown in the prefrontal cortex, you will go into survival mode. Your survival skills and protective mechanisms will rule. Your life, which was about how to live, is now about how to survive. You will have little or no feeling for the future. Your animal instincts will overtake your intuition.

There are many people alive and functioning whose prefrontal cortexes have shut down, usually because of a confusing, upsetting or traumatic experience. When you lose connection with your prefrontal cortex, you lack empathy and the ability to concentrate or focus.

What the Prefrontal Cortex Controls

Empathy: The ability to feel and to understand yourself and others without judgment.

Concentration: The ability to hold on to a concept or idea that you either understand or don't understand, which increases or decreases mental strength.

Focus: The amount of time you are capable of concentrating on a specific point.

For our minds to be developed to optimum capacity, these three prefrontal cortex components—**empathy, concentration** and **focus**—must first be linked with each other, and then connected to the left and right brain. If your upsets or traumas attach to the prefrontal cortex, your concentration and focus can go out of balance, connect to a hyper-energy and become obsessive/compulsive or neurotic in some way. If you point this energy in the direction of fear and lies, insanity is all you've got to work with.

When the left brain identifies issues, facts and patterns, and the right brain feels, creates and perceives, the prefrontal cortex is balanced, creating sanity, empathy, sensitivity, higher intelligence and intimate relationships!

If these three parts of the brain disconnect from each other, a person can become semi-aware, reactive, and driven by unprocessed experiences from the past. If the prefrontal cortex is weak enough, empathy evaporates, and no amount of love or punishment will penetrate or affect this person until he or she time-travels back to the issue that created the shutdown.

Empathy
If empathy is disconnected from truth, logic, and feelings, one can become cold, rigid, a pathological liar and in extreme cases a psychopath.

A criminal mentality—the creation of evil—is often derived from the lack of this essential ingredient called empathy. It is dangerous to be without the capability to empathize with yourself and others.

A lack of empathy happens when you shut down your feeling and intuitive sensors as a result of being scared, abused or traumatized—spiritually, mentally, emotionally, physically, sexually or financially. Blocking empathy is a way to survive an upset that you can't process. When you experience a loss of empathy, a trance state transpires. You can be fine one minute and, all of a sudden, you are triggered by a color, someone's eyes, a smell, a sound—and your psyche travels back in time, causing a shutdown of feelings and sometimes memory in present time. If this happens, chances of you reverting to the upset, shutting down all feeling and self-empathy is almost inevitable. All present-time knowledge is temporarily or permanently blocked. Where are you and who is responsible for you? Certainly not you.

No matter what, a scared or abused person will find some way to repeat the fear, abuse, or trauma, or simply shut down circuits altogether, until the trauma is understood. Every abusee copies what he or she *knows*, not what he or she likes. Abusees become abusers either to themselves or to others. If these memories are not rinsed and understood, they will repeat.

Concentration

If concentration is disconnected from truth, logic and feelings we can become obsessive/compulsive, ritualistic, acquire attention deficit disorder (ADD/ADHD) and become maniacal. We will create a spin and an obsession, culminating in depression or hysteria. A thought or concept that is not rinsed and understood becomes repressed. We feel unsafe inside and look for ways to feel safe outside our self. The repressed thoughts and feelings become neurotic, which consist of our original thoughts and feelings combined with tremendous fear and ending in loss of hope. We try to become stable and safe by creating a ritualistic, patterned process to concentrate on for control. We do not want the psyche to time-travel to upsetting memories or to trigger a fear based on a past trauma that could be easily projected into the future.

The mind is very powerful. It is capable of taking something from the past, projecting it into the future, and creating thoughts, feelings and behaviors, in present time, to make this fear come true, creating a self-fulfilling prophecy. Energetically, we could be sitting in a pool of anxiety and paranoia and not know what time zone we're in. Patterns and rituals keep our mind focused on these rituals, at a high level of concentration, so the mind doesn't wander. These patterned thoughts and behaviors are compelling, because they create a false sense of power while we are in a state of powerlessness. This highly concentrated energy is used to focus on a ritual and pattern as a way to block the truth of thoughts, judgments, memories and feelings. The fear of becoming hysterical is overwhelming. Scared and hurt, we come up with obsessive techniques as a way to process, control and survive our fear, because we have lost faith that we could ever get out of our spin.

Focus

If focus is disconnected from truth, logic, and feelings, people can become anxious, scattered, chaotic, easily confused, hyper, shut down, neurotic or depressed. Fear or lack of understanding becomes physically evident. The eyes will have a tendency to look around aimlessly. Without focus, eye contact is rare. It is said that the eyes are the windows to the soul. The soul holds the truth of our psyche. If fear, pain, or judgment sit on top of the truth, the human reflex is to block it and create an act-out to release stored-up, repressed energy. The eyes have to lose focus, or they hyper-focus on something specific and drive themselves and others crazy. An out-of-balance focus muscle can cause a person to develop body twitches, a stutter, or compulsive verbal blurts.

1. How important is empathy in your life? Why?

2. How have you lost empathy for yourself and others? How? Why? What happened? How did that feel?

3. How important is concentration in your life? Why?

4. Where and how have you lost concentration in your life? Why? What happened? How did that feel?

5. How important is focus in your life? Why?

6. Where and how have you lost focus in your life? Why? What happened? How did that feel?

7. Can you guess what a person is like who places the emotional realm above truth?

The Physical Realm

One of the ways my body used to act out my subconscious pain was by my becoming physically ill. I didn't know how to use my left brain to identify my truths; and I didn't let my prefrontal cortex empathize and concentrate on what had happened in my life. So, my right brain couldn't rinse my pain, and my creator energy created agony, slowly breaking down my mind and body strength.

I became a victim to myself, lost inside my own mind and memories. I was full of blame, self-beat, humor, and illness. I developed an extroverted personality as my mask, so that no one, including myself, knew how hurt I was inside. My inner child knew my pain, and I didn't even know she existed! My protective strength mechanisms were busy blocking my thoughts, truths, feelings, memory and conscious awareness. My pain was subconsciously running my life in every realm. I believed in pain as a way of life! I concentrated on others, sympathized with others, and focused on helping others. Who and where was I? I didn't own or take responsibility for myself. I wanted others to feel responsible for my upsets and pain, as I was for theirs. This was based on sympathy, not empathy. This is fair, don't you think?

I would get sick whenever my sadness, anger, or fear was triggered. Therefore, I was able to hold people emotionally hostage with the unstated, energetic threat that I might get sicker if someone upset me. The illness became my protective strength mechanism. My bubbly personality in the face of my illness made me appear so brave that people felt even more manipulated into being nice to me. I was a hero! Mind you, this was all subconscious. I never knew this was happening.

My idea of fun, a positive idea, had been mixed with addiction, illness, bravery, anger, blame and fear, which left me confused about what fun, happiness and joy really were. The negative energy mixed in with the fun plus the positive energy of brave effervescence resulted in an unbelievable amount of destruction and pain, and a negative outcome of illness in every realm. I needed a new energetic equation, but who knew? My surroundings were too aggressive for my inner child and spirit to withstand, so I slowly shut down spiritually, mentally, and emotionally, until this confusion all manifested in my physical realm, by my getting sick!

I had positive/negative energy mixes everywhere. No wonder I was lost and felt hysterical inside. I was a perfect victim looking like a martyr and acting like a savior at the same time. I was a good, sick, little girl, going straight to heaven. All of this was real for me, even if it didn't have to be true.

I wasn't focusing on my thoughts, feelings, and past truths. That would have required rinsing, owning, and becoming more self-aware. I was too busy concentrating on others to possibly become self-aware myself. I was too busy being a good person.

> **KARMA**: The sum of all that an individual has done and is currently doing. The effects of what you think, feel, believe and how you behave actively attract and create your present and future experiences, making you responsible for your own life. In religions that incorporate reincarnation, karma is believed to exist through one's present life and past and future lives as well. In several eastern religions, karma comprises the entire cycle of cause and effect. Karma is not about right and wrong or good and bad; it's about experiencing what you understand and do not understand. It's about what you think, feel and believe—and, therefore, play out.

So, where did I end up? In a lose/lose game. That is the karma for believing in playing with manipulation, lies and denial. I blocked any chance of closeness and intimacy with others and myself. I thought I was safer this way. Notice, my goal was safety, not truth and love.

During this time, I remember wanting my mom to understand me. I was desperate for her to feel, see and hear me. I don't mean ordinary hearing and seeing, I wanted her to read between the lines. And I do believe she attempted to do so. But if my mom hadn't done her own rinsing and couldn't "see" all of herself, how could she really "see" all of me?

My mom could only "see" in me what she was willing to understand, feel, and "see" in herself. She did read me to a point, until I triggered her own issues and blocks. Every parent, including me, deals with this dilemma.

I had always envisioned my mother having great power over me. I didn't have any understanding of empowerment, so I was subconsciously thrilled I was sick. You see, I knew I finally held the power to upset her like she did me. She wouldn't listen to me. The illness made me feel in control. My inner vindictive voice was saying "How does it feel to hurt like you make me hurt? How does it feel to not be able to control me and scare my leg into doing your bidding?" I felt extremely powerful. I mixed the negative energy of being sick with the positive energy of being powerful and created a negative and painful outcome for myself: I kept myself ill.

I sure showed her, didn't I? Rebellion is a childish process. I time-traveled to my childhood, became that age and hurt myself, just to show my mother that she was hurting me. Stay away from rebellions. They are just childish act-outs that stem from low ego. The result is that you hurt you, to prove someone else hurt you.

My power and high were coming from outside me. I had made my mother my "God." Because I had given her my power, I naturally felt that the only way to get my power back was to take it from her. I became the controller of me and I hurt me as I believed she was hurting me. I let her know I was in charge. I was worse to me than she was. I could only create what I knew, so there was no rinsing or owning. A voice inside that I did not heed was crying, "Get me out of this!"

This was definitely not just a physical problem.

After years of struggling, I finally found medical and holistic doctors to support me in addressing every realm of my life. The first question my doctor asked me was, "Why do you want to be ill, Mona?"

He said this from a left-brain, logical point of view. I gasped and said, "What moron wants to be sick? I don't want this!"

He said, "Go deep and feel what the positive reason is for you wanting to be hurt." I responded by throwing a temper tantrum, storming out and quitting that stupid doctor's program. I thought, felt, screamed and cried until I lay helpless, wanting to die!

Then, it hit me! I wanted to not feel life's hurts anymore. First, I numbed myself spiritually, and then I numbed my inner child and her memories. Emotionally, I was hyper-disconnected, manic, or depressed. I couldn't truly feel myself anymore. Every part of me became numb. So, it was only natural to physically shut down. I didn't want attention as everyone had thought.

Attention, to me, meant pressure and judgment. I wanted to be left alone. So I started to die, just to get out of the pressure and memories. My feelings began to create behaviors that protected me and blocked my memories and upsetting truths.

Through my perceptions and blocks, I wore my physical state down. I physically became what my left brain thoughts and judgments perceived. I felt, and therefore became, a broken, weak, inadequate, and pitiful piece of flesh. I created this from my inner child's perception of how I saw me in my child's mind. My brain was crippled! My body followed the only path it knew. Come hell or high water, the creative mind shall create!

How powerful is the brain when it has no awareness, no truth, and doesn't know how to own?

1. Do you or someone you know place his or her physical realm first among their realms? What do you see? How does it feel to watch that?

The Sexual Realm

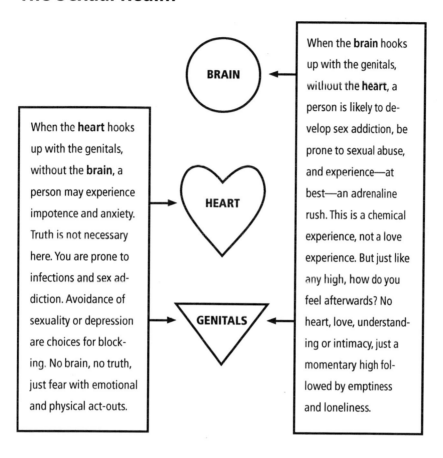

When the **heart** hooks up with the genitals, without the **brain**, a person may experience impotence and anxiety. Truth is not necessary here. You are prone to infections and sex addiction. Avoidance of sexuality or depression are choices for blocking. No brain, no truth, just fear with emotional and physical act-outs.

When the **brain** hooks up with the genitals, without the **heart**, a person is likely to develop sex addiction, be prone to sexual abuse, and experience—at best—an adrenaline rush. This is a chemical experience, not a love experience. But just like any high, how do you feel afterwards? No heart, love, understanding or intimacy, just a momentary high followed by emptiness and loneliness.

Why is sexuality listed as separate from the physical realm?

Sexuality is an expression of personality that stems from the interaction of your body, left and right brains, and the prefrontal cortex. Sexuality is felt physically, mentally, emotionally and psychically, and has its own energy. It is a build-up of all the above realms if connected fully.

We are more aware of sexuality because, however invisible its energy may be, it becomes visible when expressed through the physical realm. It can engulf you if charged with truth, love, chemistry and intuition. Within the realms, sexuality is number five for a reason. It holds so many thoughts, feelings, drives, and memories that if it is out of balance and order, it can easily become addictive, obsessive, and dangerous, resulting in threatening power struggles or deep intimacy issues.

Consider the idea of a mind, heart and soul connection during a sexual act. Isn't it possible that the physical body plays a secondary role to the energetic connection of the brain's thoughts and visuals? When mental, emotional and sexual feelings become active with no fear, shame or guilt, while using the intuition's telepathic senses to see, feel, and touch energetically with no physical contact, you may begin to tremble from all the connecting energy. This is the beginning of making love. This is why sexuality is the fifth realm.

As we heal the hurt in our hearts and evolve into a true self-love being, we can know the meaning of internal and external love... spiritually, mentally, emotionally, physically, psychically and sexually.

What were you taught about sex?

Dear Sex:
When I look at you I see... And feel... And I remember when...
I am angry with you (sex itself) because... And that makes me feel...
Sex, you ruined my life because...
I hate sex because...
I hate me and sex because...
I am scared of sex because...
I am afraid of me with sex because...
I feel bad about sex because...
Screw sex because...
I am guilty about sex because...
I am ashamed of sex because...
I am embarrassed by sex because
I am disappointed in sex because...
I feel sad about sex because...
I am hurt by sex because...
I feel sorry for myself with sex because...
I feel sorry for _____ with sex because...
I feel excited about sex because...
I love sex because...
I like sex because...
I'm happy about sex because...
This makes me feel...
I wish sex could be like...

Responsibility for your thoughts, feelings, memories, and essence is crucial when bringing others into this realm. Walking away from someone who is not a match for you is a part of your truth and, therefore, your spirituality. Any time you experience truth with understanding, you naturally use spiritual language. Make sure love and compassion are attached to the truth before you speak or make a move. Do not separate these two energies. They go together. Awareness of your truth and any others involved really matters. Don't just listen to words. You can sense what is really true, whether you like the truth or not.

A mental and emotional connection allows logical communication to connect with feelings and empathy. Even if someone else is not aware of his or her feelings, you don't get to play dumb. If that person is connected to you more than you are, speak up and set your boundaries.

Physically, everything you do to your body or someone else's body is recorded as a type of body memory. Every time you touch yours or someone else's body without the other realms in alignment, a little more pain, fear, disconnection from other realms occurs and bitterness grows in your and their minds and hearts.

I did not understand the hurt and pain I caused when I was young. Boys or men who said they really liked me or even loved me didn't register. I couldn't feel what that meant. I really hurt their hearts. Recovering from heart-breaking experiences of love takes incredible work. Recovery takes a lot of time too, that is, if one knows how to recover at all. This kind of disrespect of love can truly leave a scar. And, yes, when I got older, I fell hard and was left in a way that made me feel I was just another notch on someone's belt. I found someone who didn't connect as deeply to me as I did, and it was devastating.

I'm better now after a lot of work. I needed to understand this information—not to be punished, but to grow. This is what I mean by karma. Was I being punished by getting hurt the way I had hurt others, or was I creating from both perspectives what I knew and believed to understand and grow? Getting sexually involved without your truth and heart can lead you to lie, deny, or hurt yourself and others. If you say yes or no based on truth and boundaries and not on control, domination, manipulation or a desire to please and/or feel better about yourself through someone else, then you will ignite your body, mind, heart and soul, together!

We all have to know ourselves first before we can "see" someone else. All of our realms work this way. The more we understand ourselves, and all our realms, the better our intuition works. Once our intuition enters the equation, we can "check-in" clearly. The more we check-in, the more confident we become in knowing there is a match out there for us. Not matching isn't good, bad, right, or wrong. Sometimes people's truths just don't match and there is a reason for that too. Don't judge it. Let truth lead rather than guilt or desire.

Rather than letting your desire for sex lead you to love (which doesn't work) let your love of the truth lead you to love, and then making love! (which does work)

> **If your sexual realm is your 1st, 2nd, 3rd, 4th, or 6th realm—you are "out of balance"!**

If you make decisions based on your feelings and desires, rather than on your truth, you are destined to play out your promiscuity, sexual addiction, or become a prude and/or impotent. Remember that a need to feel good leads to addictions or highs as a protective mechanism to cover up your insecurity or pain. Insecurity and pain are simply lessons, not punishments.

Ask yourself:

If I need to feel good
then I must be feeling bad somehow.
So, why am I feeling bad?
Why do I need to create a "good" feeling
with no truth in it?

Defining Some Sexual Terms

Identification helps to create understanding if you do not judge as you are identifying. It is often very difficult to face taboo occurrences, even if they have been going on since the beginning of time. Ignoring them, or severely punishing them, does not make the truth of the issues go away. So, at least, we can renew our perspective on these age-old issues.

What is sexuality?

Sexuality is the personality of our sexual orientation. Although hormonally influenced, it is very personal. It exists in our mental and emotional realms and has a chemical (therefore, physical) component as well. A chemical reaction can come from a psychological or physical stimulus. Sexuality is interactive play, touching upon deep thoughts and feelings, and capable of stimulating and awakening the psyche for a soulful connection if so desired.

What is sexual freedom, and why does it have boundaries?

To have sexual freedom means that we are free of anger, fear, guilt, and shame. Freedom means no bondage, not no boundaries. Freedom means no strict laws are set upon you. Setting boundaries means that you matter, I matter, and truth matters. It also means that I am clear on what is okay with me, and what is not. Boundaries mean that I back up my thoughts and feelings with words, and back up these words with actions.

What does it mean to be a hermaphrodite?

According to the Wikipedia, the free online encyclopedia, a hermaphrodite is a *species* that contains both *male* and *female sexual organs* at some point during its life. In many species hermaphroditism is a normal part of the life-cycle.

What does it mean to be homosexual?

Wikipedia says that homosexuality is a *sexual orientation* characterized by esthetic attraction, romantic love, or *sexual desire* exclusively for another of the same *sex*.

What does it mean to be transsexual?

A transsexual is a person who establishes him- or herself as a permanent identity with the opposite *gender* to that assigned at birth. Transsexual men and women make or desire a transition from their birth sex
to that of the opposite sex, with some type of medical *alteration (gender
reassignment therapy)*.

What does it mean to be bisexual?

Bisexuality is a *sexual orientation* characterized by *romantic love* or *sexual desire* for members of both genders.

What does it mean to be asexual?

Asexuality is a designation or self-designation for people who lack
urges or feelings of *sexual attraction* and/or *sexual desire*. There is debate as to whether this is a *sexual dysfunction* or an actual *sexual orientation*; furthermore, there is disagreement over the exact definition of
the word. The term is also sometimes used for *gender identity* by those
who believe their lack of sexual attraction places them outside the
standard definitions of gender.

*Why are there homosexual, bisexual, heterosexual, hermaphrodit-
ic, and asexual species in nature?*

A species that doesn't have wide variations of all perceptions has no
depth, no true experience, and does not advance. Humans are all different. Our differences stimulate our collective thoughts, feelings, intelligence, and wisdom. Full lives are full of differences and varieties of
experience. If there were just one way to be, we all would live one-dimensional lives. Our very nature, as humans, is multi-dimensional.

Something in Nature Can Also Be in Human Nature!

Hermaphroditic Animals:	Homosexual and Bisexual Behaviors among Animals:	Asexual Animals:
Round Worm	Gray Whale (male)	Sea Star
Leech	Orcas/Killer Whale (male)	Sea Anemone
Seabass	Harbor Seal (male)	Sponge
Wrass	Dolphin (male)	Planarian
Earthworm	Sea Otter (male)	Stony Coral
Planaria	West Indian Manatee (male)	Starfish
Hamlet	Giraffe	Jelly Fish
	Bonobo (Chimpanzee)	Sand Dollar
	Ape (female)	Sea Cucumber
	Grizzly Bear (female)	Sea Urchin
	Bighorn Ram (male)	Tape Worm
	Penguin	Whiptail Lizard
	Fruit Bat	
	Ostrich (male)	
	Black Swan	
	Flatworm	

1. When do you feel sexually powerful? Why?

2. When do you feel powerless sexually? Why?

3. How can you be empowered in sex?

4. What turns you off spiritually about sex? What turns you on?

5. What turns you off mentally about sex? What turns you on?

6. What turns you off emotionally about sex? What turns you on?

7. What turns you off physically about sex? What turns you on?

8. What turns you off sexually about sex? What turns you on?

9. What action can you take to be turned on to yourself?

10. What action can you take to turn on your partner, or future partner, in every realm?

The Financial Realm

What's interesting about the financial realm is how spiritual it really is. There are two ways of looking at the world: I'll never have enough, or I have it all and I am very grateful. A feeling of never having enough comes from past fears that are projected into the future; a feeling of having it all and being grateful is based on faith and comes from the present.

People who feel grateful and full have faith that things will always work out. They believe that they are enough inside. The earth does not dictate who they are, or what they do. They can process anything because of their ability to be compassionate and understood inside. These people do not believe life and struggles are about punishment. Life is meant to be experienced for wisdom, not judgment. There is enough of everything for everyone. Are you one of them? Or do you expect the worst? Be aware of your self-fulfilling prophecy. Your psyche does not judge, so if you believe in poverty you have a shot of being it or feeling it, even if it's not true.

People who place their financial realm among the top five of their realms are not prepared for financial success or failure internally! They have moved the financial realm up a few notches precisely because they are afraid to see, feel and own truths based on hurts and insecurities. What does success and failure mean to you? Hint: The only thing you can take with you—is you.

Let's take some time to write to our power sources: Power, Money and then to Money and Power together. I am listing these words on the rinse paper. You can do this exercise with any concept. Are you ready?

Dear Power,
When I look at you I see...And feel... And I remember when... And I was taught...

Dear Money,
When I look at you I see...And feel... And I remember when... And I was taught...

Dear Money and Power,
I am angry with you because...
And that makes me feel...
Money and power ruined my life because...
I hate money and power because...
I hate me with money and power because...
I am scared of money and power because...
I am afraid of money and power with me because...
I feel bad about money and power because...
Screw money and power because...
I am guilty about money and power because...
I am ashamed of money and power because...
I am embarrassed by money and power because...
I am disappointed in money and power because...
I feel sad about money and power because...
I am hurt about money and power because...
I feel sorry for myself regarding money and power because...
I feel sorry for money and power because...
I feel excited with money and power because...
I love money and power because...
I like me with money and power because...
I love me with money and power because...
I'm happy with money and power because...
This makes me feel...
I wish money and power could be like...

Can you set some new boundaries in relation to money and power?*

*When it comes to my checking account and credit cards, my
    boundaries are...*
I can reduce my debt or spending by...
I can increase my savings by...
I can increase my investments by...
I can enjoy my money, without depending on highs, by...
*I can turn my powerless and powerful energy to financial
    empowerment by...*

Chapter Review

I learned...
I feel...

Summary

Seeing oneself as having a disorder, meaning out of order, is a more workable concept than judging oneself as a broken piece of garbage. First, you can find the balanced order, then you identify how you are "out of order." Seeing opposites is crucial for any type of connecting, for acceptance and bonding of opposites. I use the word "alignment" because it shows an order in which to visualize yourself in parts and a way to connect to these parts.

We all are think tanks. A think tank is a picture that lets us see all of these ideas as a type of research project, where the mistakes are as vital as the actual discoveries.

The low- and high-ego power struggle with the soul, mind, heart, body and power are as clear as can be. And each realm has its own job that can easily contradict or connect to one another. Without the judgment of right or wrong, good and bad, I can "see" and "hear" all the opposite and similar components. No more confusion. That doesn't mean I like what I see and hear, but at least I can understand it and let go!

---

*See Suze Orman, *Nine Steps to Financial Freedom.*

The brain lives by maps and rules, just like a computer. Any perceptions can create either pain or miracles. Playing dumb just makes you numb. Do you want to play dumb, or understand where we all come from?

13 The Psyche
The Depth of Our Communication

Let's look at the word psychology. Broken down, it's:

> **Psych** (psyche)
> + **ology** (the study of)
> ———————————————
> **Psychology** (the study of the psyche)

The psyche is often defined as the spiritual part of the brain.

Three Areas of the Subconscious Mind

Psyche: the spirit

Intuition: the voice of the spirit

Telepathy: energetic communication from one spirit to another

---

When we develop these aspects of our subconscious mind—our psyche, intuition, and telepathic abilities—we move beyond our earthly experience and obvious awareness. If we ignore these energetic traits, fear, superstition, paranoia, phobias, projections and even more insanity may set in.

This is why it's so important to rinse before "checking-in" with yourself. Only when you are "clean" can you be clear in your intuition.

Truth and Love Plus:	Lies and Judgment Plus:
Psyche = clarity and sight	**Psyche** = fear
Intuition = wisdom, insight	**Intuition** = paranoia & phobia
Telepathy = clairvoyance	**Telepathy** = projection

If we disconnect from our thoughts, feelings, and memories, we depart from our psyche's awareness. For example, when we worry about others, we lose faith in them. If we worry or care, we feel fear—not love—and either shut down or control, because we are much too busy carrying our victimization, righteousness and fear in our psyche to be loving. In actuality, we are no help to anyone like this. We are now making their issues about us because *we* are worried and care about them.

Traveling to Other Places and Times

When in our psyche, our face can physically change. We become faceless. We can be present, physically, yet distant in our mind's eye. We are "here," yet our mind will be traveling inside itself. The psyche can travel beyond thoughts, feelings and judgments. **Letting go of what we know is the only way to travel *beyond what we know.***

Past Lives

Your psyche knows everything about you. It holds all your memories from this life, and, if you believe in past lives, it holds past-life memories as well. Furthermore, the psyche has received and stored many visuals and telepathic messages throughout your lifetime that your conscious mind knows nothing about. Some people believe that we may have even received visuals and telepathic messages from different cultures, in different languages, that we do not consciously understand.

**Can you imagine a time-travel
to your personal past, and past lives as well?**

Have you ever awakened from sleep and were not sure if you had been dreaming or not?

Some people believe that many of us enter this life with unresolved issues from a former life or a wish to experience things for a deeper understanding through the soul's eyes. Have you ever experienced a deep understanding of something and felt a huge weight had just lifted from your mind and body? Nothing visible or physical really happened, except a change in perception? Perhaps you had a change in perception, then received some type of understanding that you have never felt before. The reason for being aware of all this is to enable us to have more conscious awareness of our beliefs. Perception is a choice.

Imagine having the capability to tap into these hidden and unaware parts of your mind so that you can make drastic changes in your life, stemming from deep wisdom and understanding, instead of defensive act-outs.

Out-of-Body Experiences

Out-of-body experiences are also part of the psyche. They sometimes happen to people in a near-death circumstance, if people are very ill, very upset, in shock, in a coma, or in a drug-induced or alcohol or dream state.

Why is the mind more ready for out-of-body experiences when in these situations? We are fully capable of having out-of-body experiences in everyday life, but to fully experience them, we would need to release our conscious judgment, fears, disbelief, and control mechanisms.

Invisible Knowingness and Déjà Vu

Have you ever just known something that you had no reason to know? And even after thinking about it, you realized that you couldn't figure out where or how this information came to you? Think about it for a minute. Could this information have been sent telepathically? Could this information have been from a past-life experience?

Déjà vu is a remembrance or sensing of what and where you feel you have been before, yet it presents itself with the illusion that this is the first time it's happening. If there are such things as an out-of-body experience, past life or telepathic communication, could these be in the same vein as a déjà vu? Is déjà vu just a feeling, or could it be a sensory memory?

If our psyche knows all, isn't it possible to understand ourselves on a much deeper level? The reason most of us are frightened or skeptical of such beliefs is because we cannot be aware of our subconscious if we are judging.

Processing our anger, fear, guilt, and shame is a must, to help us clear the psyche and intuition to become even slightly conscious of these capabilities. We are all blind until we can truly "see."

Premonitions

We've talked a lot about the past and the present. How about a little future talk?

A premonition happens when the psyche can "see" and feel through the intuition that something is coming. Does it make sense that if history repeats itself and re-creates itself, that it is possible for our intuition to sense the future?

If every thought and feeling has energy, what are you transmitting and receiving to and from others? Whatever your energy is, can it be sensed psychically by you and others? These transmissions happen all day, back and forth. How many of us have a clue this type of communication is happening? Are vibes a telepathic transmitter like a radio? Is it possible that you are receiving vibes and telepathic frequencies from other people's thoughts, feelings, and visuals every day? If so, why can't information involving the future be transferred and received as well. Anyone is capable of having premonitions.

Telepathy and Intuition

Have you ever had a question in your mind that you didn't say out loud, and someone answered it? It's a shocker, isn't it? Have you ever thought of someone, and then the phone rang and that person was on the other line? That's telepathy!

Telepathy is an energetic form of communication without words. Proof that telepathy is true and real can be discerned in the study of animals. Animals sense the environment and all other forms of life in this way. They are weather predictors. They can sense through smell, air tides, precipitation and inner instinct when there is even a slight change in environment. Ever notice how an animal can smell a hunter many feet away?

Telepathy was the primary source of human communication before we developed language skills. Our technological advancements have both helped and hurt our ability to communicate, because these developments have made us less aware and less capable of consciously using this form of communication that is still subconsciously active in our daily lives. Telepathy may have worked more easily in the past, when human life was simpler, because truth was clearer.

The desire to dominate each other has created such intimidation and fear that we don't trust each other or ourselves anymore.

We are all telepathic beings, and telepathy is an incredible language unlike any other.

Telepathy

Tele: Communication of thought and feeling energetically from one person/spirit to another.

Path: A passageway creating a direction.

Telepathy is energetic communication, from spirit to spirit, manifesting a passageway creating a direction between your life and that of others.

If you want this deepest part of your brain to function at its peak, you cannot be in a mindset where you care or judge anything or anyone as good, bad, right, wrong, stupid, or smart. Caring and judging create control and fear, which will interrupt a soul's truthful message. Only the ego seeks to control, not the soul.

What Is Intuition?

1. What is intuition? Can you feel, see or hear it?

2. Have you ever listened to your intuition before? If so, what did your intuition say?

3. What happens to your intuition if you mix it with fear, care or worry? Can you give an example?

4. If your intuition is your inner voice or your soul's voice, how can you discern it from insecure, needy, arrogant, and egotistical voices? Guess!

We cannot achieve insight by hiding from the truth. Everything that happens to us has a life lesson. Those lessons, if learned, help us take the steps necessary to lead us to our life's purpose. If we pay attention to our lessons, our purpose will reveal itself. But if we decide what our life purpose is before learning our lessons, we may miss our purpose and get frustrated, stuck, and controlling.

Our intuition is meant to be our guide and teacher as we walk through our life lessons. If you are the kind of person who wants to get to the finish line, you will be very frustrated with this piece of information, because after you've learned a lesson, guess what? There's another lesson right behind it. So, the more you let go of control, the better off you are.

To "tune in" to your intuition is to be in harmony or alignment with yourself internally. Listening means to sense and hear the sounds of the intuitive voice inside you. Can you tell the difference between your intuition, logic, feelings, and ego? These voices are all different. Just know that when your intuition leads you, you will get a sense of flow in your life.

Your intuition is an extra-sensory perception. It works subconsciously, unless you bring it to the conscious mind. Intuition is a crucial ingredient for the development of self-trust and true self-confidence, not egotistical arrogance.

The more you depend on your intuition for strength and clarity, the less you will need your ego. You will no longer lose yourself to others, nor fear others' judgments. You won't need to "check-out" with others to "check-in" with yourself. "Checking out" to "see" how you are, by asking other people for their opinions, can create openness if you process and own the truth of others' views. But if you blindly follow others, or if you interpret their truths as the sole truth, you lose your conscious intuition.

How can you have intimacy in your life with no intuition?

Intimacy—A Willing Loss of Ego Control

Intimacy

In – ti – ma – cy

In – to – me – I "see"

If I can travel into me and "see" (my soul, inner child and ego) I can travel into you and "see" (the soul, inner child and ego) in you through my psyche and telepathic mind.

Intuition

In + Tuition = Inner teaching

(Inner + (teaching) = Insight

With inner teaching you will have insight.

The true concept of intimacy can be intimidating to some people because it means a loss of ego control. Most of us have depended on our ego to lead us our entire lives. The concept of releasing egotistical control, and operating from the psyche and intuitive mind instead, is frightening. These energies are invisible and intangible. We are trained to control. Most of our institutions teach us to control as a means of leadership, rather than to enhance each other and work as a team using intuition and telepathy. Our ego wants to rule. On the other hand our spirit wants to understand and touch, because it knows that we are all connected to one another.

Have you ever heard the phrase "I am so into you?" Does this mean I am losing my truths, my boundaries and my worth *through* you, *with* you, and *for* you? Where the heck am I in this? And if I am not being true to me, who are you in love with? It can't be me, because I'm not here. We forget that we need to be in ourselves before we can be "into" someone else.

How many times have you asked yourself, "What will the neighbors think?" How about, "What do I think?" If you fear or worry about what the neighbors will think, you'll be disconnected from your own self-awareness. This is a perfect environment for controlling, addictive, rebellious, or vindictive behavior. If you do what you think others think you should do, then you become a liar, based on caring what others think. Are you sure the neighbors are even thinking what you think they are thinking? Are you creating a one-act play in your head? Are you time-traveling? Where are you?

 You cannot work with truth if you don't consciously bring it forward!

The exercise, "**When I look at you I see… and I feel…**" is used in this book for a reason. *"When I look at you I see…"* pulls up information from the left brain and sometimes from the judger or the intuition. The *"When I look at you I feel…"* pulls up feelings from the right brain and sometimes our creative or destructive side pops up, as the psyche intervenes.

This writing can be to anyone—a neighbor, a friend, a family member, a movie, a word definition, even a stranger. Pick someone who has inspired, scared or hurt you or something that annoyed you or ticked you off.

Seeing Through the Blame

This is a recall or "vibe" reading exercise, with intuition, telepathy, and blame all mixed together. In these exercises all you do first is "see" *through* the eye of blame. Then you turn it on yourself and own. This exercise consists of five steps:

1. Blame with judgment and victim energy
2. Rinse
3. Own
4. Time travel
5. Own

Here's an example of how it works. Bob, the subject of my letter writing, will never know that I am doing this.

1. Blame with Judgment and Victim Energy

Dear Bob...

When I look at you I see... *someone who holds emotions in and then explodes later. You are nice on the surface and angry underneath. You are a loser and a quitter who never loved anyone but yourself. You make me sick.*

When I look at you I feel... *scared. I feel twisted and manipulated. I get sucker-punched because I don't "see" it coming. You make me feel creepy and I want to hit you and run away.*

2. Rinse!

Write and do a physical rinse, to get clear with yourself. Feel free to turn any of your rinse letters on yourself.

Dear Bob...

I am angry because you attacked me. Screw you! You scare me and others. Why did you do this to me and others?! You hurt me and tricked me and others so much!

3. Own!

Now, notice all the "you's" in the blame and judgmental writings. Change those "you's" to "I's," "me's" or "my." This helps you see what is truly yours! (See example below.)

If the original writing says "I" or "me," keep the "I" or "me" and add the word "others" to it. This will help you "see" how you affect not only you, but how the way you think and feel plays out with others.

If the writings about "others" don't fit your truth, alter their pictures in the writings to make the story fit your own truths!

These writings and rinses will show you, through "vibe reads," how to "see" yourself in other people. Even if the pictures you write about are different, the behaviors creating your pictures have similar patterns that affect you over and over again.

Dear Bob…

When I (and others) look at ~~*you*~~ *me I see someone who holds emotions in*

and then explodes later. ~~*You are*~~ *I am nice on the surface and angry underneath.*

~~*You are*~~ *I am a loser and a quitter* (if not an exact example, alter the ex-

ample and make the story true for you) *who never loved anyone but*

~~*yourself.*~~ *myself*

~~*You*~~ *I make me (and others) feel sick. I (and others)* ~~*see someone*~~ *feel tall.*

(Since I am not physically and literally tall, I altered the example because I

feel strong which could be "tall" (metaphorically)). When I (and others)

look at ~~*you*~~ *me (and others) I feel…scared. I (and others) feel twisted and*

manipulated. I (and others) get sucker-punched because I (and others)

don't "see" it. ~~*You*~~ *I make me (and others) feel creepy. I (and others) want to*

hit ~~*you*~~ *me and run away.*

4. Time Travel

Dear Bob,

You remind me… *of my uncle Steve, who would lie to me over and over again. I felt so creepy. Uncle Steve would say loving things to me, then yell at me and ridicule me. I hated him and loved him at the same time. I felt so lost and twisted. I shut down and became depressed.*

5. Own

Now change "you's" to "I's," "me's" and "my" just like you did before. Add the word "others" to the original "me's" and "I's."

> *Dear Bob,*
>
> *I*
> *~~You~~ remind me of my uncle Steve, who would lie to me **(and others)***
>
> *   I*
> *over and over again. Others felt so creepy. ~~He~~ would say loving things to*
>
> *me **(and others)** then yell at me **(and others)** and ridicule me **(and others)**.*
>
> *   me   me*
> *I **(and others)** hated ~~him~~ and loved ~~him~~ **(and others)** at the same time.*
>
> *I **(and others)** felt so lost and twisted. I **(and Bob)** were shut down and*
>
> *became depressed.*

Now do a rinse sheet with your inner child and recall your memories and past point of view. Then end with *"I learned and feel..."* Feel free to ask your inner child questions and let that part of you answer at the end. Own everything you can! Owning is the only door out of hell!

"See" how you can consciously "vibe read" others and own at the same time?

Before you can consciously use your own psyche, you must release yourself from blame and from feeling like a victim. That means you must own!

Now, do this exercise yourself! Follow the model above. Pick out your own "Bob," and get started...

(*Dear* _____, *When I look at you I see.... And I feel....*)

Whether we know it or not, we are constantly reading everyone's vibes. We can do this in an empowered way, by using our psychic, intuitive and telepathic mind; or in a powerless way, by being paranoid, phobic or projecting.

The Psyche Dream State

One way to understand yourself and your issues, from the psyche's point of view, is to consciously study your dreams. Dreams are a way your psyche communicates with you. When your day-time protective and manipulative behavior prevents you from "seeing," hearing, or speaking to your psyche, your psyche will either attempt to stimulate your telepathy and your intuition, or it will visit you in your dreams.

With training, dreams become subconscious messages you can comprehend consciously. As soon as you truly understand a dream, you will notice that the dream will not recur. Dreams need rinsing and understanding too.

**Everything has a reason, a lesson, and a purpose
if you *choose* to "see"!**

Keep a notebook by your bed. If you can remember any parts of your dreams when you wake up, write out your visuals, thoughts and feelings. Don't worry if the dream is disappointing and doesn't make sense, or if you can't remember all of it. Don't pressure your dreams. Pressure and psyche don't mix. Little by little, dreams will begin to come forward. Welcome whatever you can! Give it time! There are awake dreams during the day as well. Those count too.

Most dreams are **metaphors** for what your conscious mind doesn't understand or is afraid to "see." By understanding these metaphors and subliminals, you will learn more about your ego struggles, which is a stepping stone to your soul's purpose.

Here's how it works. The psyche wants to talk to your conscious mind, but the conscious mind isn't listening. In order to bypass logic and judgmental defenses, it creates a metaphor to stimulate your feelings and visual mind. If the psyche can stimulate the feelings, emotion begins, pictures evolve and there is a chance of you and your intuition awakening. When you are asleep, your defense mechanisms are too. That's when you are more open to subconscious truths.

If you have an issue, your psyche wants to show you something. The psyche is the door to your enlightened awareness. The psyche does not try to protect because it does not judge something as bad or wrong. Even death. After all, isn't death the psyche or spirit's way of going home? The dream state is the psyche's turn to be seen and heard. So, your psyche comes to you in a dream to tell you a story. Remember the goal is to stimulate pictures to awaken feelings and awareness. The reason these dreams may be in pieces is because of the speed of the psyche.

Write out your story or visuals from your dreams. Then write how the story or visuals made you feel. Do not manipulate or push the story. The psyche works with the idea of faith. Have faith that the wisdom and information are already here. Just stay open in the unknowingness. The hard part about this idea is that unknowingness is where fear lives and if your ego grabs you, so will the fear. Go ahead and rinse until you can drop the fear again. If you exercise these concepts, fear will be replaced with faith more and more.

Personalize and understand your dreams to see how the dreams relate to you on a conscious level.

Let's go for it!

Directions

Write one of your dreams out as best as you can remember. Don't worry if the dream is fragmented or doesn't make sense. We're going to go *underneath the obvious to "see" the psyche messages.*

Dream

Let's say, I had a dream about...

There was a man chasing me and I was scared and I turned around, started fighting him and he kissed me. My brother walked in, woke me and then I went back to sleep where I was just swimming, going nowhere special.

To me, this dream makes no sense. Let's take it apart and "see" what the psyche subliminal message is really saying.

Circle any verb, any picture word, or any feeling word. (Those are the images your psyche has picked in order to bypass your logic and judger). Do not circle any word that repeats unless it changes the meaning of another word. You can do this circle word exercise to any writing to go underneath the surface meaning; I'm just using this technique on the dream segment.

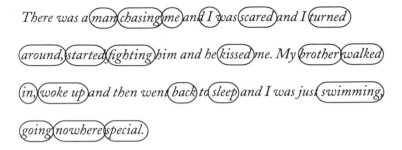

There was a man chasing me and I was scared and I turned around, started fighting him and he kissed me. My brother walked in, woke up and then went back to sleep and I was just swimming, going nowhere special.

Take the circled words in order, from the beginning of the dream to the end. List these words down the paper like a spelling list. Be sure to skip a line or space in between the words.

Example:

> **List of Circled Words**
>
> Man:
>
> Chasing:
>
> Me:

Next to the circled words, write down the first thing that comes to your mind as quickly as possible. Remember, there are no right or wrong answers. You can write a word or a phrase. These words do not have to relate to the dream. If your definitions don't make logical sense, that's okay; visuals work in energy more than logic sometimes. Keep going!

> This is a right brain, subconscious exercise. No judging allowed!

On the next page leave room for three columns:

Column 1: The original circled words are followed by the first idea, feeling, concept or phrase that comes to your head when thinking about that word. This is called free association. Your mind is free to see, think and do whatever, without judgment.

Column 2: Personalize the new words by putting "I" or "Me" wherever the other person's name is and anywhere else you can. The goal is to see and **own** as much as possible.

After completing your new words, the original words are no longer necessary. It is interesting to "see," over time, how your definitions of the same words change. Don't throw these pages away.

You're going to go "under" the original words. Use a different color pen, if possible, to help you "see" the new paragraph more clearly.

You may round off words so that they make some form of grammatical sense. But don't change the meaning!

Column 3: Own the new definitions in their new paragraph form.

**When you add "I," "me" or "my"
don't control or steer the story.
Keep it as simple as possible!
Alter any story that is not your truth.**

New Words	New Paragraph	My Owning in Question Form
(Man)— *boys*	I see *boys*	Where did I get hurt growing up with boys?
(Chasing)— *running*	*running* my	
(Me)— *spirit*	*spirit* and so my	I've ignored this and made excuses for my feelings with boys.
(I)— *center*	*center* is	
(Scared)— *hurt*	*hurt*. I go	I then have some kind of attraction or defense with boys to block my hurts.
(Turned)— *around*	*around* in	
(Around)— *circle*	*circles* inside and	
(Started)— *begin*	*begin*	How did Eddie treat or see me so my strength left?
(Fighting)— *destructive*	*destructive* thinking or behaviors affecting my	
(Kissed)— *sensitivities*	*sensitivities*.	This is not his fault, but it's my responsibility to understand and clear my defenses with boys or men.
(Brother)— *Eddie*	*Eddie* (my real brother)	
(Walked)— *straight*	is a *straight* energy	
(In)— *focus*	*focused* on me in the	
(Woke up)— *morning*	*morning*. When he	How do I self-beat or put myself down with boys or my brother Eddie?
(Back)— *front*	is in *front* of me	
(Sleep)— *walking*	*walking*, my	
(Swimming)— *strength*	*strength* goes	How do I hold myself and my gifts down and suppress me for Eddie, or boys, or men?
(Going)— *nowhere*	*nowhere* and I	
(Nowhere)— *lost*	*lose* my	
(Special)— *gifted*	*gifts*.	

Answer those questions you have posed to yourself in column three, above. (I'm not going to do it here, but I think you can get the gist of where my psyche and I were going, here.)

Rinse

Originally, this dream made little sense. Who knew it was about my brother, boys, my childhood experiences, and my inner child's perception of it? I cannot judge these discoveries as bad or wrong, unless I want to shut down my psyche again. The dream is just telling me how I perceived this part of my life and with this awareness, do I want to change a perception and alter my life?

When I go through the rinse paper I will "see" what I've been feeling in so many ways. Everyone is stumbling through this existence and to blame or hurt them just feeds the pain and chaos. To learn is to learn more about what's going on inside me. If I become a victim as I learn, I will fill up with negative energy and who is getting hurt again? Me, that's who! The goal is to "see," feel and change with understanding and self-responsibility.

1. *My dream was... And I felt...*

2. Circle your action words, as above.

3. Write out the circled words in column one, like a spelling list.

4. Free associate from these circled words. Be quick! Don't think or judge.

5. Add "I," "me" or "my" down the page of your new words in column two. Check-in, in question form, following the example above, like in column three.

6. Answer the questions you've asked. No judging answers.

7. Do the rinse!

> **Congrats!**
>
> You just did a non-thinking, non-judging, right-brain, subconscious psyche exercise. No matter how well you did, you had to have learned at least one new thing! That's all we need to begin growing! Your intuition will always show you something new, if you ask.
>
> This is one of many ways to tap into your psyche. There are different levels of the psyche, but this step will get you started.

Can you "see" where logical and mental knowledge is not enough? The logical mind doesn't begin to touch the psyche, because they speak in different speeds and languages. The left brain thinks in words and symbols. The right brain feels energy and the psyche "sees" in pictures. The psyche is constantly sending visual messages to both sides of the brain and telepathic messages are flying everywhere. If the subconscious mind is not tapped into your conscious awareness, what is actually affecting your reality? If we really understood this, what could we do with mental illness and warfare? Do we need psyche understanding for these answers? Are we barking up the wrong tree? Can we look from a new perspective without self-beating for not getting it sooner? The self-beat blame process is what really slows us down.

To check this information, if you dare, ask five people to be brutally honest with you and "read" your energy. Ask them to write out—or even better, to sit in front of you while holding your hands and looking in your eye and say...

When I look at you I see...
When I look at you I feel...
You are...
I am...

1. If this exercise feels like too much for you right now, don't skip it. Ask someone to help you by doing this in writing and

giving it to you. Read their words when you are alone, with a support group, or with a therapist.

2. Let everyone know that you want the truth and to please not hold back. Make them feel safe to be honest and not withhold their thoughts and feelings as a way to protect you.

3. When the exercise is through, find out how what was said to you is true! If you're unhappy with what they said, don't get angry and hurt the messenger. Rinse, instead! Truth can hurt, depending on your perspective and how you process it, but it can also set you free.

4. Be sure to thank everyone for their gift of truth. When you are grateful for truth, it is hard to self-beat and hurt yourself or others. Seeing yourself is crucial. This is just a way to build your "seeing" muscle.

The psyche communicates in pictures and energy that goes beyond logical strength or knowledge. Any picture the psyche sends you has the potential to show you wisdom about yourself and other people beyond your logical understanding.

Can you imagine this energy as negative?

If you pile judgment, fear and control on top of your psyche, you can develop a cynical perception. This means your ego can take over your current thought process. Cynicism feels powerful. It thinks it is protecting you from future fear and hurt, but it is actually creating present-time fear, hurt and negativity!

A trouble-shooter uses instincts and intuition to "see" trouble that has already happened or trouble that could be coming. So, trouble is what he or she "sees" and manifests psychically and, therefore, attracts. Once again, the psyche does not "see" in good or bad, so, if the trouble-shooter fixates on trouble, then trouble is what the psyche looks for. Careful!

1. The psyche needs visual awareness. Subliminals and dreams are psyche messages.

2. The intuition needs you to be rinsed to truly be heard.

3. Telepathy needs you to be clean of fear, judgment, care and worry to send and receive clear messages with others. Or else insanity begins!

The psyche needs to "see."
The intuition needs to be "heard."
Telepathy needs to energetically "talk."

So being energetically "blind," "deaf"
and "dumb" (mute) matters, doesn't it?

The psyche is said by many to
be the mix of the mind and the soul.
It exists outside logical and physical law.

Even though your ego is limited, your spirit is limitless!

Chapter Review

I just learned…
I feel…

Summary

If the psyche is your soul and the intuition is your soul's voice and we are communicating soul to soul, why are we confused, insane and fighting one another?

Can we evolve if fear is contaminating our psyche, intuition and telepathic communication with ourselves and each other? If the yin/yang philosophy is true in saying that to accept and understand opposites is a formula for balance, then it makes sense that our life experiences are lessons consisting of opposites, ego, fear and lies versus soul, love and truth. The purpose of knowing insanity is to know peace.

Just when you think you have figured out a solid process for your obvious life, you are asked to read about past lives, out-of-body experiences, déjà vu and premonitions. If life is a lesson, what is life's purpose? Could it be for the soul to understand its opposite, which is our animal nature? Life's journey is the art of traveling, in and out of the egotistical, emotional, reactive animal states to the aware, understanding and peaceful soul.

14 Insanity:
A Hostile Psyche Takeover

Are you insane? Come on, everyone's a little insane, but that concept means nothing if we don't understand what insanity is and isn't.

What Is Insanity?

Could insanity be just a state of mind? Our left brain identifies and diagnoses issues and facts. Our right brain feels and senses, and is open to creation through the psyche. Tangled beliefs inside the facts or feelings we experience will affect what our psyche creates.

When we allow unresolved traumas to affect our thoughts, feelings and behavior, our psyche, along with our telepathic and intuitive mind, may create larger and larger issues (such as paranoia, phobias, and projections).

Until we "see" this disconnection or, even more upsetting, disassociation, we are stuck in a survival mode, and we are not capable of being present in our own lives. Insanity is a reaction, not an action. The question is, a reaction to what? And what can we do about it?

There are different levels of insanity. Paranoia, phobias, and projections have different degrees of severity. The degree of insanity and hopelessness often depends on the trauma, age, environment, support or lack of, chemically altering substances such as drugs and alcohol (even sugar and caffeine). All of the examples above can add layers of confusion, disconnection and disassociation. A disconnect is a separation from our thoughts, feelings and memories. A disassociation is a separation from our conscious awareness and our thoughts, feelings and behaviors. These separations can send us into an abyss of confusion, time-travel and insanity. Add the inevitable self-beat, and suppression of our truths, and the insanity deepens. And if, along the way, we start losing empathy for ourselves or others, we may not only be mentally ill, but develop a criminal mentality.

Everyday Insanities

I want to talk about these insanities with humor and a touch of sarcasm so that you can "see" the absurdity in them, and we can have some fun with this. Our goal is not to get scared, or to self-beat. Our goal is always to "see," so we can understand.

Insanity occurs when truth and feelings are disconnected and far away from each other. Alcoholics Anonymous says insanity is, "doing the same thing over and over, expecting different results."

Here are some examples of everyday insanities:

- You fight for what you do not even like, and then you personalize everyone's reactions because, after all, it's all about you!

- You don't question yourself, ever! You don't question your beliefs, ever! Because you are always right.

- When someone brings up any point, you argue that the point is not true. Aren't arguments and debates the way to intimacy?

- You go to the "wrong" people for a "right" reaction. For example, if you want to celebrate, you go to someone who is negative and judges you.

- You live through someone else to create your own self-worth and confidence. For example, you are the friend of some celebrity so you feel that you are the celebrity.

- You believe that if your intentions are good, your words and behavior don't have to match. You think that if you say, "I didn't mean it," this means that what happened didn't really count.

- You change the subject when someone else is talking, because it keeps you from getting bored.

- You use drugs and/or alcohol and say that you are fine; it's other people who are crazy.

- You fall in love with someone's image, or fall in love with what they do, then get upset because they are not who you thought they were.

- You ruin your day-to-day life, but don't care, as long as you are successful and #1!

- You talk and talk about your issues with friends. You make your stories dramatic, filled with victimization and judgment. Then your friends get upset for you and join in the gossip. You win!

- You put someone else in charge of you and let them tell you what to think, feel and believe. Or you value someone else's opinion of you more than you value your own, and then you feel controlled!

- If you have an uncomfortable thought or feeling, you blame it on someone else so they will fix it for you.

- You avoid truths if they are upsetting to you.

- You have to be perfect. So when you make a mistake, you self-beat and punish yourself. After all, no pain, no gain.

- You live in the future because "now" is upsetting.

- Boss people around; they will like it. Show them you care.

- You say no to everything as a way to protect yourself from ever failing.

- You wait and pray. If you are a good person, maybe you won't have to do anything about it.

- You don't take any risks and when the results are in be sure to say, I told you so.

Right off the bat, *please understand:* **Going in and out of balance is natural. If you don't, you can't learn. Each time you go out of balance it's a chance to check-in and "see" yourself so that you can make a change.**

1. Can you "see" where even minor insanities can radically affect your life? If so, how?

Belief is the first step to creation. Whether positive or negative, belief opens you up to ideas, thoughts, and feelings that affect the deepest parts of your mind. The psyche, along with the telepathic and intuitive mind, creates from *all* your beliefs, whether good or bad. If a belief enters the subconscious mind, the psyche doesn't judge it. The psyche's job is only to create, giving your conscious mind the chance to better "see" and understand the belief, thoughts, and feelings through experience, whatever the belief may be.

Projection

If your memories are triggered, imagine your mind's eye as an inner camera, showing a movie of what that triggered memory was for you. Your psyche will then *project* this picture or movie on a present-time person or situation causing a type of internal double vision. You are physically in present-time and psychically in the past. Trauma trigger alert! Don't attempt to use your intuition right now. It's in a state of paranoia, phobia or projection. Projection can be a form of insanity, and it can be very destructive if you don't understand where you are in your mind.

> **Projection:** To throw; plan; cause to appear on a distant background; stick out.

Does this definition fit what our minds do?

Every word in the definition can be personalized to connect this meaning to you. Let's put "I," "me," or "my" and add "others" before or after each word, and see where it leads us.

I *throw* my *plan* on me (and others,) *causing* thoughts and feelings *to appear on a distant background.* My issues are now **projected** on me (and others) and that's what is *sticking out* when I "see" me (and others.)

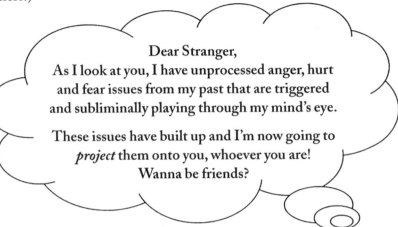

> Dear Stranger,
> As I look at you, I have unprocessed anger, hurt and fear issues from my past that are triggered and subliminally playing through my mind's eye.
>
> These issues have built up and I'm now going to *project* them onto you, whoever you are!
> Wanna be friends?

I asked my friend if I could tell one of my favorite stories about her and me. She gave me permission, but she specifically asked me to tell you that *she is not nuts!*

Little Red Mommy

My friend is an *amazing* chef. She lives about thirty minutes from me, depending on Los Angeles traffic. One day I drove to her house, very excited to see her. Or, if I'm owning, very excited to eat. How did she greet me at the door?

Friend: *(In a snide voice).* Well, I guess you can "see" it too, can't you?

Mona: *(Can I read her vibe? Probably, but I'm not going to touch it. I'm hungry.)* Uhm…what are you talking about?

Friend: In school today my son drew a big, giant picture of your son and a little red mommy in the corner that's supposed to be me. You know what that means, don't you!

Mona: Your son's favorite color is red?

Friend: No. You know full well what he's saying with this "little red mommy!"

Mona: Listen. Let's review. You're a great chef and I'm not. I'm here for free food. Okay?

Friend: Fine! We'll drop it then!

And she walked off. Phew! Looks like I got out of that one, right?

Cut to dinner! I am now eating alongside a group of people. They are not my friends, they are hers. I want the food. Suddenly, my friend says in front of everyone...

Friend: Well, Mona! I guess you can't wait to tell everyone about the "little red mommy!"

Mona: *(That's it. Her projection and one-act play, that's going on inside her head, has got to go.)* You know what? If you mention the "little red mommy" one more time, you're gonna get it.

Great! Now she runs out of the room crying, and tells her husband (who has been my friend for twenty-three years) that I've hurt her feelings. Now he comes up to me.

Friend's Husband: Mona, please handle this, you're faster than me, okay?

Mona: She's your wife! You handle it!

Friend's Husband: Mona, we haven't had dinner yet. And if I try to help her, we probably never will. But you, on the other hand...

Mona: *(Grumbling).* Alright.

I find my friend hiding in a bathroom. I don't get a chance to say anything before...

Friend: I'm a bitch. You know I'm a bitch. That's why my son is drawing this, isn't he? He thinks I'm a "little red angry mommy," a bitch.

Mona: You know, "red" means passion, too. Maybe he drew a passionate mommy?

Friend: No! It's an angry mommy! I grew up with so much screaming, I think I'm yelling too much!

Mona: OK. No parent is perfect. Work on the yelling.

Friend: Aha! So you do think I'm a bitch!

Mona: Oh no, you don't! Look, do a check-in and feel yourself. Don't set me up to hurt you. You're doing a heck of a job of hurting you all by yourself. Your kids love you and a parent's job is to continually own your positive and negative qualities and keep growing. As we grow and own our struggles, our children copy us and hopefully they'll own and grow as well. We are all little red mommies, sometimes!

My friend starts to cry. I start to cry. We embrace. And I go downstairs and help her eat.

Whew!

"Projection at Its Finest"
Sabotage: The Inner Battle
A one-act play in my friend's head

My friend's reality!	My friend's Self Talk	Me! Mona
1. Whatever I fear, I am creating (past and present enmeshing again).	1. I'm a bitch and everyone knows it!	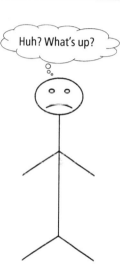
2. I don't know I'm thinking all of this. It's subconscious.	2. What's wrong with me? I feel hysterical. I'm nuts!	
3. I now care what Mona and others think.	3. Mona hates me!	
4. I project my insecurities and fears onto Mona and others, which means I'll start making stuff up from my own personal fears, memories and insecurities.	4. Mona is putting me down behind my back to everyone at dinner.	
5. As I'm thinking of all of this, notice: I won't ask Mona or others any questions.	5. Who does Mona think she is anyway, "Miss Perfect?"	
6. Now, I've decided Mona and others are the bad guys.	6. Mona and everyone ignores me.	
7. Question: Do I hate me, and the way I'm treating Mona and others, or do I really hate Mona and others? I'm lost and confused when I look at Mona and others.	7. HELP!	

I'm projecting and time-traveling all over the place!

1. Write one of YOUR projections and one-act plays! Pick a time when you were projecting your own thoughts and feelings onto someone else!

2. How did that make you feel?

3. What did you think you were doing at the time? How did you justify your thoughts and feelings?

4. How did this projection make them feel?

5. What would you do differently, now that you are aware?

6. Is it too late to revisit that situation, and own your projection?

7. Go for it!

Phobias

Here are some Webster's Dictionary definitions:

> **Phobia** morbid fear; dislike; abnormal fear; dread
>
> **Dread** attitude or anticipation of something that will be disagreeable
>
> **Morbid** gross, gloomy, sick, sensitive

Remember, you can take any definition and personalize it to better "see" what it means to you. Go ahead and personalize definitions by adding an "I," "me," or "my" and making the definition alive and active, as follows:

My **phobias** are my **morbid** *fears* that *I dislike*. This feels like an *abnormal fear* of something or someone that I **dread**. I then develop an *attitude* from *anticipating* a *disagreeable*, **morbid**, *gross* situation that makes me feel *gloomy*. This gave me a *sick* feeling and I became very *sensitive* to life!

When we experience a truly frightening ordeal, fear becomes our automatic decision-maker. That means we have three choices. We can freeze, run or attack others or ourselves. The creative mind may use feelings from the trauma to paint or act out a metaphoric thought, feeling or behavior. The subconscious mind will hide the truth, while the conscious mind plays out a thought or behavior, reminding us that something upsetting has happened. The phobia will stay until we are ready to deal with the original traumas.

Can you "see" how the phobia is not there to hurt you?

It is there to hide your upsetting truth as a protection and be a messenger, to remind you, when you're ready, to get help.

The subconscious may replay the trauma over and over again by surfacing unprocessed life experiences, which repeat and repeat as a signal for attention and become obsessive thoughts, feelings or behaviors, until we break that pattern. For example, many people who were hit and beaten get into fights later on in life without consciously knowing why. They are not aware they are in a trance or pattern from misunderstood life experiences that will keep happening until processed. The brain is repeating what it knows and remembers, not what it likes. By the way, people who are in a pattern or trance, hurting themselves or others, are not bad or stupid. They are survivors, stuck in time.

Another option is to shut down and isolate from everyone as a way to protect themselves. A shutdown feels safe, if you don't want this trauma to ever happen again. The people who are shut-down may have metaphoric phobias, such as a fear of doors, going outside, or someone strangling them. These make sense if you know how to associate a picture with the upset or trauma. It may not be the exact trauma, but it is a feeling or an aspect of it. Maybe you weren't strangled, but you couldn't breathe when your parent, a peer or sibling put their hand over your mouth. A phobia is sometimes an obsessive/compulsive repetitive thought, feeling or behavior representing a previous trauma. The repetitive obsession will, at the least, release the anxiety for the moment, but without acknowledging the truth of the event. You are now psychically blind.

When a phobia is obvious in our lives, it reminds us to revisit the trauma and rinse it. The trick to phobias is that the trauma and true feelings are often hidden, so the trauma doesn't become conscious; yet, every time the trauma is triggered, the phobia becomes active with no conscious memory of the trauma. What a confused mess. Since hiding the truth was fear-motivated in the first place, and fear is one of the best blockers of truth, how can logic and intelligence help us without our first acknowledging the truth? And what are the chances of truth popping easily on this one? Intelligence cannot help this problem. It is a feeling, a psychic issue. If the intellect can't see it, the left brain will often defer to a judgment. The judger can easily call you a bad name and you shut down. Is someone phobic, broken or are we investigating something in the wrong place?

**Many people self-medicate with drugs or alcohol,
or sleep and isolate or over-work,
to block a phobia and the fear attached to the trauma.**

**But what's important to know is that
the trauma holds the truth and, therefore, the cure!**

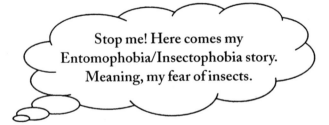

Stop me! Here comes my Entomophobia/Insectophobia story. Meaning, my fear of insects.

My Entomophobia

Falling asleep was nerve-racking. Am I nuts or could I be having a body memory? Just lying down can affect my breathing. I get hot and sweaty. I panic and start hitting my arms and legs. I swear I feel bugs crawling all over me! Then I look around for the bug, but I can never find one.

This is one of my past fears. As time went on, I even started "seeing" bugs on my arm. I was awake. It wasn't a dream. There was no real bug there, but I could swear I was looking at one. It was a roach in case you wanted to know the type of bug tormenting me. This started to freak me out.

If this had affected me a little more strongly, I might have developed an obsessive/compulsive behavior. Maybe I would have compulsively washed my hands. The point is, my mind gave me delusions instead of obsessions. I mean, if I see bugs that are not there, that's delusional. At least I wasn't obsessive too.

I never told anyone about these bugs, because I was afraid they'd lock me up! The fear of fear gave me no hope. But, by my mid-20s, the phobia became so annoying that I finally broke down and told my mom. She said,

"That's so strange. When you were six weeks old, your father and I had no money and lived in an old, dirty, disgusting apartment. I cleaned it from top to bottom; but one afternoon, I went into your room to check on you while you were taking a nap, and you had roaches crawling all over you and your bassinet."

My mom said she screamed and threw every piece of furniture she could out on the front lawn. She packed up the car and said to my dad, "We're moving back to my hometown! Today!"

If my psyche could remember a trauma from when I was six weeks old, what else can the psyche do?

After my mom told me this truth, I stopped feeling and "seeing" the roaches. The truth set me free again! Writing, family research, rinsing, sobriety, and not judging myself became my path to clarity and peace.

When Insanity Arises from Protective Behavior

Let's say someone yells at you as you're sitting behind a desk. You may react by getting upset or hurt, or freeze and time-travel to your childhood and feel, with little or no adult information available in this instance. If you are centered in this moment, you will not personalize someone's upsets. You may time-travel with awareness to the past to achieve wisdom and to not get lost in time. You may ask questions to better understand the person yelling. If you react by becoming paralyzed or attacking back or running away, there's a good chance you will not get what you need to know.

Suppose you were physically here but your mind was nine years old and had only a nine-year-old's awareness? That would mean this adult yelling at you was the authority figure controlling you in that moment. What rights does a nine-year-old have without adult backing? Probably none. When you were young, did your parents or siblings trap you in a corner and scream at you? Or hit you? And because you were so small, there was no way you could fight back? Did you feel trapped then and was today's feeling similar to those memories? Were you in actuality being trapped today? Or was that a feeling and body memory from a long time ago? These feelings are real, but not necessarily true in present time.

So, when someone yells at you today and your psyche receives a subliminal picture from a memory stored in your subconscious mind of a yelling person from your past, a visual enters your subconscious mind and is immediately attached to past memories and visuals of yelling scenes. Because, as a child, you managed to survive by freezing up, your present-day instinct and reaction is to respond in the same way. In this moment you have lost your adult life information and remember only what you knew and did at that young age. Your body is in the present, but your mind is in the past.

But does it have to be this way? Do you really want or need to feel small, helpless, and unable to function every time someone yells in front of you?

This is where you rinse the present-time person, and then time-travel to past traumatic experiences. When finished, don't forget to find a way to understand the person who upset you. This takes you out of the powerless position. Whoever was yelling at you or hitting you was an off-center, upset person. If you can feel and understand yourself, set boundaries around what you can and cannot invite in your life, and be empathetic, you will achieve self-trust and empowerment. You will be able to hold your center by depersonalizing. Just know, the yelling person is probably time-traveling too, and doesn't consciously know it. Do you want this kind of person to be in charge of you and any decisions you make?

What's your method of prevention the next time a yelling person is in front of you? What can you do differently without being reactive? You don't want to freeze, attack yourself and/or others, or run. Write

new ideas down and role-play them mentally, emotionally and physically with yourself, a friend or a therapist. This is when you can create
new body memories by seeing and acting out the original pain, and
then create a new ending. If you don't "rinse" you can get lost in your
psyche, lost in the past, and forever live in fear of the future when a
memory is triggered. How are you going to know what is happening in
present time if you are in every other time zone but this one?

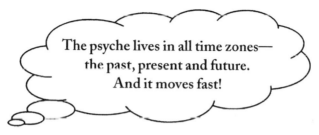

The psyche lives in all time zones—
the past, present and future.
And it moves fast!

**Now we're going to pick one of your everyday insanities,
understand it, find the trauma behind it, rinse that trauma,
and pick out a new behavior. Ready?**

Fill in the blanks:

1. *I know that it's insane because every time I do it, I still believe
   that the result will be....*

2. *I remember when...*

3. *But the truth is...*

4. *I remember when...*

5. *And I feel...*

6. *My prevention is...*

Now, lie on your back. Relax. Create a visual in your mind of your old
memories and then your new ideas. Sit with it. Feel it and breathe.
Now take the old memory and feelings and, in your mind, see it and
exchange it with your new ideas and pictures.

It's time to celebrate a new beginning. Another insanity just became a little weaker. If you have more energy, do another daily insanity, phobia or projection and go back to the top!

Fear Exercise
Back to Webster's Dictionary:

Fear—distressing emotion, aroused by an impending pain, danger, evil, or by the illusion of such.

Distressing—severe trouble; mental pain; pressure of hunger or fatigue or want.

Impending—imminent threat

Now, again, we personalize the definitions:

My **fear** keeps me in **distress** *emotionally*. I am *aroused by an* **impending** *pain*. I live feeling in *danger* and *evil*. I live in *illusions of such*. I live in *severe trouble* from *mental pain*. It's the *pressure from this hunger* causing *fatigue* and *wantingness*. I feel that there is an **impending** *imminent threat* to come.

1. *Fear now means to me...*

2. *Fear affects me by...*

3. *And I understand...*

> Our "triggers" are never gone forever. The goal is to be triggered less and to process faster. That's as good as it gets! Your brain holds all of your memories. Any of them can be triggered by fear at any time. The only alternative is a lobotomy!

Pick a phobia! Any phobia!

Do you think you have a phobia? Check-in! Everyone has everything! Are you scared of the night? Loud barks? Heights? Public speaking? Spiders? Find a phobia somewhere!

1. *My phobia is...*

2. Now do some research on this subject. Do an Internet search, call an expert, go on a field trip. Study. Then write, *I have learned...*

3. Now rinse your phobia. Go through the anger/rinse sheet and the physical body rinse. *I learned... And I feel...*

4. *And my phobia reminds me of...*

5. *I am triggered because... I am reliving...*

6. *Next time I'm in a phobia, I will...*

7. Lastly, lie on your back. Relax. Create a visual in your mind of your old memory and then create a new memory with a new behavior. Sit with it. Feel it. Breathe through it. You are replacing a new subliminal with the old one. To heal this body memory re-enact the old behavior and then create a new reaction, physically. Repeat it over and over, until it becomes a body memory and becomes part of your subconscious mind.

8. Now find a way to celebrate a phobia getting weaker! If you have the energy, pick another phobia and go back to the top!

9. Now take your old memory, visualize it while feeling it, and switch to your new visuals and feelings.

How a Phobia Becomes a Self-fulfilling Prophecy
by Mona

My family and I used to tease my father because he was terrified of dogs. We didn't understand that his fear had come from an incident in his past, and that it felt real in present-time to him. We judged him as ridiculous. Here's my dad, an athlete, six feet tall, a strong man, sitting on the roof of his car because a toy poodle was barking his little head off below!

I now know that my father was bitten and hurt by dogs when he was young. And, in my father's case, his phobia has become a self-fulfilling prophecy. Dogs aren't innately dangerous to someone like me, who has no fear of dogs. But to my dad, there can be a danger, because his fear of dogs makes dogs dangerous and reactive to his fear and therefore, him.

Remember, fear in you begets fear in others and then creates anger, right? Dogs are frightened of my dad, because my dad sends his fear energy to them telepathically. The dogs react to the fear and become afraid, so they respond with anger. Even a totally peaceful dog might be "triggered" by my father's trigger, and start to attack.

Now, here's the next problem. My father won't rinse or understand this. So, his phobia grows. Now he has developed a phobia of loud noises. Any loud noise makes him leap out of his skin and get hyper. He's been triggered; he thinks that the dogs are coming to get him.

So my dad continually asks, "What is that?" "Did you hear that?" "Is that a dog?" and on and on it goes. People around him pick up on his fear and hyperness. And this makes them hyper and annoyed or agitated. So where do you think this is leading?

Take a look at the phobia you rinsed during the last exercise.

1. *If I don't continue to rinse this phobia, it can become a self-fulfilling prophecy by...*

2. *Or it will expand to make me phobic about other things because...*

3. *It might spread to behaviors such as...*

4. *But not if I...*

5. *This makes me feel...*

6. *My prevention is...*

Paranoia

Paranoia is a trigger caused by a time-travel. When it happens we are in the past, future and present at the same time.

The psyche hopes you will "see," feel and process the memory of living in paranoia to understand it and turn it into wisdom. If not, you get to be insane instead. So that movie stays in your subconscious playing and re-playing. There's a good chance you will think, feel, and act from the age you were at the time of that memory, in present time. You can feel as if it were happening now and act it out accordingly. Insanity comes into the picture when you don't know that your psyche is in the past and your body is physically in the present.

The truth is, the memory is not happening now. You are triggered. Your triggered thoughts, feelings, and actions are about to be judged ridiculous. You may not feel totally crazy because somewhere inside, your intuition tells you this thing has truth in it. The truth is, it is real; it is just not true, now. But who knows this transference is happening?

The subliminal memory projects itself onto today's trigger. The subconscious mind superimposes these pictures in the style of trick photography. You are now in two places at one time—mentally, emotionally, physically and psychically.

If you are paranoid that someone is following you and there is no one there, it's likely that someone did follow you sometime in the past. The boogie man in the closet you fear could have been someone who had been sneaking into your room, when you were younger, who scared or hurt you. You just consciously forgot the trauma and did not connect the boogie-man fear to the sneaky man-in-your-room memories. So the sneaky man in your room is blocked, but the fears from that memory are not blocked.

Now, the fear creates a metaphorical picture and paranoia is born. The action of going to bed at a certain time triggers a message to the subconscious. The memory is brought up from the subconscious files of your memory. The mind says: This is where the sneaky man used to enter my room. Fear enters and transmits energy to your conscious mind in present time with no consciousness of the trauma memory.

The subliminal memory ignites fear of a sneaky man, yet there's no sneaky man here right now. You're nuts, especially if this keeps repeating over and over again, right? You may even be afraid to sleep in your room. Do you prefer a couch? Sleep in clothes versus pajamas? "Well, that's ridiculous," says your logical, judgmental mind. Now what? The fear is still there. You will probably self-beat and shut down, develop self-hate and anxiety, because you don't understand what's happening and people are re-acting to you in a shameful way. So you try to hide it.

Notice that the more you try to hide it, the worse you feel. This would be a good time to start some ritual blocking techniques or put the fear on something more tangible, such as fearing small places. Now we have a phobia called claustrophobia. Well, we're really lost in our mind now. You have the original fear of the sneaky man from the past, with a fear of going to sleep in present time, on top of a fear of your room, on top of a self-beat for being ridiculous, logically, on top of other people's voices telling you, "You're nuts! Get over it! There's nothing there!" All of this craziness is attempting to block so-called irrational fears. Wait. Don't forget the new phobia we just created, claustrophobia. And the list can go on.

These fears can create self-loathing from the anxiety caused by the fear. Just a touch of paranoia added to other fears could drive anyone over the edge. Remember, paranoia is a symptom reminding you that something upsetting did happen, and is a way of reminding you to process or live in anxiety. The triggered memory, stored subconsciously, attempts to surface hoping you are ready to deal with whatever fear memory is in there. Paranoia and phobias are messengers. We just need to learn how to de-code the blocks so the messages can get through.

1. Where are your irrational thoughts and feelings that you or others do not understand and deem crazy?

2. Why is your world a scary place to you?

3. If you use an absolute with an upset you are about to be hysterical and depressed. Are you using any of these absolutes, like "never," "always" or "forever"? How can an absolute send you over the edge? You're never going to be happy.

4. Why is there no hope? Finding a paranoid moment in your life is the way to understand and rid yourself of it. It's obviously not going away by itself.

5. *I am paranoid when... (or I have been paranoid when...) And this makes me feel...*

6. When did this paranoia begin?

7. What happened before the paranoia first began?

8. How is this fear or memory projecting into your present life? Was it a self-fulfilling prophecy?

9. *I am learning that...*

10. Now rinse your paranoia. Go through the anger/rinse sheet.

11. *When I am triggered, I am reliving...*

12. *Next time I end up in that trigger and paranoia, I will choose to...*

13. Lie on your back. Relax. Create a visual in your mind of your old memory and then replace it with a new picture and behavior idea. Sit with it. See it. Feel it. Exchange the two pictures in your mind and hold it. Breathe.

14. Celebrate the beginning of the paranoia becoming weaker! If you have the energy, pick another paranoia and go back to the top!

Bipolar Disorder

Many people who are truly bipolar have a strong right and left brain. If "bi" means two and "polar" means opposites, could "bi-polar" be a fight between two opposites? And as we've learned "disorder" means out of order. Could the left and right brain be considered opposites? And don't they often disagree with each other, making one's self argumentative and out of order?

Could this create paranoia about one's self? How would you like the bad guy to be in your brain? Could the manic depression be from an internal fight where one side of the brain will become suppressed, one side will dominate the other side shutting it down? Many people medicate with drugs, alcohol, career moves, or obsessive/compulsive behavior to calm this fight. Some people will act-out to "see" the pain as the result of this fighting, by making it physical. They cut themselves, pull out eyelashes, develop eating disorders, or torture others in one way or another depending which side of the brain is active.

In the battle between the brain hemispheres, one side of the brain dominates the other. If the logical left brain loses to the right brain, it becomes shut down and depressed. The right brain, now uninhibited by the left and disconnected from boundaries, has acts-outs and becomes an out-of-balance addict or obsessive nightmare from the big feelings, flailing with no sense of truth or self-responsibility.

Eventually, the out-of-balance feeling right brain gets so out-of-control that the left brain wakes up in a fury. The left brain begins berating the right brain. (Or self-beat). Now the left brain takes control and the right brain shuts down in shame knowing it's out-of-balance and it is depressed. The righteous left brain is now in control. Functioning in tunnel vision, it becomes a drill sergeant. The left drill sergeant is anal, obsessive, compulsive, and without empathy. Empathy needs feelings, feelings are in the right brain and the right brain is suppressed and depressed. The left brain is going to bring order and fix the right brain's addictive chaos.

After the left brain has functioned, using fear as control to the point of pure misery, the right brain wakes back up and strangles the left-brain with hysteria or a suicidal threat. The right brain is angry and rebellious. Freedom from rigid rules, rituals, barriers and suffocation is the right brain's goal. Unfortunately, these brain parts that are out of balance kill truth, boundaries and self-responsibility. The right brain screams at the left brain to "get out of the way, or else." The right brain doesn't want to live if it cannot feel. The left brain knows this is true and gets out of the way, for now. Victory! The right brain has won again! It's addict time, until next time!

Can you "see" why this person is always either on a high, in a depression, or is a demanding control freak? One side of the brain is always down and suppressed. The active half berates the suppressed side and keeps it weak and down. The self-beat is constant, just flipping sides.

A person suffering in this way needs self-processing skills. This type of person needs to slow down, rinse the crazy voices and write: *My logic says… and feels. My feelings say… and think… or believe…*

The idea is to teach these two strong sides of the brain to hear each other, one at a time, with no interruptions from the other. Treat them like a Congressional hearing. The Senate speaks and feels and then the House of Representatives speaks and feels. They both have a point. No point/counterpoint is allowed, especially inside yourself.

 Have you fought with your logic and feelings? Have you ever ignored your logic and reasoning in order to act-out on an addiction or a feeling? Have you ever ignored your feelings and intuition in order to control your image or righteousness?

1. *My right brain takes over and my left brain shuts down when…*
   And this feels…
   And this creates…

2. *My left brain takes over and my right brain shuts down when…*
   And this feels…
   And creates…

Making the Subconscious Conscious

Subliminal messages in movies, music, and advertisements are often illegal because of their subconscious power. So imagine your internal voices and memories as subliminal messages playing out with no control or consciousness from within. "See" why we need to rinse and remember?

For example: Notice when an advertiser puts yummy, sexy feelings on a chocolate bar, you start wanting chocolate. Chocolate is now yummy and sexual.

How about the smell of your ex's cologne or perfume. You could be at a bank, dressed in sweats, bored out of your mind and the aroma hits. You tell me what happens next. Oh, by the way, tell your logic to stop seeing and feeling whatever it is you're seeing and feeling. Good luck.

We don't have to remember and process every memory or every voice.

All thoughts, feelings and memories are connected to each other. Therefore, every time you understand one thing, that understanding automatically affects everything that aligns with that point. It's like a domino effect. The moment you knock one down, they all fall down. To clear one memory is to heal many memories that connect with that one. Like spell-check on a computer, if you fix one word, the computer gets set to clean up the entire document. If you rinse and do your time travels, your past will connect to your present, and clarity will appear. This understanding will calm the fear voices living in the future, but only after the past is rinsed and understood and the present is altered in thought, feeling and behavior. Let the truth lead!

Rip Van Winkle

Do you think that, after years of sleeping, Rip Van Winkle woke up and was happy? I think not! If he fell asleep and his life consisted of horses and buggies and then he woke up to cars and airplanes, I imagine he would be frightened. If everyone he knew was dead, I imagine he would feel angry, sad, and out of control. Is he happy to be alive? Who knows, but I imagine he wouldn't be right away.

Once he makes friends and understands his new environment, he might begin to adjust, and the understanding of how things are might start to dissipate his fear of the unknown. But if Rip doesn't deal with his fear, trauma, pain, hurt, and sadness, he'll develop paranoia, phobias, and projections.

Could Rip become paranoid or develop a phobia regarding going to sleep, or not waking up? Maybe he'd be afraid that his new friends might die like the old ones. Can you see how this could create paranoia, or an overly protective insomniac? If he's still angry or scared while he is awake, he might develop new phobias. Suppose Rip's fear is triggered by warm breezes and trees? If warm breezes and trees were in the environment when he fell asleep he might not want to go near a tree and not know or remember why. Poor Rip doesn't know his fear comes from past trauma, from years of sleeping under a tree. His conscious, logical mind acknowledges only what is real today. This is fertile ground for paranoia, phobias and projections.

Logically, if you ask Rip about trees, he'd probably say he's just fine with trees. When he feels a "tree fear" coming on, he might emotionally ignore the feeling and logically say, "I'm crazy. It's in the past. It's over!"

And maybe it is over, logically. But, not psychologically. If he has an irrational fear such as that of his friends dying, he'll likely become controlling, shut-down and then paranoid or phobic about death.

Poor Rip's mind is full of time-travels, awake and asleep. Dream writings could help. If there is no rinsing of his psyche, he can easily fill up with thoughts, memories and feelings and become anxious with no consciousness of why. He needs to empty his head. He may have trouble breathing while sleeping because fear has a tremendous effect on the breath. He might end up having a stroke while asleep because of the internal pressure he's created subconsciously for himself. Or his friends might actually get aggressive or controlling with him, because they sense the fear in him and that makes them angry. Unless he takes what is subconscious and makes it conscious, he may create terrible, self-fulfilling prophecies and craziness in and around him.

Don't be a Winkle!

1. In what ways is your reality distorted?

2. How does that make you feel?

3. Can you be in touch with yourself and others if you are even slightly drugged or high, prescription or not? Why do you think so?

4. Can you be true to yourself, if you don't face your truths? Why?

Drugs and Alcohol—Chemical Disconnection

Drugs and alcohol help you live *in* your pain, not process *through* the pain. If you are in a state of emergency, drugs are a useful tool. Sometimes we need an emergency stabilizer as we begin to learn a processing technique. However, relying on a drug as your cure and savior can keep you from developing faith in yourself. Instead, learn about and study yourself and your history. **Have faith in you, by believing in you and your truth, until you trust you!**

After this, you will become a person who touches the planet, rather than a person who fears or needs to conquer the planet. Do you want to work with life or against it? Wisdom enables us to create what we truly "wish" for in this life.

Many people believe they can get more in touch and become more vulnerable by using drugs or alcohol. In a way this can be true short-term, but what about long-term centering. Drugs or alcohol can bypass judgmental, crazy voices, momentarily. But drugs and alcohol do not understand or cure your issues and feelings. It is possible to drop into your feelings with sensitivity because you're in an induced state, numbing the self-beat/judger. But you cannot achieve true, psychic peace while drugged, because your judgmental voices will come back when the intoxication wears off. The opposite may happen as well. In an induced state you could act out your traumas. Either way, you are out of control.

When you are healing your insanities, and "seeing" and feeling your psyche, consider seeing a nutritionist, Chinese doctor, holistic doctor, homeopath, or acupuncturist. Learn to feed your body and align your chemistry. Western and Eastern medicine and healers all have a purpose in our earthly recovery.

There are incredible cleansing programs, amino acids, and nutritional supplements you can take to realign your chemistry. Your body and mind may have become very challenged and depleted of their nutritional balance. Of course, your mind has a chemical problem if you are full of chemicals! You have thrown it out of balance. Cleanse and feed it!

Every cell in your body dies off long before you do; most regenerate. It is very possible to realign your chemistry through a physical, mental, and emotional detox. Re-fill your body, mind and beliefs with new thoughts, new feelings and the ability to understand.

Just as you can die at any time, you can also be reborn.

Superstition: A False Sense of Security

Superstition is smoke and mirrors—in a subconscious, fear-based belief system. It causes you to process *outside* yourself in order to feel safe. The question is, safe from what? Why can't you come from *inside* yourself with faith in the truth? Superstition is a protective strength mechanism, but the sense of self and safety it gives you is false. Superstition is a kind of mind manipulation, as a result of past fears and loss of self-understanding. Superstition keeps feeding the lifespan of your fears. Any time you check-in by checking on something *outside* you, you lose intuition and, therefore, self-trust, self-confidence, and faith. Fear becomes your ruler and god again.

When you lose your intuition, you become powerless. As a survival skill, you create power outside yourself, without using your intuition. You look for ways to give you a feeling of power and control without inner awareness. Isolation and withdrawal are protective behaviors as well. Are you really in control? If so, how? Dominating fear or submitting to fear still feeds fear. Understanding fear and changing your beliefs and habits releases fear's grip on you.

When we're playing the **game of superstition,** we:

1. Don't check-in to "see" how we feel or what we think.

2. Don't question belief systems.

3. Don't tell scary or hurtful truths.

4. Believe that secrecy is a must.

5. Do not rinse.

6. Never time-travel with conscious awareness.

7. Have no understanding of our crazy voices.

8. Self-beat often.

9. Judge everyone and everything.

 Have you ever done something subconscious to keep something bad from happening? Have you ever given money to a homeless person because you were afraid that if you didn't, you might be punished? Have you become or stayed religious because you were afraid that if you didn't, it meant that you were "bad" and bad things might happen to you? See if you can find your superstition. We all have a few.

1. *I am superstitious about...*

2. *I became superstitions because of my ... (who and why)*

3. *My superstitions hide my fear of...*

4. *Now rinse this fear*

5. *I'm scared of God or the Universe because...*
   So I act like... to protect myself from...

6. *The truth is...*

Fear of Happiness

There is a superstitious vibe I see in so many people. It is a fear and light paranoia or phobia about happiness. I often wonder what kind of a sucker-punch instigated this kind of protective strength mechanism. Look at what Mikaela wrote about this. She is fifteen years old.

I Don't Trust Happiness
by Mikaela

I have a superstition about happiness, which means that I will never let myself be happy. I think there is some trick involved with happiness. I don't trust it. I always think there's something else that I'm not getting and I can't be happy until I get it all!* When I have it all, then I'll be safe. And then maybe I can be happy. Until then, I keep pushing myself to do more and be more* — allowing myself no gratitude or praise along the way!

I feel miserable and hate myself. I compare myself to everyone and never measure up. I self-beat and then my big fat pusher energy comes out. Keeping myself upset keeps me on guard. Happy would make me not pay attention. I would get hurt. I would get bored and I wouldn't learn anything. Fear and misery keep me motivated.

If I let myself be happy, then that would be it! My life wouldn't get any better, ever. I would just stay the same forever. I will have betrayed myself. I won't ever be able to connect with anybody.

If I was happy, I wouldn't be able to jump into people's heads, where I am able to judge things and see things coming for safety. I use jumping into other people's heads as my check-in to see if everything is okay with me.

I used to be happy. So was my sister. One day the two of us were so happy; and then the next day my parents were fighting badly. Then my parents got divorced and our world fell apart. I never want to be happy and not see bad things about to come and get me! Ever again!

---

*"All" is an absolute setting up of hopelessness.

*"More" is an endless, out of control word because there is no end to living in the "more" word.

1. Are you afraid to truly be happy? If so, why?

2. Were you ever caught off guard while content or happy? When and how?

3. How did you feel? Did you feel sucker-punched? If so, what do you remember?

4. Has your psyche accidentally connected the bad, hurt, or scared memories with being caught off guard and with happiness? How can life not have any upsets in it?

5. Do you feel upsets are a punishment? Is life about experiences, or punishments and rewards? Explain.

6. How do your fear belief systems make you feel about your life?

7. Can you find where you or your inner child is jealous of others and their life or happiness? Explain.

8. How can you change your fear to faith?

Homework!

One of the best movies to show how insanity is created and how to get out of insanity is *Sybil*. This is an intense movie, so I would like to take it apart with you. It will give us a deeper understanding of insanity.

Please note there are some painful scenes in this movie. If these scenes are too painful, fast forward. You'll get the point without the play-by-play blows.

I'm assuming that you have rented the movie, so it's processing time.

1. Notice when the swing starts to squeak in the beginning of the movie, Sybil disconnects in a subliminal time-travel (shown as a flashback in the movie) but pulls out of it the first time. The second time, she is already triggered and more susceptible to a bigger time-travel. More of the visual occurs. We "see" her mom pulling on a rope that squeaks this time. Sybil becomes disconnected. Still, she pulls out of her time-travel again momentarily. **What psyche time zone is she in? How old is she in this moment?**

2. When Sybil leads the children in "follow the leader," her inner child is already triggered. This is the third trigger so her inner child is close to the surface this time. The time-travel takes her over and she consciously disconnects and disassociates. She becomes disoriented causing a momentary loss of memory in present-time awareness. The memory is operating alone with no consciousness of where she was and is. She returns to present time and finds herself standing in the water, confused. **Why water? What happens with the pulley and squeaks with momma? Is water involved in the enema and a loss of control of her bladder? Explain.**

3. Notice that there is no accent when she is the art teacher. **What could have caused the accent to come and go? What caused this disconnection and disassociation?**

4. Noises hurt her head. **Why?** Sybil goes into a trance and is actually in physical pain when she hears the noise. **Isn't this illogical? Or are body memories real and this strong? Explain.**

5. Have you ever heard of ghost pain, when someone has had a leg amputated, yet they can feel pain as if the leg was still there? These are mental and psychological body memories that send neurological signals that actually hurt. **How does this work? How strong is the psyche? Guess.**

6. The noise triggers the scary, shame voices and talents of her mother. Just the subliminal memory of the violence takes over her psyche and body. Her left-brain logic disconnects from her right-brain feelings. She psychically time-travels back to her subliminal memories. She reacts as if she's back in time, a little girl, with no adult information. When there is no present-time awareness, this is called "disassociation." Sybil is no longer associated with her child memories and her adult, present-time awareness. This is stronger than a disconnection. Her body goes out of control, and she is in body-memory hell. She does not know she's okay in present time. **How do you see disassociation versus disconnection? And why would this happen? Why is disconnection and disassociation necessary for some to survive life?**

7. Sybil's voices split when she takes on her mother's punishing voice as well as her own, scared, little girl's voice and creates a conversation between them. This looks schizophrenic. She's time-traveling again. Her brain is remembering and copying what she knows and psychically sees. The disassociation allows the split. **Why would she start doing this split conversation?**

8. The doctor gives Sybil things to smell to trigger a body memory through scents. She wants to "see" if Sybil would time-travel to her little-girl self with a little girl's voice. The doctor wants to "see" if the voice was conscious and aware, or subconscious and unaware. As soon as the doctor calls her on the little girl voice, she pulls out of it, but is disoriented. This proves adult unawareness. **What makes Sybil pop in and out of these behaviors?**

9. Sybil reacts in fear and trauma when she thinks of her mother playing the piano. However, when Sybil plays the piano as another personality, she separates from her mother's memory of pain and becomes light, artistic, gleeful and fun. There are two piano memories. One with her mother, playing piano, mixed with abuse and another memory of Sybil playing piano with joy as another personality. If she succeeds in a disassociation from her mother, the piano and herself, she can actually enjoy the piano without remembering the pain. Both are real experiences and need to be separated. **Why?**

10. Cut to the scene with the father at lunch. When Sybil asks for permission to see the doctor, and the father responds in a negative, non-understanding way, he uses religion, God, the devil, and Armageddon as his rebuttal. His conversation traps her energetically because there will be no way of getting her father to understand. **Is the lack of understanding from the father just as detrimental as the abuse of the mother? Why?**

11. When she feels trapped and bad with her dad, she time travels and gets stuck until her movie finishes playing. When her anger is over, she pops out, just as her mother used to do. Both mother and daughter are brilliant at time-traveling. Is this chemical or is it a generational and learned behavior, or both?

12. Watch what happens when her father goes to touch her. He is unsafe because he cannot see or understand her. The body memory of the physical pain inflicted by her mother, in the past, still feels real in present-time even though her father is not physically hurting her. He mentally, emotionally and psychically has. **What do you understand here? How does this scenario feel?**

13. Even though the mother is dead, the memories and insanity are not. Sybil has been programmed and, therefore, brainwashed. Although this is not her fault, it is her responsibility to recover or live a life of hell. This is not about good, bad, right or wrong; it is about a spiritual understanding to understand insanity, in order to develop wisdom and appreciation for sanity. Sybil has to "own" it all or stay insane forever. She time-travels and runs. **Why does touching hurt spiritually, mentally, emotionally and physically? Explain.**

14. Memories are kept in different ages by different personalities that have developed in Sybil, in order to be able to pull different pieces of information and talents to the surface, without remembering mother. This is the only way she can momentarily pretend she is okay by being someone else. This is a self mind manipulation, so as not to time-travel. The survival goal is to keep positive or happy experiences safe and away from trauma memories. **Does this sound like an ignorant person, or a brilliant person? The amount of mental capabilities needed to mind manipulate is quite developed. The question is, who would these people be if they understood this? Explain.**

15. Sybil is afraid of people, piano sounds, language, painting and hands. She is afraid of everything she loves. Different personalities act out Sybil's anger, protections, hatred, talent, language, extroverted personality, suicide, and tomboy. Sybil is actually brilliant and well educated. **Why would she want to die?**

16. Suicide is about killing the pain. Often suicidal people don't consciously realize they are connected to the pain. Sybil wants to die to go to her love source—the one person who showed her love. She wants to go to Grandma and Grandma's dead.

How could Marcia, the suicide personality, be bad? Bad is a perception. If we would understand things outside of logic and judgment, we could see more and go deeper. Marcia, the suicide personality, wanted to kill Sybil's pain and take her to her love, Grandma.

17. If Grandma's dead, then love is in death. **Explain in your own words what this means.**

18. Vicki, another one of Sybil's personalities, who is logical, usually stops Marcia or gets help, but Marcia is the savior of Sybil's honor. **Why is Vickie so important?**

19. Richard's sharing and owning was crucial for Sybil. She touched his hand and kissed him back. Intimacy came from Richard's understanding and owning of his pain. Truth and vulnerability bring love feelings. But Sybil is still missing self-love. So when Richard kisses Sybil it hurts, love hurts. The presence of love triggers what she never had and very much needs. If Sybil has no real love experience, or never saw love as strong, how would she know how to accept or build love? Love does trigger non-loving memories. Love does not hurt us but can bring hurt to the surface. True love needs understanding to heal the hurt associated with love . **How could someone wanting to love Sybil scare and hurt her?**

20. **Do you think Sybil's mom was tortured and abused? Is it chemical or is it taught?** The mother is smart and talented. She speaks in poetry when she tortures Sybil. She, too, speaks in other languages. The mother often speaks in a baby voice herself. **Is this relationship child to child or mother to daughter? Explain.**

21. Someone tortured Sybil's mother and she is merely copying what she was taught. Sybil's mom was in a ghost trance, and now, so is Sybil. Sybil's dad admits that her mom was diagnosed as paranoid/schizophrenic. **How can the father be in such denial? What might have happened to him as a child? Did he miss identifying abuse in his childhood? Make it up.**

22. If it is true that you attract what you are, what you are used to, or your misunderstood issues, then her father has experienced abuse in his past that he has not owned or allowed to surface. Maybe he was ritually abused, religiously tortured or beaten. Something shut him down and made him very comfortable with insanity. During his threats of fear concerning religious beliefs and repercussions, he robotically rattled disconnected, scary information to Sybil. The sins of the forefathers are passed from generation to generation, again and again. **Who is going to stop the madness?** Madness is suppressed truth, fear, anger, guilt, shame and pain. Rinse! **Notice the word mad is in madness. Could madness be anger towards suppressed truth? Explain.**

23. When you mix God with punishment and shame, a child has nothing greater to believe in. If parents make God scary, punishing and bad, there is no hope. The parent becomes God. Fear, pain, and a scary God equal insanity from the hopelessness and helplessness of it all. Insanity is a survival technique that becomes a process for people in fear, traumas, memories and the pain of abuse. Notice how busy the psyche is in Sybil's dream state. Truth does not go away. **What is the psyche trying to show Sybil through her dream state?**

24. Kids are intuitive, psychic and telepathic. They are not full of judgments or brainwashing yet. If you deny your thoughts, feelings and mistakes, a child can feel and sense the lies. Without truth, the child's psyche and intuition are ruined. Truth is the language of the psyche and sanity. Drop the ego and own. If not, "nuts" and rebellions are the outcomes. Children just "see" and speak truth, if you let them. The child, Matthew, knew Sybil was not the personality that showed up at dinner with him and his dad. He was aware Sybil had many personalities. **Why would Matthew, a child, see Sybil more clearly than the adult father?**

25. Because of anger, fear, guilt and shame people deny that their pain ever happened, even after the truth has surfaced. These

feelings can be overwhelming if there is no understanding of how to process them. People fear truth and pain, because we have not come up with strong enough processing techniques for the right brain and the psyche. Most people will get stuck and lost in the pain and never come out. Then people feel guilty for betraying the abusers or upsetting a loved one who is upset by the truth. This kind of back-door guilt will take any-one to a kamikaze leap towards insanity to bury the upsetting truth forever. The truth will then be locked up and safe inside the twisted mind of the nuts person. **How can this create in-sanity and depression?**

26. **Are these insanity splits all to prevent Sybil from time-trav-eling? What do you think?**

When you "see" the red car, with the voiceover of Sybil and the doctor, notice that Sybil complains about all the green. Too much green. Green grass, green trees. The doctor says, "You meant the green kitch-en." This "green" obsession is a typical protective mechanism. Sybil is putting her uncomfortable feelings on something other then the actual trauma. She has a phobic and paranoid claustrophobic feeling with the color green. The color green is the trigger to go into the paranoid epi-sode to keep Sybil blocked from conscious awareness of a subliminal memory that is flashing forward. The paranoia is releasing energy, without dealing with the truth of the trauma. Green isn't the trauma. So yes, you release the energy that comes up from the memories for a moment through blaming the color green, but the issue still remains. The body, mind and soul remember it all. Her body reacts to any past visuals. The abuse was in the green kitchen. When Sybil goes in and out of her personalities, her body, voice and information change ac-cordingly. Sybil would say, "The people, I am scared of the people." The people are the phobias, which truly represent her mother. The people meant mother. Sybil's body would time-travel and she would crawl, react, flinch, scream and run away. She would say, "Ouch! The people are coming." Or was it, her mother was coming and she did not want to admit this abusive person was her mother, so she made up a new reality that it must have been someone else. No real mother could do this, right? The question is, what is today and what was yesterday, and is there a way out?

The mother was diagnosed as paranoid/schizophrenic. If paranoia causes time-travel while in the present time, and a schizophrenic is a split personality, is her mother's behavior what caused Sybil's multiple personality and paranoia, phobias and projections? Is it really chemical, or is it psyche abuse that has been passed down and we use chemicals to control Sybil? Is the brain just a copy machine or are we truly helpless when faced with insanity? You know, there was a time when the thought of flying was considered "nuts," too.

> Sybil became a professor of art at a university, and came to understand truth and love!
>
> Can insanity be cured? I don't want to work with someone if that person does not believe we can get to the other side. I know our traumas will never go away, but if we believe in life as a spiritual journey on which we experience good, bad and ugly, can truth, with love, take us beyond what Earth provides for us?
>
> Can we create what we let ourselves believe? Are insanity and miracles about processing and perceptions? It worked for Sybil!

Is There Hope Through Truth and Love?

Everyone has a different personality. If we are not disassociated then the distinct parts of our personalities are just energies and perceptions. Can we identify ourselves to better understand our contradictions? Feel free to name your separate personalities or voices. We are multi-dimensional creatures trying to be black and white. Could that be lie #1? Crazy voice rinses are great, to let yourself go, on purpose, with no fear or shame of what comes out. No logic allowed until you're finished. No judgment is allowed at all. You can name your different sides, people's names, or energy names such as Joe, Susie, Fred or Maniac Madness, The Old One, Desperate Energy, Fearful One, Control Freak, or other names.

My personalities are...

1.
2.
3.
4.
5.
6.
7.
8.
9.
10.

The personality of _____ is there because...
This part is showing me...
And I remember when...
And I feel...

Name as many of these sides as possible. Get to know all of you, and you will not be bored anymore!

Chapter Review

I learned...
And I feel...

Summary

Insanity is a state of being in which truth and feelings are far away from each other. Insanity is about time-traveling and disconnecting and disassociating from our thoughts, feelings and memories. Insanity is about surviving life. It's about mind manipulating. Insanity happens when there is a physiological mass, tumor or deformity or when fear enters the psyche, as well as the telepathic and intuitive mind and turns into projections, paranoias and phobias. When insanity occurs, low- and high-ego overtake and dominate the soul!

15 Vibeless One: Wake Up! You Are in a Trance!

If you are unaware of your energy, and you give it no understanding, no vocabulary, no processing, then you are ignoring yourself.

Flatness: Intellectually Stimulated, Emotionally Dead

When we feel "flat," we can be intellectually stimulated, but not emotionally. Another option is to shut down in a suppressed depression. Being vibeless keeps us invisible so we cannot be truly seen intuitively. Obviously, somewhere in our life being "seen" was not allowed or scary. Vibeless people develop a type of poker face.

1. Was it ever unsafe for you to be "seen" when you were a child? Explain.

2. How did this feel? What do you remember?

3. Do you ever have trouble expressing your own thoughts or feelings? Why? When did this first start?

4. Now own and rinse these memories!

Suppression: The Art of Ignoring Yourself

Suppressed energy can surprise-attack you or someone else. It lies dormant until it becomes overwhelmed with built-up anger, fear, guilt, shame, or hurt. Top it off with a big aggressive judgment—good, bad, right, wrong, stupid, or smart—and look out! The explosion or implosion will be something to see.

> **Explosion:** Aggressive or passive energy that attacks, freaks out, and blames everyone, usually catching others and ourselves off guard. So the explosion is full of blame. Since there is scrambled truth inside the information now exploding, we feel righteous and arrogant and refuse to rinse or own anything!
>
> **Implosion:** A person is fine one day, then enraged or even dead the next (from cancer, a heart attack, suicide). If you do not own your energy and your memories, if you don't process them with words, feelings, and actions, you can create an energy that attacks yourself.

The listening capability of a vibeless person grows weaker every day, because he or she is listening to a mob of mixed voices: internal opinions, fears, worries, and projections. The vibeless person's past bleeds into all present-time situations. By the time a vibeless person speaks, he or she is so afraid, frustrated, and angry, that passive-aggressive energy spills out or fragments. This scares other people, which scares the vibeless person even more. So, shut-down, here we come...again. If you don't trust or like yourself in your communication, you can easily shut yourself off again.

The Vibeless One is shut down and passive/aggressive. Is there a part of you that is vibeless? Let's check a few vibeless traits.

- ☐ Flat
- ☐ Demeaning
- ☐ Belittled/Pitiful
- ☐ Apathetic
- ☐ Arrogant
- ☐ Condescending
- ☐ Monotone
- ☐ Perfectionist
- ☐ Loveless
- ☐ Blank
- ☐ Intellectual only
- ☐ Petrified
- ☐ Someone acting in a role

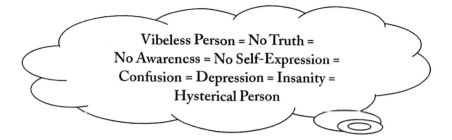

Vibeless Person = No Truth =
No Awareness = No Self-Expression =
Confusion = Depression = Insanity =
Hysterical Person

Understanding Opposites—
Finding Our Balance

A shut-down, vibeless person is the opposite of a hysterical person; yet, as we're learning, these opposites have the same issue.

The vibeless person is emotionally hysterical on the inside while spinning and emotionally flat on the outside!

The hysterical person is emotionally hysterical on the outside while spinning and emotionally flat on the inside!

Vibeless and hysterical people are scary because they are spinning, but don't understand why they're spinning. One is imploding and one is exploding! These two people often attract and then repel each other because they are so similar and in denial.

Vibeless people can't "see," feel, or sense themselves. Therefore, they can stay stuck, indefinitely. Energetically, vibeless people are scary because their aura resonates with their judgments, self-beats and past pain. Afraid of themselves, their shutdown protects them by blocking their energy altogether. This fear of self does show itself to many people through vibes. In fact, some people will often say yes to the vibeless one, and say whatever they believe the vibeless person wants to hear, just to get away as soon as possible, even though the vibeless person appears harmless on the outside.

It's always the *inside* that counts.

Be careful, extroverts! Just because you appear to be energized on the outside doesn't mean that part of you isn't vibeless on the inside. For example, your truth and vulnerable inner child may be shut down. It takes a lot of insight and bravery to be in touch with all aspects of ourselves.

YIN YANG: A symbol that represents the ancient Chinese understanding of how energy works. It has an outer circle that represents "everything," with black and white shapes within the circle that represent the interaction of two energies—"yin" (black) and "yang" (white), which cause everything to happen. They are not completely black or white, just as things in life are not completely black or white, and they cannot exist without each other.

While "yin" is dark, passive, downward, cold, contracting, and weak, "yang" is bright, active, upward, hot, expanding, and strong. There is continual movement between these two energies, yin to yang and yang to yin, causing everything to happen, just as things in life expand and contract, and temperature changes from hot to cold.

According to this theory, when we evolve to the point of understanding and accepting all opposites, we lose any desire for righteousness, war and ego. Accepting and understanding opposites is the beginning process for peace and balance.

If you are a vibeless person and you appear flat, what you need to do is to find and understand the opposite energy, then come to the middle for balance. That means you need to find your hysteria and your suppressed rage to be balanced with passion and inner peace.

The reason I use the word *rage* instead of *anger* is that rage is *present-time anger* mixed with *pent-up anger and hurt* stored inside you, haunting you from the past. But the fact is, if we are alive, we did make it through the past upset, didn't we? The truth is, we are safe but maybe not psychically. So what are we afraid of? Hint: check your self-beat, guilt and shame to find out.

Save yourself from yourself and self-beat!

1. Rage feels like... and it creates...

2. When someone starts to rage at me, I shut down my thoughts and/or feelings, because I remember when...

3. If I let my mind and feelings go, I am afraid of...

4. Now—time-travel and rinse!

Human Nature: Seeing Ourselves in Nature

As we discussed earlier in this book, human nature is constantly reflected in our planet's nature. Take, for example, the tornado. A tornado's phenomenal energy comes from the rapid mixture of warm air from one direction meeting cold air coming from the opposite direction. "Seeing" ourselves in nature, metaphorically, is a great way to understand ourselves in a different light. Let's call the warm air love and compassion, and the cold air judgment and/or indifference.

When two invisible and opposite energies conflict inside your mind, heart and soul, you end up with torrentially mixed thoughts and feelings that spin and destroy everything in their path. In the wake of the storm, we or those nearest to us end up disoriented, wandering off in different directions, like wounded animals after a tornado.

The Tornado

Before a tornado forms, the energy is twisted, conflicted with itself. The air becomes flat and dead. Animals can feel the environment change and start to react. Birds stop moving. There is a deep and scary silence. The air feels warm, but empty. When the cold air hits, so does a kind of suffocated moisture, creating hail. When the suffocation is released, hail and rain begin to fall rapidly. When the freight-train sound of the tornado forms, chaos and destruction take over. Any animal wishing to be safe has to go underground and wait, anxiously.

Now, turn this story on yourself.

My Personal Tornado

Before my internal tornado forms, my energy gets twisted and conflicted within myself. My energy is flat and dead. People can feel my energy change and they start to react. Others stop moving. I have a deep and scary silence inside. I feel warm, but empty. When my cold air of indifference hits, so does my suffocated moisture (from withheld hurt and tears) creating hail (cold, icy tears with fast attacking aggressiveness). When my suffocation is released, hail and rain (hysterical and aggressive tears) fall rapidly. When the freight-train sound of anger and rage begins, my tornado forms. The chaos and destruction take over. Any person or animal wishing to be safe has to go underground and wait (don't forget waiting is an anger word due to passive suppression), anxiously.

Do you see how different pictures can be used for the subconscious mind to "see" yourself, others or life in a new way?

This metaphor can help us better understand how a vibeless person becomes or attracts a hysterical person, and vice versa.

1. Close your eyes. Can you feel, and describe, the indifference and fear that is felt when your air or aura turns flat and vibeless right before your tornado? Explain. How does this feel?

2. Can you "see" and describe the hysteria and destruction that are felt when a tornado hits?

3. Can you feel and describe the fear that develops inside you when you or others are flat and void of energy?

4. Can you "see" and describe the hysteria and destruction that develop in you when you or others are hysterical and destructive?

It is your *choice* to learn about your essence. A life that is misunderstood or a life with unprocessed traumas becomes trancelike. It will keep you vibeless, or in a lifelong tornado. Just as you inherited ancient traumas from your parents energetically and behaviorally, you will pass traumas on to strangers, friends and children, unless someone, somewhere, breaks the trance. Will that someone be you?

1. *My own personal tornado is...*

2. *My tornado feels like...*

3. *My tornado destroys...*

4. *I can recover by...*

How Invisible Energy Works

This electromagnetic spectrum shows how invisible, vibeless energy works:

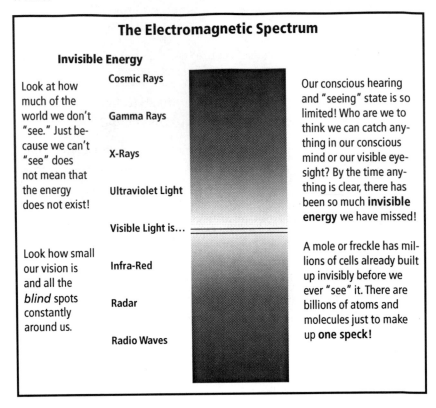

The Electromagnetic Spectrum

Invisible Energy

Cosmic Rays

Gamma Rays

X-Rays

Ultraviolet Light

Visible Light is...

Infra-Red

Radar

Radio Waves

Look at how much of the world we don't "see." Just because we can't "see" does not mean that the energy does not exist!

Look how small our vision is and all the *blind* spots constantly around us.

Our conscious hearing and "seeing" state is so limited! Who are we to think we can catch anything in our conscious mind or our visible eyesight? By the time anything is clear, there has been so much **invisible energy** we have missed!

A mole or freckle has millions of cells already built up invisibly before we ever "see" it. There are billions of atoms and molecules just to make up **one speck!**

Exercise:
If human feeling and thinking are like electromagnetic waves, they are mostly invisible. What are we not "seeing?" How strong, yet invisible, are these light rays?

We are trained to rely on our intellect; therefore, denying and losing faith in things we cannot "see," taste, hear, touch, or smell is inevitable. Is there not miraculous information to be understood and sensed by things not "seen"? Traditional sensory perception is limited. If invisible energy is already difficult to understand because we are blind to it, then imagine the fear levels regarding our invisible sensors: our psyche, telepathy, and intuition.

If the electromagnetic spectrum graph is an example of how much is going on in this world that is invisible, why aren't we more open to invisible ideas? Science also shows us that before something becomes visible, a tremendous amount of invisible energy has gone into its creation while still invisible to the naked eye. In order to understand what is visible, we have to go back and comprehend its opposite, the invisible energy, which is what created the visible.

Scientists make most of their discoveries by studying patterns. At first, researchers start with the most obvious patterns and then work their way back to invisible or less obvious patterns. In the same way that scientists use magnifying glasses and microscopes, you and I use rinsing, crazy voices, reflection exercises, and letters of absurdity to *magnify* our thoughts and feelings. Through this energetic magnification we can "see" and understand our "invisible" patterns.

Homework!

The movie *"What the Bleep Do We Know?"* (for the DVD, go to www.whatthebleep.com)

This is just another perception of life and how we work. Remember, there are many ways to "see" and understand ourselves and life itself. This movie is about quantum physics and how the world exists from a more spiritual and scientific perception. Don't judge this subject matter if you do not understand it yet. Open up to the unknown to **go beyond what you know.**

"Quantum physics" sounds like big words to me. I, personally, need to take them apart or become overwhelmed by my lack of faith that I am even capable of understanding this subject matter. This can easily shut me down and flip the "on" switch for the judger. Whenever a word has a charge to it, take it apart. See differently what you think you know.

> **"Quantum"** comes from the word quantity, meaning how much or how many. It means a desired or required amount. **"Physics"** is the root word of physician and pharmacy. So physics is the study of medicine. It is a science and understanding of the elements of nature and energy and doses of medicine both outside and within the body. Quantum theory is about the amount of energy from a discharge of electrons that is not continually being discharged. The body has its own, natural medicinal chemicals. Suppose we truly knew how to tap into them.

So this movie is about you as energy and how your mind and heart affect your chemistry and the world around you. Everything has a reason.

Did you watch the movie? If so, write:

1. *This movie was like... And it made me feel...*

2. The power of thought is about its effect on our physical reactions and our chemical stimuli and manifestation capability. Our likes or dislikes do not matter. It is based on feeling and belief. **What does the power of thought mean to you?**

3. Reality is a perception. It is not necessarily based on truth. It comes from decisions and behaviors based on our subconscious beliefs and protections. We actually create our life and reality. And yes, with a change of perception and belief, you will change your life. **What does reality with the concept of perception mean?**

4. We are trained and programmed by the age of eight. The rest of our life is about de-programming. We are in a trance, reactive and defensive. **How much does our conditioning block what and how we see?**

5. If we saw ourselves in the third person, we would watch ourselves and wake up to our manifestations. If we could watch ourselves with no judgments and listen to people's thoughts

and jokes about us, maybe we could hear truth and see reality through the world around us without personalizing. **In what ways can you be more of an observer of your self?**

6. To not be curious is to not be open. It is to be shut-down, trance-like or a replica of the people who raised or influenced you. **Who and where are you?** *"To not be curious is to be ¾ dead," means…creates…*

7. The self-beat of the character of Amanda affects her entire life. The self-hate manifests itself in physical pain, popping pills, drinking too much alcohol, attacking tones of voice, defensiveness and shut-down/hysterical explosions. **Wonder why there are no real relationships?** There is no faith. She is a pessimist with a bad habit until her mind opens. **How does the self-beat affect Amanda's (Marlie Matlin) perception and attitude?**

8. Notice that positive thinking is not necessarily based on truth. Thinking positively can discount you from reality. **Why is thinking positively not real? Is it true?**

9. Every thought and feeling can tap into the mind, heart and body. Certain feelings cause chemical releases and a rush of peptides. That's why thoughts and feelings affect the body, especially when they are working overtime. If you are depressed or shut-down when you make love, the chemical rush that you get from those feelings can become a craving. Depression is a miserable existence, so finding ways to create a rush is vital. So, fake fun, domination, drinking and drugs, sugar and any other addiction feels really good, because you can feel for a minute. Whether the feeling is positive or negative. Positive energy is the new oxygen and who cares about tomorrow when today feels awful? **Can one thought or perception cause enough chemicals to release a feeling rush that can create addictive behaviors if you long to feel? Explain.**

10. Have you ever felt butterflies in your stomach? Have you ever felt your heart race when feelings hit? Have you ever felt

faint, when there is nothing physically wrong? Why does your head ache when there is no tumor? Do you ever get excited and start running or jumping around without wanting to behave that way? Ever get sick or achy when there was an upsetting experience? Ever get tired and overly sleepy when you have had plenty of sleep? **Can you think of an example of how your feelings and thoughts have affected your neurons, neuro-peptides, amino acids, and cell receptacles? How about your immune system?**

11. Why do we bless water in many religions? Does concentrated thought and feeling affect the molecular pattern of water causing temperature and life change under water? Search the internet, research new concepts. Stay open, let's see. Ninety percent of our bodies are water. **How do our thoughts and feelings affect water? How do you think your thoughts and feelings are affecting your body chemistry?**

12. Notice how much Amanda lives in her past. Some people live in the past because they felt proud or were over-achievers. Some people are stuck in their pain from the past. They are either shut-down, defensive or attackers. Either way, they are not living in the present time. **How does living in the past create a fearful, pompus or negative attitude?**

Could we be avoiding healing and understanding ourselves to avoid a chemical withdrawal?

What is a nervous breakdown? A nervous breakdown is a breakdown of your nervous system. A nerve can be rejuvenated physically and emotionally. These breakdowns allow confusion or misunderstood pain to come forward, to be seen and re-built for a more solid foundation. If you would welcome and not resist a breakdown, in fact, see it as a release and a new beginning, you create so many possibilities versus same old, same old. You can use many rinsing techniques to clear your thoughts and feelings, and develop wisdom and clarity for a stronger foundation. Cleansing the body and feeding it healthy foods would support your re-building as well.

We can either create possibilities or live in a ghost trance as many have lived before…

We Are Ghosts in a Different Dimension

The vibeless one, truly a result of invisible warfare, is in an earthly trance, shut-down from self-awareness; in a robotic, habitual state, doing the same thing day after day. The trance of the vibeless or hysterical one is a similar existence to that of a spirit or ghost who is stuck in a time-travel. Like a ghost existing in a different dimension this person struggles to grasp an understanding of its past-life confusions. The "vibeless" or hysterical one and/or ghost is stuck existing, spinning and repeating what he or she knows, but does not understand. The real question is: Do either energies even know they are spinning in a trance?

Both the "vibeless" or hysterical one and the ghost are re-experiencing some traumatic event from the past, repeating the misunderstood occurrence over and over again. The ghost and the "vibeless" or hysterical one often don't realize that they are the walking dead. Most ghost stories portray the ghost as an energy or life force that has to learn and understand a lesson before the ghost can move on. A ghostly trance and an earthly trance are both indicative that there is a need to "see" oneself more clearly to live in the present and move forward.

In a trance our subconscious minds circle insanely to attempt to find an answer, the anger, fear, guilt and shame feed the circling, like a hamster in a wheel, going nowhere fast.

Hauntings stop when patterns are interrupted.
Once our patterns stop, there is room for new and changing thoughts, feelings and ideas, creating the openness to "see" differently. Then, we can break the trance!

1. What is a trance?

2. What is the repetitive pattern of your trance?

3. When did your "trance" begin? Why is it there?

4. How does this trance feel?

5. How could you break this trance?

It's a choice: We either pay attention to the lessons, or let the trance begin!

Understanding "What Is"

Everything that appears in our lives is there for a reason. Therefore, if you intentionally ignore something, you'll keep attracting it, over and over again. A trance or pattern is not about whether you are right or wrong. It's about "what is" that you need to understand. If something is repeating in your life, you are overlooking a message.

Maybe you attract the same kind of person that continually sets you off, or you always lose jobs and believe it's the boss's fault, or that it's everyone but you.

We all repeat experiences in our lives. We all get stuck in the same old thoughts, feelings and behavior! But do we know, when that happens to us, that we have played a part in the happening?

Instead of looking at what you think others are or aren't doing, look at what you are or aren't doing!

Ghost Trance Story

I remember watching a ghost story on TV about a couple who died from a misunderstanding that resulted in murder. The husband accused his wife of cheating on him, even though she had a sweet, innocent energy and would never do such a thing. This is obviously a projection on the husband's part. What do you think could have happened in his past that would blind him to the point of no longer "seeing" the essence of his wife's aura? Some trauma was triggered regarding cheating that was strong enough to turn him into an attacking, accusatory murderer. He did love her very much.

What was happening? He was overtaken subconsciously with rage, old anger from the past, and became suspicious. He was in a trance. His wife did not stand a chance, because he was in another time zone psychically. He could not truly "see" or hear her. She became someone from his past and his subliminals came forward and created a temporary insanity. He needed a time-travel rinse!

Years later, a live human being comes to visit this haunted house. Of course, the house was haunted by the husband and wife we just spoke about. Every night, at the same time, the husband ghost chases the wife ghost through the wall, as she shrieks, "No! No!" The husband then throws her onto the bed and wrestles with her. She escapes his arms, but can't get out of the room. She's trapped. He rushes at her, she cries and yells, and he stabs her. She falls and dies, he drops the knife and falls to the ground sobbing in remorse and disbelief, and then the ghosts fade away.

Minutes later they come running through the wall again and repeat the same behavior over and over again. Several times a night. Every night, the trance continues. The ghosts have no conscious awareness of their ghostly trance and existence, until this human "sees" the ghosts coming through the wall. First, the yelling, the trapping, murdering, crying, and then fading away. When the "trance" happens again, two minutes later, the human is appalled. He can't watch the trance again. He tries to stop the ghosts by yelling at them. But they can't hear him.

Finally, the human physically steps between the two ghosts. As the husband goes to stab his wife, something changes. The presence of the human's body interrupts the feeling and pattern of the stabbing. The human doesn't feel the stab but he does, energetically, interrupt it. The husband stays in the trance and plays the same scenario by himself, but the wife suddenly pops out of the trance. She is able to "see" the human. She asks questions of the human. What did he "see?" What did he think and feel? After the human shares everything with the ghost wife, she "sees" life from a new perspective, which is a miracle.

She is saved from her own trance-like state because her end of the trance was broken. She had been in this trance hoping to find understanding of why her husband did what he did. She understands her past and is finally free to come forward in time!

How many times has a spouse, child or other family member tried to break a "trance" by coming forward with a question or a different perception, only to be shamed, rejected or hurt for such a behavior?

Understanding Our Own Trances

In order to understand how trances form, think of the mind as a photocopier, programmed to record and comprehend whatever it sees and feels with no judgment. If you have an experience that creates strong beliefs or feelings, your mind will take a picture of it, store it subconsciously and make a copy of it to play later. The copy becomes a subliminal picture. Then your brain starts to study this picture, again and again, until it is understood. The brain will keep repeating the image until it makes sense. Over time, the subliminal will continue repeating as you begin to lose recall of when and where this picture originated. As a result, understanding becomes very difficult. Get ready for a pattern and trance to begin.

Unless you consciously step in and help your subconscious mind make sense of these subliminals by finding the original experience that began the trance, you will live on autopilot.

Every time you repeat a pattern
you make the pattern stronger.
Ask yourself, is this a pattern I want to keep?
If not, find the pattern, time-travel,
rinse it, and cut it loose!

1. Examples of Autopilot Trances
- Freezing when someone yells at you
- Growing enraged when you are stuck in traffic
- Staring at a TV screen whenever it is on and zoning out

Let's create a formula to find our trances:
My trance is... And it makes me feel...
It reminds me of...
I do this when...
I just learned...

2. Examples of Mental Obsessions That Can Be Trances

- Over-thinking
- Bossing people around
- Being anal or picky
- Repeating the same thing over and over again
- Worrying
- Procrastinating

My mental habit/trance(s) is... And it makes me feel...
It reminds me of...
I do this when...
I just learned...

3. Examples of Emotional Hysterical Habits That Can Be Trances

- Freaking out
- Crying incessantly
- Attacking someone with little provocation
- Projecting
- Berating yourself

My emotional habit/trance(s) is... And it makes me feel...
It reminds me of...
I do this when...
I just learned...

4. Examples of Physical Habits That Can Be Trances

- Always smoking at a certain time
- Compulsively talking when nervous
- Laughing at inappropriate times
- Cutting oneself when upset or depressed

My physical habit/trance(s) is... And it makes me feel...
It reminds me of...
I do this when...
I just learned...

5. Examples of Sexual Habits That Can Be Trances

- Picking up one-night stands
- Masturbating to fall asleep
- Romanticizing every relationship you have with someone you find attractive
- Running scared from anyone you might actually like

My sexual habit/trance(s) is... And it makes me feel...
It reminds me of...
I do this when...
I just learned...

6. Examples of Financial Habits That Can Be Trances

- Overspending
- Incessant shopping
- Being cheap
- Obsessing about the stock market
- Avoiding bills or forms as if they carry the plague.

My financial habit/trance(s) is... And it makes me feel...
It reminds me of...
I do this when...
I just learned...

7. Examples of Spiritual Habits That Can Be Trances

- Praying relentlessly
- Putting a false god on a pedestal and waiting for it to save you
- Hurting yourself because you think God or the devil is punishing you
- Debating religion whether someone wants to hear you or not.

My spiritual habit/trance(s) is... And it makes me feel...
It reminds me of...
I do this when...
I just learned...

From a spiritual viewpoint, the human experience itself can be seen as a trance. Many believe that our spirits have created this human existence to feel the opposite of what the spirit is. If the spirit is free, then it needs to feel the opposite experience of being trapped, stuck, punished and judged.

So, with this thought, the spirit created its spiritual opposite, a false god called the ego. In the yin-yang struggle, the spirit's remarkable understanding capabilities are challenged in every moment of life by the opposite of understanding—judgment. Judgmental perceptions have little or no faith in the spirit's insight, intuition and telepathy. Therefore we live in a state of invisible warfare, as life is an experience of these polar opposites. How can we not be angry, scared, embarrassed or hurt with this internal and external battle between the low and high ego, and the gnawing tug of the spirit's intuition inside. This gnawing intuition is continually pulling us to the other side—a side we cannot "see."

Are the hummingbird's wings really invisible, or is this an illusion? This phenomenon is about mass and speed. It's a miraculous equation, that creates the mirage of invisibility. The hummingbird's weightlessness, combined with the incredible speed of its wings, provides the illusion that the wings are invisible. The hummingbird's body looks like it is stationary while in the air. In reality, the body is moving back and forth so quickly, that it looks like it's standing still.

Our egotistical struggle goes in and out of balance as fast as the hummingbird's wings and body. Depending on our mind's mass and speed, we, too, create invisible wars and lifeless existences. Our psyche moves so fast, our level of imbalance may actually seem balanced. But flipping from low ego to high ego is still processing from the ego. It is impossible to see, because our ego is operating at a speed and wavelength we cannot comprehend; yet, we must keep ourselves in flight.

When the spirit is done with its earthly experience and has learned its lessons, the life-long trance is broken. The spirit then sheds the body like a snake shedding its skin. Have you ever seen a snake do this? First, the snake slows down a little at a time, then more and more. It appears as though its skin itches and is uncomfortable and heavy. Finally, it shakes off the skin, leaving it all curled up behind, and takes off, moving much faster and lighter than before. Does that sound like a metaphor for the transition of death or the spirit going home?

1. Is death bad? Or is it simply sad for those still living?

2. What is frightening to you about death? Is this fear true?

3. How do you think your life would change if you embraced the concept of death, without fear?

4. How can understanding and accepting the concept of death, which is inevitable, teach you to live differently? If you knew your time was about up, how would you think, believe and act?

In my belief system, death is not bad or wrong; it's simply inevitable. The only way for the spirit to travel to the next dimension (whatever that may be) is to shed the body, which is too heavy and slow to bring along.

When I was younger it disturbed me that some people died old, and some died young. Eventually, I came to accept the idea that life is an experience, and that people who die have simply had their experience. Therefore, life and death aren't about age. The idea that an early death is some kind of punishment is an opinion, not a fact. If death isn't bad, then the fact that someone dies young doesn't mean that he or she was bad. The spirit had its experience and moved on. A lot of so-called bad people live a long life. A lot of so-called good people do not.

The more we evolve, the less we want to go back in time, and the less we want to be young again. Every age brings its own enlightenment and wisdom. When we understand our past, it's easier to live in the moment and not fear the future.

If we live in the past or the future, we live in fear, in a trance, and miss the here and now. If we live in the past, we dwell on anger, guilt, shame or old egotistical successes or failures. People who avoid living truthfully aren't living lovingly within themselves or with others. People in a trance are spiritually dormant. When we live fully in truth and understanding we have no regret, and don't fear death. Ultimately, fear of death is simply regret about how we're living.

The Inevitable, Invisible, Dimension Travel Called... Death!
Good-bye, Vinny—Until We Meet

I met Vinny Gambino two-and-a-half years ago. He was a strong, funny, typical Brooklyn Italian. His heart was so big he had the capability to genuinely love you instantaneously. Saying good-bye and letting go of this lovable man was gut-wrenching to everyone. No one could say good-bye.

It was Vinny's forty-ninth wedding anniversary. I walked into his home and saw his eyes bugging out, his face white, sitting up, shaking, holding on to a metal triangle above his bed. The music was blaring through the house speakers, playing songs he and his wife had danced and kissed to for many years. He was very sick. He'd had many heart attacks, a pacemaker, emphysema, asthma and a fungus eating his flesh.

We were aware that Vinny feared two things: dying and leaving his wife and family. This fear was so strong, he wouldn't pass. He saw himself as the one completely responsible for the family. He taught love through care and control, not empowerment. This love not only crippled the family but it was a tremendous burden to himself. Every child and grandchild was standing around his bed in a ten-by-ten-foot room, sobbing hysterically. The wind was blowing through an open window. Dear God, this was way too much energy for a spirit trying to let go. No one knew or understood.

The strength of love or fear is death-defying. He had almost died for nine years, all of which centered around his wedding anniversary. Don't think feelings don't affect your life and drive. He had become frightened of sleeping and frightened of the dark. He feared falling asleep and not waking.

Months earlier, Vinny had begun to speak of spirits and family members who had already passed. If you talk to hospice people they will tell you how common this is. When he was in the hospital months earlier, a friend of his from church was in a room, upstairs, in a coma. He said this friend had come and visited him. This was impossible physically, but not spiritually. Could that have been an out-of-body experience from his friend?

The powerful energy of Vinny's adult children and young grand-children would jolt him every time someone walked into the room. Their life-force energy was strong—so strong that he could not rest in peace. No one in the family understood how to bring their energy down to let him go. There was so much love and so much pain. There were energetic tornados everywhere.

I decided to help Vinny pass. I had hoped the family would leave the room, but no such luck with this Italian group. I hesitated for a moment with my own fear about what the family would think. They were not used to death. Would they understand?

His physical pain mixed with his fear of dying was keeping him bound to Earth. I knew I had to release the physical pain first. Was the family going to watch me? You bet! I opened my mind to hear Vinny tell me where the pain was. I opened myself to telepathy. This meant that I could pretty much pick up what everyone else was thinking too. Believe me, it wasn't all nice. What was I doing? After all, I wasn't even family.

I blocked the family's voices and began. I knelt over his body, put my hands on his chest, and began to breathe deeply. I said to him, "Give me your pain." Vinny grunted. I spoke back in Brooklynese, "Give me your pain, now! It will pass through me."

Then came the miracle! He began to let go. I felt his pain run through my body. My left leg went numb. I instantly knew the pain was not coming from his leg but from his heart. I moved my hands slowly around his heart while I was breathing deeply. I began to cry, my voice and body shook as I physically felt his pain. I thought, "Where's the morphine for me?"

As his heart calmed down, I went to his stomach and did the same. For the first time in a long time, his muscles stopped jerking and calmed down.

As I cried, he stopped letting go. He wouldn't give me any more pain. He was protecting me. I said, "Give me your pain." He grunted, "Um hm, no!" I said I was okay. It would pass through me. Do it! He mumbled and let go once again. Mind you, he was not awake or fully conscious, yet he could hear in these moments. My back almost went out. The pain was everywhere. I followed the same procedure with his back and neck. Soon he was calm and so was I. He was breathing without a breathing machine or any pain-killers. He fell into a deep sleep with no pain for the first time.

He soon opened his eyes, just for a moment and said gruffly, "Put me to sleep." I said "Okay. I'm going to turn out the light." He allowed it. Remember, he was afraid of the dark. I lay down next to him and began to softly speak in his ear. I spoke half in a spiritual language and half Brooklynese. After all, he hadn't passed yet.

I spoke about "the Light." I asked if anyone was by "the Light." He said yes, there was a man. I said, "Can you go to him?" He aggressively said, "No!" So I asked, who else did he "see"? He said his grandparents and Aunt Mary. Everyone was there but his parents.

I told him I had been to "the Light" when I was twenty-five years old. Could I take him to "the Light?" He said, "No!" I couldn't figure out why he would say no. Then I remembered. What strong Italian man is going to follow a woman to a gas station, let alone "the Light?" I changed my approach. I asked if he would take me to "the Light." He mumbled, "Okay."

I spoke of "home" as the other dimension. This went on for hours. When he fell deeply asleep, I left the room. It was 1:00 A.M. He was going to go this time.

His wife had asked me if he was in a coma because he was so still. I said, "No, he's just in a deep sleep."

Early the next morning, I walked into his room and he was awake, holding on to the metal triangle, staring at the ceiling, body shaking, eyes bugging out and white-faced. I touched his chest and said, "Let go." He let go of the triangle while staring at the ceiling. He was definitely "seeing" something much different from the ceiling. He fell back onto the bed and yelled, "I am!" As I touched his chest gently, yet firmly, he went back into the "sleep." Still no machines, no pain-killers and the body stopped shaking.

His wife said he had not spoken of his mother or father yet. I said, "There is only one person stronger than an Italian wife and that is an Italian mother. He can't say no to the Italian mother. So he's not going to 'see' her until he's ready to go. When his mother says come, he will come.

"When he speaks of his mother, know the time is near. Please, don't let everyone in this room at one time. He needs low energy for peace. If everyone is physically watching him and crying, they can energetically hold him here. Please don't touch him! He won't let go."

His wife told me later that someone had touched him and he yelled, "Don't touch me!" He knew. He was finally getting it. He had begun speaking differently. He used the same words I had whispered in his ear the night before. He said to his wife, "I want to go home." She said sweetly, "Go, my love." He then said to his wife, "Honey, make some food for momma in the sky." She looked at me, understood and bravely said okay, and proceeded to say what food she would make. He was happy and said, "Good, good," and went back to sleep. The time was approaching. Momma was here.

The adult children had all said good-bye, they loved him and he could go. There was one more breath, he gasped and said to his wife, "Hold me," and then it was over. He had passed on. He was free, home, and not alone.

Chapter Review

I just learned…
I feel…

Summary

If the vibeless are not connected to their truths, thoughts and feelings, connection to others in intimacy is hopeless. They can share a camaraderie through similar interests and intelligence, but there is no self-connection. So, life easily becomes a platonic trance.

Being shut-down from a pressured self-beat feels uncomfortable, so they steer away from too much awareness or feeling surrounded by fear, self-beat and confusion. This is a survival state. The question: What shut them down and when?

To see ourselves only in each other can be convoluted; to see purely is to see our reflection through Earth's nature.

The vibeless one's suppressed truths, thoughts and feelings, over time, can become hysterical and trapped inside. The vibeless either crack, become a rager or hysterical. Opposites attract and repel. The trick is to hook up opposites for balance, understanding and peace. The yin and yang need each other for balance. All this energy is expanded to try to self-balance from the outside in instead of the inside out. This flat energy is heavily charged. The electromagnetic light spectrum shows us how much we don't "see" in our lives. Does it take a dimension travel towards death to understand our present existence?

1. Do you want to live life or merely survive?

2. Do you want to fear death as you live dead inside or understand life and its purpose? Why?

3. Is a fear of death your intuition telling you that your life was lived in regret?

4. Why are you here?

5. Do you matter? If so, why?

16 Spiritual Warfare:
Living in Spirit Rather Than Ego

Belief is stronger than truth, unless you believe in the truth! A person who questions beliefs is considered a trouble-maker. Are you a trouble-maker?

What is good? What is right? What is love? What is bad? What is wrong? What is hate? What is fear? What is punishment? What is forgiveness? These are questions that are answered according to individual perceptions. Every family, culture and religion can answer these questions and alter these words to fit their beliefs. There have been many fights, disagreements and wars as a result of these words.

Perception is a choice. The action and belief of the perception you choose will be the point from which you create. God is a creator and does not judge; therefore the creator part of you does not judge.

At War with Ego-Based Indoctrination

Hell is sometimes described as a place below Earth, in an eternal inferno of flames. Is the concept of eternally burning hopeful or forgiving? If forgiveness is real and possible, and God forgives you before you even attempt to sin, how are we supposed to understand and forgive ourselves and those who have hurt us here on Earth? How can the word *forever* be true or a part of the concept of recovery, no matter what you've done? What does *forever damned* do to the concept of evolution and forgiveness? Is this concept what keeps us judgmental and punishing instead of understanding, forgiving and recovering? So this is what happens to me if I'm not good? Is "good" an illusion that can, at best, last for only a moment?

Is good something I will only fall short of, with no recovery techniques? Is this the failure formula that creates our stress disorders? Is this why we fear the other shoe dropping?

The shoe will drop. That's life. But what punishment must I receive for making mistakes? If someone won't punish me, how will I punish myself? Don't these outcomes—the swinging of good to bad and right creating wrong—derive from an effort to balance? Isn't balance the middle? So, is hell a state of mind flipping to the opposites, still out of balance? Is it a part of our own creation? Is this the scare tactic we use on ourselves and each other to control? Is hell a projection of our reality of what is right here on Earth? Are our answers and cures the very things we believe are not true?

Since the beginning of time we have punished and damned. Is it working yet? Isn't insanity doing the same thing over and over, expecting a different result? Do we not come up with recovery and forgiveness techniques because so-called good people would need to break image, own where they are bad, and recover themselves?

Let's face it, when we're hurt and upset, we want to kick someone's butt. We need a release without having to understand the jerk who upset us. Is that why we won't heal and recover? "I need vindication! I am upset, damn it! Now die, hurtful one!" Punishments are good, as long as you recover and forgive me if I hurt you. Yes, this represents a double standard, but life's not fair, is it? Welcome to hell! We would rather die or hurt ourselves than change. We keep repeating the horrors of yesterday. **Is hell really a place below Earth, or is hell the suppressed energy that sits below our truths, where there is no love?** Depression is the result of suppression of truths, thoughts, and feelings. It exists, below our spirit's understanding. The fires of hell can either burn us if we live in a victim state of fear, lies and anger, or the fire can warm us in a loving, understanding acceptance of truth, therefore creating heaven on Earth. Must we die to get this lesson, or can we learn it now so life doesn't pass us by?

If hell is merely a state of mind, a belief, then is heaven too? Can we really create a state of mind that resembles our perception of heaven? What would it be for you? A light of understanding, openness towards truth, the understanding of lies without fear, a clear mind? Would this bring peace? Is this what peace of mind means? There would be no judgment in the state of heaven, no anxiety, because there is no fear. There is only understanding of all things. This is my heaven.

It's your turn to write about your heaven and hell.

My hell looks like...Feels... And creates...
My heaven looks like... Feels... And creates...

Every day of our lives, we have a choice whether to live in heaven or hell. If we live in our ego, our state of mind consists of care, worry, fear and pressure. No wonder some of us desire an early death. With acid burns in our stomach and even in our muscles, is this the fire of hell in which we could forever live? When we live in our spirit, where truth, love, understanding, acceptance, and forgiveness are, we can let go of our ego and experience true intuition. Our intuition can guide us to understanding all truths, with no judgment, which creates peace. This sounds like heaven to me.

Spirit/Heaven	**Ego/Hell**
Spirit is represented by:	Ego is represented by:
God, Higher Power, Universal Energy, Spirit, Essence, Allah, Natural Force (whatever name works for you)	Devil, Satan, Evil, Demonic, Darkness, Savage, Mongrel, Iblis, or Bad Guy (whatever name works for you)

Because these forces are opposites they give us a vision for free-will choice:

God is Truth	Devil is a Liar
God is Light	Devil is Darkness
God is The Way	Devil is Lost
God is Love	Devil is Indifferent
God is the Creator	Devil is the Destroyer

Now I'm going to personalize these definitions by putting them into sentences:

> **God/essence** is **truth**, which **lights the way** to **love**, and we **create** from this.

> **Devil/bad guy** is a **liar**, living in **darkness, lost** in **indifference**
(needing to rinse hate, judgment, and fear), **destroying** self and others.

**We are all made of both of these energies.
We go in and out of Liar/Denier and Spirit/Essence all day.**

Do you think the devil, anti-Christ or evil attacker is someone outside you? Do you think that God is someone or something just outside you? For you to have a real experience of who you are and who you are not while living this life, would you question that these energies are also inside you?

Unless we can "see" all of our truths, we can't learn or grow, which means we can't complete our purpose on this planet. Ego and spirit are states of mind and perception. The more time we spend in ego, the more we develop neediness and greediness. The ego distorts truth, because it leads and makes decisions based on fear, control, wants and desires. This is a monster living in the depths of the dark abyss. It lives in all struggles—powerless and powerful. The spirit, however, is fearless and feeds on truth. If the essence/spirit is fed, then empowerment grows.

So how do we learn to live in our essence/spirit instead of our ego? The first lesson to unlearn is the self-beating we do every time we slip out of our spirit state, and into a low- or high-ego state. The fear of hurting one's self or being punished and judged by others is gut-wrenching. It doesn't help us grow and improve. It affects us in a "give up" or attacking sort of way, keeping us from coming forward and even attempting recovery. We don't want to expose our mistakes. We want to lie and hide behind an image or someone else's rules, because if we follow others and there's a mistake, we can blame *them*. This is the self-preservation state of mind from hell. This is fear, not love.

Loving Through the Essence/Spirit

Let's picture three forms of love:

Lovers
Journey partners
Soul mates

Lovers are brought together by chemistry, by a physiological and chemical reaction that happens when two people are together. Sometimes the physical and chemical surge is all there is, and other times a mental and/or emotional bond occurs simultaneously. Nonetheless, this is a human and earthly connection that can easily trigger low- and high-ego struggles from the lack of inner awareness and truth.

Journey partners can be friends, children, animals and/or lovers. Journey partners go through struggles together. They are together to create and teach one another wisdom if their free will allows it. Journey partners can either stay and feed any struggle and live in a ghost trance, or learn from each other by seeing and owning what is happening and then break habits and patterns to interrupt the trance so they can evolve. This is a very strong bond. The feelings of hurt, anger, fear and shame are superglue ingredients that hold these relationships together until the learning begins or the running away ends it. Journey partners need processing skills to see what is going on or the pain will spin and continue.

Soul mates are in a psyche relationship. They can picture and sense each other whether they are physically near one another or not. Their intuition communicates through telepathy. Their connection stems from a "knowingness" of self and the other person, with no explanation. If you are feeling anger, fear, guilt or shame, the intuition won't work; you're back to being lovers or journey partners.

All of these relationships are equally valuable and have a purpose. It is possible to experience one, two, or all three of these types of relationships with the same person or with different people.

Which relationship have you experienced and what do you think was the lesson and purpose of these relationships? Repeat with as many people as possible.

My lover relationship is (was) with _____. (name)
   And it is (was) like...
   And I felt...
   It was for...
   I remember when...
   I learned...

My journey partner is (was) with _____.
    And it is (was) like...
    And I felt...
    It was for...
    I remember when...
    I learned...

My soul mate is (was) with _____.
    And it is (was) like...
    And I felt...
    It was for...
    I remember when...
    I learned...

In relationships love has two spiritual components. One is to be understanding even when understanding is not being reciprocated. The second is to be connected by mutual understanding.

Sometimes "understanding love" is a one-sided relationship. No expectations or needs are allowed with the person you are loving. This applies to people who do not own, "see" or understand themselves or someone else, but whom you want to love.

So your job is to understand yourself and create self boundaries regarding what you can or cannot do or say with these people who are closed internally. This is your spirit loving someone in low or high ego.

A connected love happens when you understand your own truth and that of someone else who is connected to him- or herself and you both connect to each other spiritually, mentally, emotionally, physically, sexually, financially and psychically. You may connect fully in one or all the realms.

What would your life be like if you understood how to love through your spirit and understand your ego's connections inside yourself and with others?

What It Means to "Spare the Rod"

What does "spare the rod and spoil the child" mean? Society has taught us that this means disciplinary punishments are essential if you care for a child's development. In other words, if you spare punishment, your child will be spoiled.

If a child touches something he is not supposed to touch, and the goal is to teach him why something's not to be touched, teaching the fast way is to hit and scare with a "Don't touch that!" What happens is that the child is scared and sucker-punched. He still doesn't get why he shouldn't touch. He just knows he can be hit at any time. Now he is crying and hears, "Stop crying before I give you something to cry about." Is he thinking, "I thought I did have something to cry about, because I'm crying."

When you say, "This is going to hurt me more than it's going to hurt you," is the child now supposed to feel sorry for you, because you feel guilty for hurting and hitting him? This is an emotional, confusing disaster! Isn't there another way? Is the guilt a voice from your intuition, saying there is another way? Guilt, like all thoughts and feelings, has a message. The true message of these statements is: You do not have to believe or do what you've been taught. Picture yourself in the role of the child. How do you wish you would have been treated? Let's create something new.

Rods were once the symbol of *leadership* and *teaching*. Moses led his people through forty years of life in the desert with his rod. The only time he used his rod to hit was when he was very angry and struck a rock to produce water. But my question is… If God is an immediately forgiving and non-controlling God, did Moses' guilt and self-beat for getting angry keep him out of the promised land, or was it really God?

So the phrase "spare the rod and spoil the child" has nothing to do with hitting or punishment! It means that if we fail to *teach* and *lead* our children, we ruin them.

The goal of hitting and shaming—spiritually, mentally, emotionally, verbally or physically and financially—is to release pent-up energy from the person hitting and shaming as a way to frighten and intimidate people. This puts the people who are hit in low ego, makes them easier to dominate and control. Hitting and whipping were used in the development of slaves. Many people will argue and defend their being hit as something they needed in order to learn. They do not recognize that they fear everyone and everything. They suppress themselves and then implode or explode. Many flinch or withdraw if you go near them, even for a hug. Is this brainwashing? If they are young enough, they may actually run back to the abusive situation because it is comfortable and what they know. Remember, we behave in ways we know, not necessarily in ways we like.

As you'll recall, powerful leaders who are in high ego prefer their children, slaves or followers to exist in a state of low ego and powerlessness, so children or followers do not feel enough self-worth to challenge someone acting in a role of power. Such leaders want their followers to check-out, not check-in to see if they are okay. The powerful parent or leader will then tell them who they are, how they are and what to think and feel. People in these powerful and powerless roles often are consciously unaware they are playing these roles.

Powerful leaders cannot dominate empowered people. Empowered people can't be controlled because they are not being driven by their ego. Empowered people, motivated by inspiration, are in a state of spirit. They check-in with their intuitions for guidance rather than checking-out for leadership. Even if an empowered person is imprisoned, you can dominate the body, but not the mind and soul.

I call America the "Runaway Shelter." America was built by many people who were running away from something. This mentality can create part freedom and part master-slave dynamics. These people wanted to create equal rights, but if they did not own the pain they were running away from they still created what they knew. They would need to rinse and own their abusee and abuser selves to the point of such understanding and with no shame before they could truly create something they had never seen.

There are obviously other ways to raise a child, outside the master-slave, powerful-powerless dynamic. For example, how is the Dalai Lama raised or taught?

The Dalai Lama is the spiritual leader of the Tibetan people. "Dalai" means ocean and "Lama" means monk. A monk practices deep thought as he meditates. So, the Dalai Lama continually sails in an ocean of deep thought and prayer and experiences boundless compassion through understanding. The Dalai Lama is believed to be a reincarnated soul. Tradition says that two years after the "old" Dalai Lama dies, the Tibetan monks search the land for a "new" Dalai Lama. They find a two-year-old boy who shows, through a series of tests, that he has retained the memories and soul of the previous Dalai Lama. Then, this boy becomes their spiritual and political leader. He is raised in a spiritual way, with techniques for inner development and wisdom. Whether he is a reincarnated soul or not, he is raised in such worthiness, depth and honor that he becomes spiritual.

How to Raise a Spiritual Child

The Tibetan monks take the boy away from society so that he won't be influenced or corrupted by egotistical beliefs. They raise him in a secluded environment, so he is exposed to nature. He learns to know himself and others by observing and feeling nature's ways. There is no ego in nature. Nature is what it is—clear and simple. Is this a way to find and understand our nature? The nature in human nature?

In modern America, if we want to teach a child about a tree, we show him a tree or a picture of a tree and tell him what a tree is. We name it. We describe its qualities. "It is wood. It is green and brown. It is alive." If the child has questions about the tree, we answer them until he is saturated or bored. Then, later we test the child's knowledge to make sure that the information we've provided has been taken in.

When the child Dalai Lama encounters a tree, and asks his teacher, "What is that?" the teacher responds patiently with a question, "What do you think it is?" The child may look more closely and ask more questions or throw out ideas that come from observing the tree. He may interact and climb the tree.

He may ask if it is alive and wonder how to feed it. These questions and answers create curiosity while generating no fear of being wrong. The teacher, without judgment or coaxing, asks him, "What does the tree mean to you?" The teacher asks the child to teach *him* about the tree.

By treating the child as a teacher, instead of as a student, the child is empowered. His intuition and creativity are stimulated. Eventually, as he plays with and nurtures the tree, he will learn what he needs to know about the tree's essential existence and purpose, reaching way beyond the moment of this lesson. But he will have done so playfully, experientially and openly. With this form of thinking, the boy may find uses beyond what the teacher had originally thought. He will then teach his teacher, as all children, students and friends do.

If we know how to listen to them, we learn too. Questions becomes the child's form of processing and self-talk.

True listening requires patience. Patience is not a thought or a feeling, it is an energy, the soul's energy. Patience is a spiritual experience . It aligns with your breath. Breathe and let go of care, worry and time pressure. Try it.

When we integrate patience, in the long run, the lesson is deeply learned and seldom forgotten. There is no fear of exploration and learning. The gift for teachers is that they will continually learn as well.

And that's the secret to stepping out of the ego and into the spirit. It's an exercise in patience and being in a state of not knowing, even when you think you know.

So in guiding and teaching life, which are you? Patient? Or impatient? And why?

We can learn to teach and think as the Dalai Lama is taught, by teaching ourselves the art of self-talk and questions.

1. Why teach in questions?

2. Were you taught to think and feel with your own ideas and intuitions? If so, how? If not, why do you think you weren't?

3. How would you be different if you were raised the way they raised the Dalai Lama?

4. Write a way you would have liked to have been raised.

5. What do you think it means to be spiritual?

6. How can you re-parent yourself now?

Parenting Your Inner Child

There are a bunch of things that many of us weren't taught to think, feel or do when we were children. But that doesn't mean that we *couldn't* have been taught, nor does it mean we can't learn them now. Here are three of them.

1. Most children aren't taught to process anger.

Most kids aren't taught to process hate and anger; they are taught to repress them! How crazy is that! As we have learned, thoughts and feelings need detoxing, just like the body does. Spiritual parents are able to teach their child that hate and anger are energy and messengers. The processing, not act-outs of hate and anger, is essential for wisdom. No one is allowed to be harmed in any processing.

If parents have done a lot of work on themselves, the rinsing methods in this book are easy for their children. Children at surprisingly young ages can be taught to rinse on their own. If they are too young to rinse or emotionally out of control, or stuck and confused, children can rinse or "air out" with parents, if parents can be non-reactive. The idea is not for children to abuse parents by verbally vomiting on them in an aggressive way; but if parents understand rinsing with boundaries and see the child's words and feelings as a rinse, without personalizing those words, parents can create miracles and provide wisdom for the entire family.

Parents, be aware, if you are unprocessed or unprepared, listening to a child's "air-out" can easily trigger your childhood hurts. Look at your children as mirrors of yourself; therefore, every lesson your child encounters is a lesson for both of you.

The raising of a spiritual child requires that a parent stay in his or her spiritual awareness. When children "air-out," they are off center. Don't both of you be off. Kids blame parents. Learn to hear underneath the blame and understand the message without personalizing it. We blame them for our lives, too, if we're honest with our crazy voices. These complaints are feelings, not necessarily facts. Don't forget to practice what you teach. Find a truth in whatever someone says. As your child is upset, own something about yourself.

Don't even attempt to listen to a child if you haven't rinsed and owned something too. Treat the child as you would have "wished" to be treated when you were the child. Create that wish. What is it?

Can you imagine how different you might be if you had been allowed to process with your parents when you were young? If you had learned not to judge, feel shame or suppress while your mind and heart were developing, how would you think and feel today? So, if you weren't raised this way, don't beat yourself up for the time it takes to learn how to re-do it. At least you are learning it now! Better now than never!

2. Most children are taught selfishness or selflessness rather than self-love.

Many of us were raised with an underdeveloped sense of self that keeps us either in a state of high ego, needing to selfishly control our vulnerability and therefore that of others, or low ego, needing to selflessly please others or isolate.

We are taught to lead or to follow, with little awareness of what we are doing. We are not only unaware of others' situations or truth, but often clueless about our own. Boundaries? What are those? Barriers I can do.

Fantasy Time!

If we were surrounded at birth by people who truly knew the gift of understanding and the art of loving themselves, then we would have copied that. There would be no need for this book.

If you aren't centered, don't look at anyone else, especially your own parents. Rinse your parents. Don't live in angry thoughts, blames and feelings, which will only hurt *your* heart in the long run. Your parents just copied what *they* were taught. Self-help was not even a thought. If they had an emotional upset, they were locked up, drugged or had electric shock treatments. If that didn't work, there was a lobotomy. I would have suppressed and controlled everything too. Wouldn't you? The things we are capable of doing to each other is terrifying. And the idea of punishments is too.

3. Most parents and children have an "I want it now" mentality.

It takes years to teach depth and wisdom. Whenever I teach my children or myself a new concept, I know it may not manifest for years. Concepts begin as a thought. Then a feeling which conjures up a picture. If you don't judge this concept, you can connect to a behavior and ignite a creative plan to implement it which creates a habit. Then you may screw it up. If you have developed patience, you may continually brainstorm new ideas and behaviors until you find one that works, or develop a low or high ego and quit. A new concept may not be dead if it doesn't work right away. It may just be lying dormant, until something triggers your memory of it. Who knows when this seed will sprout and become a tree? Relax! If it is meant to be, it will be. No controlling allowed. When we attempt to control, we can create only what we know. You and I are trying to **go beyond what we know**.

Homework!
Time to Rent a Movie!

We all have a child inside us. The child energy holds our truth and is the closest connection to our soul and soul's purpose. So parenting and re-parenting ourselves holds many keys to wisdom and spirituality. The more we learn about parenting, the more spiritually aware we become of ourselves. That's why I'd like you to rent the movie *The Karate Kid* (the first one!). This is actually a movie on parenting and spirituality and features both Eastern and Western styles.

   After you watch the movie, answer the following questions:

1. In the opening scene in the car, we hear the mother and son (Daniel) talking. The mother is selling the idea of California to her son. Mind you, she has already made the decision to move to California without involving Daniel in the process. Therefore, Daniel has no curiosity about California; in fact; all he has is bitterness. **How could his mother have handled the move differently?**

2. In the first scene of the Karate class, the American teacher

teaches students to chant aggressively and powerfully. "Strike first! Strike hard! No mercy!" Chanting and repetitive self-talk can easily become subliminal and create brainwashing. Children are very susceptible to chanting because they are looking for their truths and essence by following someone else. They are powerless, hoping to survive by finding something powerful. Kids are looking for someone or something to emulate. Unless taught, empowerment is not even a thought. Master-slave roles are perfect for the powerful, powerless struggle. **How could this class have been taught differently, in order to empower instead of enslave and dominate?**

3. After Daniel is pushed down a hillside on his bike by the other bikers, he finally loses it. His suppression and depression explodes. He yells at his mother, saying that she doesn't want truth. (All his mother wants is to create a positive existence for him. But she does this by debating, arguing, and selling him on her concepts. Her subconscious messages to Daniel say that his thoughts and feelings aren't as important as his acting happy.) **What is she accidentally teaching him about the truth and love?**

Miyagi

Miyagi, like many wise leaders and teachers, speaks in constant pictures, because pictures and metaphors speak to the subconscious mind and stimulate the psyche. The psyche and subconscious mind bypass thinking and judgment. Thinking can trigger judgment, which can trigger fear, time-traveling, and self-doubt.

If the psyche grabs a picture along with feelings, it will instantly begin creating from the pictures for a deeper understanding. This is why metaphors work so well. Metaphors help create pictures that don't activate a self-beat. A metaphor doesn't hit a point directly, so it avoids defensiveness. A metaphor helps us "see," feel and understand, through someone and something outside us.

Miyagi: "To make honey, young bee needs young flower, not old prune."

Miyagi is seed-dropping: initiating a thought or feeling that will stimulate ideas, thoughts, and feelings to create new pictures and beliefs at some point in the future. Miyagi plants pictures and ideas as he bypasses defensiveness and denial from the ego. Miyagi is not in a hurry to "see" results. He enjoys the process of learning and revelations.

Miyagi: "No such thing as a bad student—just a bad teacher.

When Miyagi speaks he makes us "see" and question. We must listen, feel, "see," and question to truly understand anything.

4. Miyagi cuts a bonsai tree in front of Daniel, so he says, "You already know how to cut bonsai trees." Daniel has never attempted such a thing. If Daniel has seen a bonsai tree cut, could it be that his visual mind has recorded the information and so he does already know how to cut a bonsai tree if he sees it internally? **What is Miyagi teaching Daniel about the power of visual images?**

5. **What kind of listening and believing in himself is Miyagi talking about with Daniel?**

6. Miyagi tells Daniel to close his eyes to "see." When you close your eyes to "see," you internally "see" through your mind's eye. This is where your true self lives. But Daniel's habit is to stop himself from "seeing" and creating through his psyche and intuition, because his fear of messing up or being wrong keeps surfacing. **When you close your eyes to "see," how does this affect your perceptions?**

7. **How does your psyche's inner voice differ from your ordinary self-talk?**

8. Miyagi says, "Clean everything out of your mind…only think and 'see' the tree. If it comes from inside, it is always right." When information comes to us from our intuition, it is always right, because it is always true. **What did Daniel need to do to trust his intuition?**

9. What do you need to do to trust yours?

10. In the second Karate class, what energy does the American sensei teacher use for his karate students?
    Check all that apply:
    A. Wisdom   ☐
    B. Empowerment   ☐
    C. Fear   ☐
    D. Intimidation   ☐
    E. Rage   ☐
    F. Strength and Domination   ☐
    G. Ego   ☐
    H. Spirit   ☐

11. **Where in your life do you use these tactics or similar tactics?**

12. **When in your life were similar tactics used to teach you?**

13. Miyagi focuses a great amount of attention on breathing. Breathing is very important in order to center the body. If you breathe from the diaphragm (that means, when you inhale, your lower stomach goes out and as you exhale your lower stomach goes in, but your chest doesn't move) you will "see" your focus and stability increase. **Can breathing affect the way you handle a situation? How?**

14. Miyagi made Daniel repeatedly wash the car, clean the floor, and paint the fence. **Did you notice he developed subconscious body memories? Explain.**

15. Daniel's fear develops during a karate fight; the fear could block his mind, and he could forget what he knows. If the karate moves were dropped into his subconscious mind with no thought or judgment, he has body memories that will take him over. This is a type of positive brain washing. **Can you think of instances where a body memory stepped in and took over, whether in a positive or negative way? What happened? What was or is it like for you?**

16. Miyagi teaches Daniel the importance of eye contact. He teaches Daniel to keep his mind clean and clear in order to openly receive and read energy from others and sense his own intuition. Eye contact enhances focus and concentration. High levels of focus and concentration stimulate the psyche for intuitive messages, subliminal pictures, memory, and telepathy. All of these activate spiritual empowerment. **How does eye contact affect the way you listen, and the way you are heard?**

17. Notice that Miyagi himself goes "in" and "out" of center. It is easier to "see" him on the outside, rather than the inside. When Miyagi drinks, what he is running away from becomes apparent. He is running from thoughts, feelings, and memories of his past love that haunt him. Miyagi knows how to stabilize mentally; he is struggling emotionally. He uses isolation and drinking to disconnect from his thoughts, feelings, and memories. The movie shows how the Medal of Honor

failed to take away his pain. Life's accomplishments cannot heal emotional hurts. No logic can help with emotional pain. Miyagi's emotions need to be rinsed to open his energy and heart again. **What does this mean to you?**

18. **What is the difference between the karate sensei and Miyagi? Is the sensei in low and high ego? Is Miyagi in spirit? If so, both are talented, yet they are very different. Explain.**

Everyone Struggles with Ego

Just because this chapter is about living in spirit rather than ego, it does not mean to imply that living in spirit is easier than living in ego. In fact, it is the challenge of a lifetime.

Jesus was a spiritual leader, yet he had feelings.

1. In the temple, Jesus became **angry** with the merchants for exchanging currency in the temple. He had already warned them to stop. When the merchants returned, he yelled, overturned their tables. He was spiritual *and* human.

2. In the desert, Jesus prayed, "Father, pass this cup if it be your will." He wanted the responsibility to be passed over him. He was **fearful** of being captured and taken to his death. Who could **blame** him?

> Feelings are energetic messages and releases. Experiencing our feelings is not "bad!" Acting out on our feelings? That's another story.

3. Right before Jesus was taken prisoner, he came back from praying in the desert and found his apostles were asleep. Jesus said, in essence, "No, don't get up. After everything I've done for you, you fell asleep in my hour of need. You guys just sleep."

Ahhh. **Guilt**. Is it possible that this guilt was based on his **fear** and **hurt** feelings? He felt abandoned and **suppressed his sadness**. This caused a **self-pity** energy to bleed into his words. He was trying to be strong in the anticipation of horror. He fell into a low-ego position because he didn't want to be alone in his pain.

Can a Muslim Understand Jesus?

The word "Muslim" means one who has submitted one's will to God (Allah). Muslims are considered to be a people who have let go of their egos, their false gods, in favor of the True God. Mohammed preached that God sent Moses to save the Jews from paganism. He believed that the Jewish rituals were followed too strictly because the Jews were carrying, instead of processing, the guilt from previous generations. The Jews had lost touch with understanding and forgiveness. So God, Mohammed believed, sent Jesus to save Jews from themselves. Mohammed believed that Jesus was the ultimate teacher and forgiver. His compassion mixed with forgiveness created metaphysical healing. He was a prophet, someone who spoke in God's language, like Mohammed.

Thus, God sent Mohammed to teach the Arabs that they did not need to worship *anyone* or anything to get to God. They could go directly. Mohammed believed that people could "see" with faith, truth, and love and have compassion for themselves and others. He believed that people should *not* look at the world in terms of "believers" and "non-believers." And even after he died, that is what most believed. Today, that is what many still believe, just as today there are still many Christians who, like Jesus, practice forgiveness and understanding. But what happened when judgment and segregation emerged? If Jesus and Mohammed were to come back and see what we have done to each other, I'm sure they would be horrified.

Many religions have slipped away from the beliefs of those who first brought people to the faith. Most religions at their core believe in forgiveness and love without judgment. What keeps happening? Judgment, maybe? Could understanding these truths stop the wars?

When you lose faith in truth, love and forgiveness, you automatically look to the world to save you because the world is physical and visible. Yet, what world are you looking at? You can often receive immediate, visible results which temporarily calm fear and pain or cause more. Faith doesn't always offer immediate, visible results. It is an invisible energy that you need to believe in first, and then it manifests, later. The ego is rarely satisfied by delayed gratification. Thus, the struggle between ego and spirit goes on.

A spirit is...
> *Feels...*
> *Creates...*

An ego is...
> *Feels...*
> *Creates...*

Your ego cannot be balanced within itself. It can only flip from insecurity to arrogance at a very fast pace and create an illusion of confidence. Only the spirit can create balance.

Spiritual Leadership

We don't need to go back 2,000 years to find an example of someone who may have struggled between spirit and ego, but managed to inspire others to live in their spirit. How about Dr. Martin Luther King, Jr., who understood subconscious energetic creation as well as any leader in history. He believed that we create and attract what we believe, feel, and think.

Like Mohammed, Moses and Jesus, King personally traveled in and out of his ego and spirit. He was human with an inspiring soul. His inspiration was not driven by his will and ego. When he was inspired he was empowered. Therefore, he was able to inspire and empower others.

When King advised people to understand rather than fight, to own rather than hate, many thought he was crazy. They felt that oppressed people should protect themselves and fight back.

But he had a vision:

Does vision mean insight, psychic seeing, soulful communication?

When we create from what we *wish*,
rather than from what we *know*,
we create something unique!

If we create from what we know, we become reactive, and mirror what we do and do not like. We become what we know. If we *react* to a behavior we don't like, we *become* or feed the behavior we don't like.

If people are bigoted, hateful, or angry, and we *react* to that behavior, we become a reverse bigot, still hateful with a righteous cause. We are full of passion with anger, fear, guilt and a victim's shame. The trick is to not become what they are.

This is easier said than done, or there would be more, everyday Martin Luther Kings, wouldn't there? A leader does not bitch, judge or retaliate. A leader, who is humanly imperfect, still leads in belief and example.

1. Martin Luther King, Jr. dreamt that he might someday hear the people cry, "Free at last, free at last, thank God almighty, we are free at last." Did he mean personal freedom in social circumstances? Or internal freedom? What kind of freedom might he have meant?

2. In what ways are you not free inside your own mind? And what could you do to truly free yourself?

3. If you were to free yourself, internally, what kind of an impact could you have on the world around you?

Like many other spiritual leaders, Martin Luther King, Jr. had many opportunities in his life to take a safe route toward success, security, fame and fortune. He was a college football quarterback. He was highly educated, charismatic, and attractive. Any number of stable professions would have welcomed him and provided him a lifetime of comfort. **Why did he choose a path that might lead to his being killed?**

King's ideas, feelings, and words changed people's perceptions, and changes in perception can create miracles. He left a profound impression on the collective consciousness of this country and the world. At the core of his beliefs, he wanted all human beings to "see" themselves as one people. Isn't everyone someone's baby?

An inspiring leader has a different presence from that of a powerful leader. A powerful leader works from will and drive. An empowered leader works from faith and inspiration.

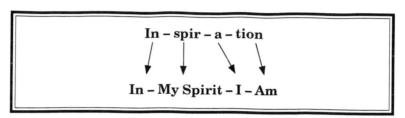

1. *Inspiration means....*
   Feels...
   Creates...

2. *Drive means...*
   Feels...
   Creates...

Drive is motivated by past or present anger, fear, guilt, shame, self-beat, hurt, or insecurity. Many people, aware that their drive comes from these sources, are still afraid to give up their drive because they fear that, without it, they might become lazy, inadequate, failures. The drive often comes from the thought that they or their families were failures in the first place.

But the truth is that if we let go of our drive, we can open ourselves up to being truly inspired. Drive is heavy and exhausting because it carries pain in it. Inspiration is light and limitless. That is why writers, artists, academics, theologians, and scientists depend on the muse, the collective unconscious, and inspiration for their energy.

1. When was the last time you accomplished something purely out of drive and effort? Was it easy or hard to do? How did you feel when it was finished?

2. When was the last time you were inspired to do something? Was it easy or hard to do? How did you feel when it was finished?

Taking a Stand

Did Dr. King take a stand by **standing up** for a cause? Did he take **no stand**? Or did he **stand in** himself?

There are three ways to support a cause. **Standing up** for a cause comes from high ego. That's when you become aggressive and fight to prove righteousness. This is being powerful. You can be difficult to listen to, unless I am as righteous and angry as you are. If you take a stand for others, you claim to know what's best for them as well. Is this intimidating, controlling and arrogant? Is this how you want to deliver your message?

If you **follow** a cause without purpose, then you have put yourself out on a limb for reasons you haven't totally owned and understood yourself. You are in low ego, being led. You are powerless and passive. You are a martyr, sacrificing yourself for what? To take **no stand** is to hold no truth and have no self. You are invisible and easily controlled and dominated.

If you **stand in** yourself, you hold truth without pushing or judging. You are empowered and centered. You are in your spirit, letting your spirit's truth lead with compassion for all perceptions.

Martin Luther King **stood *in*** himself. He used non-violent techniques and boycotted businesses that promoted segregation. Because he was in tune with himself, he led by using boundaries and empowerment versus barriers and aggressive domination.

> Before you treat someone a certain way, "see" if you want to be treated that same way. If the answer is no, you're not going to do it, are you?

Many civil rights activists believed in Dr. King. But was it truly King they believed in? Or did they just feel the message of truth that Dr. King was feeling and believe in the same truth that inspired him? King himself was reluctant to take credit for his leadership as all spiritual leaders are. He considered himself a servant of God—a servant of the Truth. He knew that his actions put his life in jeopardy.

Dr. King was clear that there is nothing "wrong" with death; it's merely our spirit or inner energy shedding its skin and going home. The understanding of truth, with love, is a risk and a lifestyle. Truth and love can become threatening to those who are afraid of truth because they aren't willing to love all truths. We can believe in fear and lies and hope for power and safety, or live for truth and love and hope for nothing but another day in which to do so. The choice is yours! Either way, no one can escape the inevitable dimension travel that we call death.

How Do You Want to Live?

We invent our fear of death because we lack control of it. It is scary only if you can't process and understand life. Death is letting go of the ego.

Pick your "F" Word

Without processing and understanding life, **faith** is impossible. Without faith, you will live in **fear**. When we are in ego, we fear. When we are in spirit, we have faith.

The more you love and understand yourself in life, the less you will fear death. When we exist in lies, confusion, fear, and anger, we are in a trance, and energetically dead. When we exist in truth and understanding, we are most alive.

It takes concentration, focus and empathy to come back from the brink of a life-long death. Be patient and wake up that prefrontal cortex.

Help children not fear death. Also let them know they are here for a reason and that death happens when it is meant to happen. Death is the ultimate experience of "letting go" and a conscious awareness that control is an illusion.

Chapter Review

I just learned...
I feel...

Summary

If we understood that life is an experience for the spirit to see and understand itself through the experience of its opposite, the ego, how would our perception change and therefore our life? If your God or divine power is truth that lights the way to love and you create from this, why do you lie and shut down and take yourself and others to darkness?

Intuition is the voice of truth. To question what you know opens your psyche to new perceptions that cause miracles. Understanding all your logic and feeling truths allows you to listen, understand and achieve wisdom. If you are living in fear, you cannot experience faith, patience, understanding or spiritual love. How can you **grow beyond what you know** if you are scared of what you know? Fear is always of the unknown, and still I am asking you to question all you know and go to the unknown and travel there in peace. This state of peace while in the unknown is based on your faith in truth, not fear of outcomes!

Jesus, Moses and Mohammed represent men, who carry an awareness of their human as well as their spiritual sides. They accept all of themselves and shame no part.

Parenting children means to understand and re-parent yourself first. Know your inner child's upsets, dreams, essence, traumas and mistakes and talk yourself through it all as you "wished" someone would have done for you.

Ask questions of yourself and children and let yourself and children answer from within. Be patient. Don't push.

In the movie *The Karate Kid*, wisdom and parenting are shown in such a deep and understanding way, yet seem so simple. Drop seeds, don't force a tree to grow.

The more you "see" into yourself, the more you will experience intimacy. In-to-me-I-see with you!

To be inspired is to "see" through your spirit. This state of being may come and go. Let's understand, not condemn—others, as well as ourselves. We all have issues. We either admit them or we don't. Every abusee is an abuser who has turned on oneself or on others. Be fore-warned. History is a picture of *what is* and what could be if we don't own and change.

17 Enlightenment:
The Awakening

The Meaning of Light

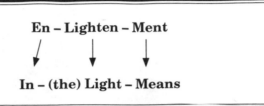

En – Lighten – Ment

In – (the) Light – Means

> **Light:** A natural agent where things are visible; a window; bright and pale, not dark
>
> **Light:** Little weight; gentle, easy, little effort; to take fire

Let's personalize this definition, as we have done before. Let's insert "I," "me" and "my" into dictionary phrases and create a new paragraph:

When I am in the **light** I can *naturally be an agent* to make things *visible*. I am a *window* that is *bright and pale* yet *not dark*. This creates *little weight* in my life and I am *gentle*. I *am easy* and life requires *little effort*. I have a *fire* (my passion and my pain) inside.

When you've been in the dark for a long while, and a light comes on, it can be uncomfortable and actually hurt your eyes at first. Your natural impulse may be to squint and try to block some of the light. This is also true of spiritual, mental and emotional light, otherwise known as truth.

As I have become more clear and let my self-beat go, I can "see" people with my spirit's eyes, instead of using my ego's judgments. My ego compares. My spirit connects. My ego judges. My spirit understands.

The Middle Way—
Connection of the Mind and Soul

Siddhartha, the man who would eventually be known as the first Buddha (meaning "the awakened one"), came from a rich and royal family who lived in India, 566 B.C. At the age of twenty-nine, he abandoned his wife and son. He left behind all his possessions in order to wander, search, and find himself from within. Our Western world would define him as a deadbeat dad. However, in his time and considering the breadth of his geography, this was common and acceptable. His parents (and many parents in similar circumstances) took responsibility for extended families, wives and children.

Siddhartha's self-discovery required that he forsake everything that represented his ego, meaning his money, family, palace, and human desires. He forced himself to experience opposite lifestyles, including physical and financial deprivation through starvation. He had been raised rich and privileged. His father protected him from knowing and seeing any form of suffering. So, he chose the opposite of this kind of life, an ascetic life, a strict lifestyle denying pleasure of any kind.

Siddhartha's father had protected him not only from suffering in itself, but from the suffering of others. When Siddhartha left the confines of his palace, he was psychologically unprepared to encounter the depth of sadness and hardship people faced. He experienced deep and unmitigated sorrow for the first time. So shocked was he to see what his people were enduring, that he became determined to find a way to end suffering, not just for them but for all humankind.

If his shock had merely triggered his guilt and shame, he might have become absorbed into his ascetic lifestyle and focused on an absence of comfort to punish himself for having been born rich. But he wasn't triggered. He was inspired. His goal became the desire to find a path of understanding and depth for everyone, not just for himself. He began to search for a meaningful process rather than replacement of suffering with more suffering.

It is said that Siddhartha overheard a music teacher explain how the strings on a musical instrument cannot be too tight or the instrument will not play harmoniously. On the other hand, if the strings are too loose, it won't play music at all. It was this metaphor that enlightened Siddhartha's life journey toward "The Middle Way."

He realized that suffering was a state of mind. Living a worldly and superficial existence wasn't the easy way. However, a life of total denial was equally unenlightening. If the soul takes refuge in the body for this lifetime, it must have something to learn from the body. So both body and soul should be cherished. Our spiritual and human characteristics should be celebrated, not denied.

Furthermore, Siddhartha felt that the way out of suffering is through concentration of the mind. To not nourish the body affected his concentration and made him think and feel unclear and weak, which sabotaged his ultimate purpose. Therefore he determined that the body, mind, and spirit all need attention and nourishment, for the enhancement of insight.

In-sight: The "sight" that comes from looking within. When you see the why's you are wise.

Do We Need to Lose Everything in Order to Know Anything?

Deprivation often does enable people to "let go" of judgment, self-beat, and ultimately, control. For example, some people learn how to "let go" while passing through a near-death experience.

Experiencing deprivation takes away egotistical desire and, therefore, the need for control. It is a way to "kill" the ego. It may only be a kind of egotistical death, but it is an experience of death. The "near-ego-death" experience of deprivation does show people how to let go.

Deprivation is not necessarily the best or the only way to learn how to "let go." It is only one way. It was how Siddhartha did it. But it wasn't necessarily the way he taught others to do it.

Each of us has our own path to enlightenment. Yours may or may not involve deprivation. Don't follow someone else's path! Don't pick deprivation to martyr yourself and prove bravery or worthiness. Your inner self-judger and destructive voices may be asking you to suffer as a technique to prove a point. Don't listen to them! Listen to your intuition. Only your intuition knows the path you are to take.

Inner Peace and Four Noble Truths

During his intellectual and spiritual travels, Siddhartha/ Buddha "saw" four kinds of people with his "seeing" eyes: an old man, a sick man, a corpse, and a monk.

Siddhartha was in touch with his psyche, which meant that he could read energies. He could "see" the pain and sadness in each of these men energetically. The old man and the sick man were still alive, but they were in pain and had found no peace. The corpse had found peace, but was not alive. The monk, however, knew peace even in the midst of pain.

The monk had taught himself to thoroughly understand pain. Knowing and understanding pain so clearly, the monk had been able to achieve peace of mind from inside himself. No earthly experience could change this. If he was living in his spirit energy, possessing no ego desires, he became immune to the loss of integrity that we often experience with physical pleasure and pain. The monk had accomplished the very goal that Siddhartha sought, to end suffering altogether!

**The more our psyche understands our animal side,
the deeper inside us the soul can "see" and understand itself.**

Siddhartha came up with a formula called the Four Noble Truths. These four truths are the foundation of all Buddhist beliefs:

1. All human life is **suffering** (*dhukka*).
2. All suffering is caused by human **desire**.
3. Human suffering can be ended by ending human desire.
4. Desire can be ended by following the Eightfold Noble Path:

   - Right understanding
   - Right thought
   - Right speech
   - Right action
   - Right livelihood
   - Right effort
   - Right mindfulness
   - Right concentration

> **Suffering:** Means undergoing or sustaining, experiencing, enduring, and permitting.

Let's personalize the word suffering. Add "I," "me" and "my."

Suffering means *undergoing* or *sustaining* myself as I'm *experiencing* life. I *endure* what I *permit*.

So does suffering mean "to experience?" The question is: How are we experiencing?

> **Desire:** Means to wish, request, long for, or have an appetite for.

Desire means what I *wish* for, I am *requesting* and *longing for* because I have an *appetite* for.

So does it matter if desire is feeding your ego or spirit?

> **Right:** Means conformable to justice and morality, in accordance with the truth; appropriate; most favorable; in satisfactory condition; and in good health or order.

Being **right** means to be *comfortable* with a *justice and morality* in *accordance with the truth*. If I am *appropriate* and *most favorable*, I am *satisfied* with my *condition*. So I am *in good health* because I have *order*.

Doesn't right sound like having an "acceptance of truth created from the body, mind, heart and soul," aligning yourself in an order stemming from your realms?

So let's restate the Buddhist principles in light of these understandings:

1. All human life is an experience.

2. Learning experiences are caused by ego drives and spiritual inspirations.

3. Suffering is a perception of ego drives or failures. The acceptance of all truth aligns with the order of your realms.

4. The egotistical life can be ended by following the Eightfold Noble Path:

    • Acceptance of truth creating clarity from understanding.
    • Acceptance of truth creating clarity of thought.
    • Acceptance of truth creating clarity in speech.
    • Acceptance of truth creating clarity of action.
    • Acceptance of truth creating clarity of livelihood.
    • Acceptance of truth creating clarity in our effort.
    • Acceptance of truth creating clarity for mindfulness.
    • Acceptance of truth creating clarity for concentration.

Dharma—Trusting in Now

Dharma consists of the duties, such as those in the Eightfold Path, that are required by the Hindu code of behavior. Living according to Dharma involves trusting that the way things are right now is the way things will always be in the universe and in nature. In other words, "What is, is."

From a metaphorical standpoint, Buddhism maintains that everything in the universe is connected. Everything has energy and has an effect on everything else. Nature, animals, air, people, and inanimate objects are all made of energy and each has an impact on the other. Truth of nature cannot change; nothing in essence ever really changes. Therefore, the idea is that energy just moves around. Could this be what the yin/yang concept is saying as well?

Note that Siddhartha's goal was not religious. He merely wanted a way to rid humans of suffering. The Eightfold Noble Path was designed to eliminate desire and attachment to the ego self and to get rid of suffering, not necessarily to find God!

The idea was to live with no care and no worry, and to let go of the insecure and arrogant battles of the ego by living and loving the truth through the understanding of all truths. But, because truth is a "God-word," and Buddhism helps people become more connected to their truths and, therefore, souls, perhaps Buddhism truly does ultimately reveal God.

Awakening the Soul's Energy and Mahatma Gandhi

We need to:

1. Wake our inner selves from a shutdown and inner sleep.
2. Choose to "see" all truths without judgment.
3. Stimulate our confusion and become comfortable with not knowing.
4. Awaken from our personal trances.
5. Break patterns.
6. Feel and process rather than avoid.
7. Know our past and present selves.
8. Know our spirit and animal selves.
9. Rinse.
10. Think and speak in questions; then answer each question, only to ask another question.
11. Stop repeating untruthful and unloving thoughts, feelings, words and actions.
12. Change our self-talk and beliefs with conscious awareness.
13. Stop punishing and condemning ourselves and others.
14. Own.
15. Connect to our psyche, intuition, and telepathic minds.

Then we can know our soul's goals and energy!

Mahatma Gandhi was born to a middle-class family in India in 1869. He was married at the age of thirteen. He hoped to follow his father, a bureaucrat, into government service, so he studied law in England, but he was not a thriving student. He soon became a lawyer with no placement. During his first appearance in front of a judge, he was unable to utter a single word.

Ultimately, the only place he could find work as an attorney was in

South Africa. He couldn't even afford to bring his family with him. He went to South Africa hoping to make enough money to come back and support his family too. Notice that Gandhi left his family. Many times men had to leave their families, and their leaving was not considered abandonment. Gandhi's departure was a necessity to find work to provide for his family and it was considered an act of strength and love to do so. There was often no work in the area. The unbelievable pressure to be sole provider and leader of the family, for the male, has been historically difficult. To find ways to support families or discover themselves, men left, to learn and later lead their families.

Gandhi was about to find a way to lead his family, not necessarily support the family, as he had originally set out to do. Was Gandhi being led by choosing to follow truth and not live by his original goal and desire?

Shortly after arriving in South Africa, a prospective client sent for him and he took an all-night train from one side of the country to another. Halfway through the ride, a white passenger boarded the train and objected to the presence of a colored man. Gandhi was ordered to move to a car at the rear of the train. He refused to leave the cabin. The attendant threw him off the train, without his luggage, and he spent the night in a train station, in the middle of winter.

The next time he traveled, he did so by stagecoach. If it is your destiny to be of truth spiritually, the lessons and messages will not go away. You cannot run. If truth keeps banging at your door, I would just surrender to it. The stagecoach was no safer than the train. There were more white people and Gandhi once again refused to behave as a proper inferior. When the white passengers insisted that he sit outside next to the driver, he again refused. This time the driver beat him severely, until even the passengers begged him to stop.

Gandhi was inspired to **stand in** for himself and others, not **stand up**. He called a meeting of fellow Indians living in Pretoria, mostly Muslim merchants. He began to organize them so they could develop acceptance of their human rights. Gandhi began planting seeds that would lead hundreds of millions of people, thousands of miles away, to free themselves from the most powerful empire in the world, the British Empire.

> Are failures a part of our journey, guiding us to where we
> belong? Are failures part of leading us to truth? And who
> decides what a failure is? Could a failure be your guide
> that leads you to your destiny, if you don't give up? Failure
> is a judgment thought; there is no such word in the
> language of spirituality. Everything has a lesson and a
> reason.

1. Can failure be a part of leadership? How?

2. How have you failed in the past? How did it make you feel?
   What did you learn?

3. Think of an area in your life in which you are currently "failing." Is there a new way to "see" this experience and turn it
   into wisdom? How?

Gandhi gave up his career, money and title. Eventually he would become celibate as well (rumor has it that celibacy took a few tries to
master).

His goal was to live with and in poverty, to internally know and
understand poverty. He owned no material possessions and wore only
a homespun loincloth and shawl. This kept him feeling and questioning to understand the pain and struggle of slavery so that his inner
wisdom would develop. You cannot truly understand something if you
cannot "see" and feel it first.

So much empowerment is in these choices. People living in poverty were often too beaten down spiritually, mentally, emotionally, physically, sexually, and financially to understand the concept of empowerment. They knew about the powerful/powerless dynamic, and that was
it. They needed someone like Gandhi to help them see what they
could become. Gandhi needed these people in order to understand
himself as well. Did poverty mean failure? Shame? How was Gandhi
the same as those living in poverty? Could it be they were the same inside? Were Gandhi and those in poverty shamed for what they knew
and didn't know, and for what they had and didn't have? What does

this have to do with who someone is? Who you are has nothing to do with any of this. The soul inside us all "sees" and knows all.

When compassion and wisdom mix with inner strength, anything and everything becomes possible.

In India, the British had enslaved many ethnic groups and dominated the people of India. But Gandhi *did not react* to the people's act-outs of pain, blame, and rage. He used the non-violent technique of holding the truth with love and understanding. He sought to understand why those who were hurting these people did so. He communicated through acts of centered resistance, via hunger strikes, peaceful marches, collective prayer. Gandhi and the others who believed in truth, love, and understanding did not "fight back" as others had attempted in the past. He focused on acts of civil disobedience, which he called *satyagiaha* (holding to the truth).

Because he and his followers refused to fight back, the British were forced to "see" themselves and their own behavior. The rest of the world was able to "see" the truth as well. If Gandhi had fought back and reacted, both sides would have behaved in the same manner, and finding the truth, which was the real message, would have been lost in the mutual fight. When anyone participates in a fight, the "good guy" "bad guy" images become distorted. Everyone fighting begins to look the same. Who is right and who is wrong is blurred by all the pain and fighting. When truth surfaces, love re-emerges. When the fight is over, all that remains hopefully is understanding.

> Gandhi: "I am not conscious of a single experience that made me feel that East is East and West is West. On the contrary, I have been convinced, more than ever, that human nature is much the same, no matter under what clime it flourishes, and that if you approached people with trust and affection, you would have ten-fold trust and thousand-fold affection returned to you."

Gandhi used the words of Jesus when he said, "Father, forgive them, for they know not what they do."

Because Gandhi searched for ways to hold "the truth with love" in a peaceful way, he often took opposing sides of the same issue. Gandhi couldn't take a side and remain true to himself. For example, he actively supported the British during World War I, then opposed them strongly for their behavior and beliefs about the Indian people. He spoke out in truth concerning the British, but objected more strongly when one of his people killed a British man. At many times during his life, even his own people felt that he was disloyal for understanding both sides.

1. *Loyal means...*
2. *Loyal feels...*
3. *Loyal creates...*
4. *Honest means...*
5. *Honest feels...*
6. *Honest creates...*
7. Is it possible to be both loyal and honest? Explain.

Loyalty Doesn't Always Welcome the Truth!

Being loyal doesn't necessarily mean welcoming the truth. If I'm a member of a certain political party and I disagree with the party's agenda, I must be disloyal to the party to stay in my truth. I can still understand both sides and their perceptions, as I choose what is true for me. I cannot follow blindly. I cannot go deaf or live mute.

If I love my parents and they tell me to hug someone who makes me feel uncomfortable, I won't hug that person. There are reasons for my being so uncomfortable. Maybe it is something I am intuitively picking up or something is being triggered inside me. Either way, I need to respect myself, to check-in with my intuition. This may make me appear disobedient or disloyal. Look at the Commandment to honor thy parents, not necessarily to obey. Could honor mean to understand? I have "seen" some parents who should not be obeyed.

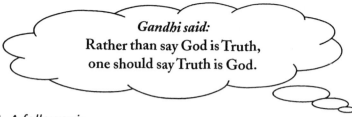

Gandhi said:
Rather than say God is Truth,
one should say Truth is God.

1. *A follower is...*
2. *A follower feels...*
3. *A follower creates...*

Now, personalize your answers above. Go back to your writings and insert an "I" in each one. When I follow, I am... When I follow, I feel... When I follow, I create... Own where and how you are a follower!

1. *A leader is...*
2. *A leader feels...*
3. *A leader creates...*

Now, personalize your answers above. Insert an "I" in each one. When I lead, I am... When I lead, I feel... When I lead, I create... Own where and how you are a leader!

Gandhi, while trying to free India from British rule, said, "Poverty is the worst form of violence." Why would he say that?

1. *Poverty is violent because...*
2. *Poverty means...*
3. *Poverty feels...*
4. *Poverty creates...*

Now, personalize this as you did above. Take out the words "Poverty means" and replace them with:

My spirit is impoverished by...My spirit feels...
My spirit creates...
I'm mentally impoverished by...I mentally feel...
And I mentally create...
I'm emotionally impoverished by...I emotionally feel...
And I emotionally create...

I'm physically impoverished by...I physically feel...
And I physically create...
I'm financially impoverished by...I financially feel...
And I financially create...

I Am Going Home to Egypt
by Amr

I am not strong enough if I go back before I am ready; I will allow the darkness to overcome me.

My darkness is poverty and the fear of poverty. Poverty is shame. When I have shame, I have no understanding, I have no self. I lose my self. I will follow anyone or anything. I will not be able to tell the difference between the light and the dark.

Poverty leads to ignorance, poor health, fear and then darkness.

The Fear of Poverty is like this: you have enough food in your house for one maybe two days. But the Fear of Poverty consumes you and you can no longer "see," "feel" or even taste the food in your house. Unless your faith is strong enough, you will shut down, go insane or both. When you go insane, you can kill, destroy, lie, steal, cheat, rape, pillage, plunder until you are satisfied. Since you are blind you will "overkill." That means you will take far more than your fair share of what you really need *and* your *ego* will *drive* you to continue to take more. It will never stop because the fear will never stop.

If I shut down, the darkness will surround me, engulf me and I will lose all hope. I will surrender to death and welcome it, maybe to bring it to myself or others because death or surviving become too much to bear. You can become obsessed with death.

I know and feel that I am not strong enough to go back. My own darkness in poverty will engulf me. I am afraid I will allow the *guilt* of having lived well for a few years to win and I will cave in. I will shut down, go insane.

You can see where poverty breeds violence. Is the war about poverty? Please don't send me back. If we could get one person to show us that we have worth and teach us how to have boundaries, everyone on the planet will want to live in Egypt.

$\sim$

How can we all learn to check-in and ask questions?

Asking Questions

Asking a question instead of making a statement opens us and those we are communicating with to think and feel from within ourselves. It keeps control and projection out of the conversation. For example, instead of saying to yourself, "I feel depressed," ask yourself "How do I feel?" "Why do I feel this way?" "When did this start and why?"

Here is an example of a statement turned into questions...

Statement/Judgment With No Understanding

"You treat me like garbage."

Question: Do you feel uncomfortable with me?
Did I make you mad?
Did I hurt your feelings?

WARNING: When you ask questions, no guilt is allowed. Questions are not supposed to be loaded with opinions that backhand someone, causing fear, guilt or shame. This is not being open and understanding. Questions are meant to truly understand someone or something. Your perspective is not the issue in these moments. Look inside yourself as you see and understand someone else.

When you ask a question, you create a way for people to "check-in" with themselves. A statement can cause arguments, defensiveness and debate.

Questions cause a check-in of thought and feelings for the purpose of understanding if your energy is open and not aggressive.

If you would like to be understood by someone, remember that person must understand him- or herself first. Don't ask questions of someone until you have rinsed and checked-in with yourself and can hold a center in case the person answering your questions attacks or hurts your feelings. Careful!

> A wise person asks questions and
> does not react or personalize.
>
> With every response there are ten more questions!
>
> Don't quit until understanding arrives for all!

Write your own statement or judgment about yourself or someone else. Then turn that statement or judgment into questions. Use feeling and picture words in your questions to create a conscious or subconscious visual, so that your question can stimulate more thoughts and feelings. You agreeing or disagreeing is not a factor when understanding and asking questions.

1. *Dear _____, when I look at you I see...*

2. *When I look at you I feel...*

3. *I judge you as...*

Now, take the statements/judgments from above and turn your thoughts, feelings and judgments into questions:

4. *Dear _____, may I ask you a question?*
   (You can ask any piece of information starting with question words: Who, what, where, when, why, how, could and would can take you anywhere.) *Why are you... When did... How did it feel when... What does it remind you of...*

   - The process of questioning keeps your mind open to explore new information for a deeper awareness.
   - When we ask questions, our goal is to genuinely want to understand the other person, even if we or that person are upset.
   - We proceed with one understanding at a time.
   - Agreeing does not matter.
   - Right and wrong do not matter during this exercise.
   - Rather than perceive ourselves as different from the person we are talking to, we "own" where we are alike or similar.

- Listen with empathy, not sympathy.
- Learn to hear what you do not want to hear.
- Be surprised by new perceptions instead of validated by righteousness!
- Must we dominate each other or submit and be dominated?

If I am looking in the mirror and you stand in front of me, who am I seeing? You, that's who. If I am to see and understand myself, get out of my way and let me see myself. Every time you are reactive or controlling, I cannot see myself, I see you.

If you haven't rinsed your judgments and crazy voices, your pain and issues will bleed into your questions and you will not see. If your questions have anger, fear, guilt, and shame in them, understanding and truth will be blocked. And the result will be a fight, and more invisible warfare. But if you come from an acceptance of truth-with-clarity, with no right or wrong, then you will find the truth and achieve enlightened understanding.

If we don't understand *all* of ourselves—the good, as well as the bad—we are not...

En – Light – End

Being In   the Light   I can "see" in the "end"
(which ends fear and indifference)

When the Light Turns Green

> Pursuing spirituality means pursuing truth with love and understanding, and creating from this belief. When you love the truth, even if you don't necessarily *like* the truth, you understand its light.

Many rich, powerful and famous people feel alarmed and cautious concerning the word "limelight." The limelight brings out the "See-Saw Game." The light turns green because of the unevolved, egotistical perception of adoration. Judging, self-beating, selfless and envious people will judge themselves as well as the "limelight" person, as the limelight person may judge him- or herself as being someone inferior or superior. This creates great pain for all involved. People who judge are not owning their issues, feelings and behaviors or they would not judge so harshly. Neither would they so adoringly praise themselves or others.

Lime = green and envious
Light = seer

Being in the limelight means to be "**seen**" with **green envy**.
It is very easy for this light to be used in egotistical ways.

How are you using the "Light"?

When a person first starts to think that he or she has won the battle between spirit and ego, ego is still in control. This opinion creates moral superiority.

> **Moral**: Right conduct or duties; ethical, virtuous, chaste, discriminating between right and wrong, verified by reason or probability; the underlying meaning; fables
>
> **Superiority:** Higher in place, position, rank, quality; surpassing others, above, beyond, power of influence; too dignified to be affected by snobbery

Let's put these two definitions together, and personalize them with the word "I," "me" and "my." Ready?

When I am **moral** I perform the *right conduct or duties*. I'm *ethical, virtuous*, and *chaste* because I'm *discriminating between right and wrong* with a *verified reason* or *probability* that I know the *underlining meaning* of mine and everyone else's story or *fables*.

And if I am **superior**, I am *higher in place, position*, and *rank* than everyone else. I am of *quality, surpassing others*. I'm *above* because I go *beyond*. I have *power* to *influence*, and I'm *too dignified to be affected* by anything. This creates *snobbery*.

Still want to be moral or morally superior? The desire is clearly ego-driven, and the attitude is that of a controller. Because we feel powerless inside, we act powerful on the outside. Fear is the motivator of arrogance and high ego. And don't think it doesn't show.

Many disciples of different spiritualists become so jaded and twisted that they often repeat information with righteousness, not inspiration. They are just rationally repeating information with no ownership of it from their own self-processing. They are needy for the information to feel important and strong. They run with it, causing the message or the religion to be taught through their ego, not through their own experience and spirit.

If we have not owned this information, yet are excited about the idea of this information, will we want to save and control everyone for their own good? Is this freeing or controlling?

Movement from light to darkness can happen fast. Be careful of the ego's judgment of goodness and righteousness. If you are judging others as less enlightened than you, you are not in an enlightened state.

> **We can't fight darkness.**
> **We can't conquer darkness.**
> **We can only understand how darkness works**
> **and allow the fear around the darkness to dissipate.**

> *"Through* the valley of darkness you shall find and understand the light."
>
> Do not live avoiding or denying the darkness and its role in your life. It, too, has a purpose!
>
> We all must understand and own our darkness to understand and not fear it. To be truly in the light, while in darkness, hold the light within yourself for yourself and others—and enlightenment will begin.
>
> It is *through* darkness that you will travel deep! Hold the truth lovingly and you will live in the light.

They say that one day the Devil approached Jesus on the mountain. The Devil said, "If you're so powerful, prove it! If you can, I'll give you all the power you desire." Jesus didn't even respond. He didn't fight. He had no egotistical desire to prove his point or prove his worth to someone closed, not asking questions. Fighting or arguing with someone closed is useless and intrusive. The Devil wasn't open to changing his point of view. The devil was operating in high ego, so there was nothing to talk about.

If someone in the darkness challenges you and you play into his or her pain and defense mechanisms, his or her darkness will follow and manifest within you. Standing "in" your truth with boundaries lets you understand that person and yourself. This is all the strength you need. Believe me, this is easier said than done. Try it. Trust your telepathy to communicate for you and remain centered.

Do not let people who are off center throw you off center. If you hold your center, you give them a chance to find their own center. This is called holding the "light" while someone is triggered and in the "dark." We all need this support sometimes. If you do this consistently, it's amazing how many people will be able to do it for you as well. They learn by watching you, not obeying you. They do not learn when you preach or shove it down their throats.

How to See Ourselves as Perfectly Imperfectly

Before I leave this chapter, I'd like to suggest a present-day example of a spiritual, humanistic leader. Oprah Winfrey. Why Oprah?

When I do the "when I look at you I see…and feel…" visual exercise, and change the "Oprahs" and "you's" to "I's," "me's" and "my's"—I can visualize any aspect of Oprah and create a picture for me to integrate into my life and behavior. I see no leader as perfect, just inspired and therefore inspiring. Here is how I do it.

       I   my

1. ~~She~~ struggled during ~~her~~ childhood.

       I   own   my   my

2. ~~She~~ "~~owns~~" ~~her~~ childhood struggles, all of which affected ~~her~~ heart, body, mind, and soul.

       I   own   myself

3. ~~She~~ "~~owns~~" and understands ~~herself~~ and, therefore, others.

       I   share   my

4. ~~She shares~~ and exposes ~~her~~ thoughts and feelings.

       I   celebrate my   my

5. ~~She celebrates her~~ courage through ~~her~~ own humanism, not perfection.

       I   allow

6. ~~She allows~~ everyone to be "seen" without judgment.

       I   my

7. ~~She~~ had to stand in ~~her~~ beliefs and truths to create an honest,

                                    life

loving, and healing ~~show~~.

       I   have   my

8. ~~She has~~ used ~~her~~ survival skills to teach the opposite of survival. How to live and take responsibility.

       I   keep

9. ~~She keeps~~ growing and changing, sometimes up, sometimes down and, yes, sometimes even sideways.

I   do not

10. ~~She doesn't~~ quit and shut down. (At least, not for long.)

I   surrender my

11. ~~She surrenders her~~ ego and image to find truth with love and understanding.

To me, Oprah is perfectly imperfect, a human being who owns her human/animal side as well as her spirit. Her faith in truth created a spiritual path, which accidentally has led so many of us along her personal journey of owning with understanding and compassion.

Your turn. You can use a fictional or non-fictional person. An actor. Anyone you perceive, be it true or not, as your picture.

My perfectly imperfect person is: _____

Dear_____,
When I look at you I see...
And I feel...

Now, change the person's name to "I's," "me's" and "my's." You are not to be this person, just "see" these parts of yourself in this person and start understanding more of "you."

Don't be envious or judgmental if you don't think you match. If you "see" this person in that way, then you "see" some aspect of yourself that way, which means you are already on your way.

No one is above or below, we are just mirrors of each other.

I am grateful for Moses, Jesus, Martin Luther King, Jr., Gandhi and Mohammed because each of them challenged the world's previously held perceptions and helped us to **"see" beyond what we "know."**

I could be a spiritual leader if...

And I would feel...

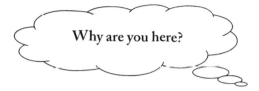

Why are you here?

Chapter Review

I just learned...
I feel...

Summary

Being in the "light" is seeing truth effortlessly. When the light of truth is seen there is no struggle. There is clarity. If you mix this clarity with your psyche, you can subconsciously develop clairvoyance, the ultimate of "seeing" truth in all time zones, past, present, and future.

In the beginning stages of an awakening, you will see and feel what you do not like or understand. That is the journey. Just know this is a stage, it is not forever. Anyone understanding an awakening of a soul knows this journey.

Siddhartha/Buddha found the Middle Way. For balance, our reflex is to flip from one side to the opposite side. Two opposites of the same are still out of balance. You must understand and unite these opposites to find the middle path for balance. It is through the understanding of yourself and your opposites that you will have the "insight" to find the middle for your own balance.

Gandhi moved through an earthly struggle that affected the planet just by holding onto truth with no reactions or judgments. How brave, yet simple. Happiness is not the goal here. Freedom from judgment by understanding all perceptions of truth is the goal. Happiness is an outcome, not the goal.

Truth, even if masked as failure, is guiding you through life's lessons to arrive at your soul's purpose if you don't quit and lose faith along the way.

Asking questions, openly with no control, creates deep understanding and wisdom. This vision is enlightening, "My being (spirit) is in the light, so I can "see," rather than judge and project.

Poverty is violence because it changes you to a state of survival that can process and overwhelm you, turning you into someone you abhor. Could poverty have been the culprit of abuse in the beginning of time?

If anger, fear, guilt, shame or jealousy hit the light, it becomes a limelight consisting of an invisible vibe and warfare between low and high egos. This sets up moral superiority and religious or righteous teachings. A spiritual leader attaches no ego to truth, wisdom and insights. A spiritualist just "is" and sees "what is." No judgment, care, worry or control allowed! **How do you "see" now?**

18 What Happens Next?
Visualization Is the Beginning of Creation

The end is the opposite of the beginning. So the end of this book is actually just the beginning.

The way we perceive the world around us begins with a thought, then a feeling, which creates a picture. As the picture unfolds, it becomes clearer. As we "see" the picture, it becomes even more visible. Then the picture changes and evolves. These evolutions represent the different views we perceive each time we think, feel, and judge the picture. This picture becomes an experience, and the experience becomes our reality.

When we intentionally create a picture in our mind, we call it conscious "visualization." And since we know that our thoughts and feelings have an impact on the world around us through vibes and behaviors, we know that the pictures we conjure up are instrumental in affecting how we can and cannot "see."

Visualization, therefore, is a magical thing.

Belief Is Stronger Than Truth

Remember, each of your perceptions of reality is spun together with your own unique thoughts, feelings, and judgments. For example, if you think, feel, and believe that all women are selfish air-heads, you will "see" them and act toward them as if they are. Those thoughts, feelings, and judgments can be telepathically transmitted in the form of subliminal pictures. The women around you can pick up on these vibes and pictures, and this energy creates an idea in their minds that can affect them according to your belief if they do not know how to hold a center.

However, if you perceive women as beautiful, deep, enchanting beings, then that telepathic message is the one they receive, and they can be influenced, subconsciously, and act according to that belief. Thus the psyche and subliminal visualizations work together to send messages telepathically that create energy that can develop into beliefs and behavior without you consciously knowing it.

Your beliefs are full of thoughts and feelings manifested from life experiences, which means your belief system is limited without the understanding of the subconscious and conscious visual mind. You carry your life's energy with you wherever you go. Since God, divine energy, and your spirit create without judgment, you are able to create from what you have experienced and from what you believe *whether it's good or bad*. Even if it's not the truth!

Many spiritualists believe life was created simply to be an experience—not good, bad, right, or wrong—just an experience. So, if you self-beat or pressure yourself, that is the way the world will treat you—that is the reality you will create.

Throughout this book, I have asked you to do exercises that show you how you look at yourself and others. The exercise:

- *When I look at you I see…* is your logical and psychological perspective, mixed with your life experiences and judgments.

- *And feel…* the feelings from the adult and inner child's perspective, personalizations, projections and inner intuitions.

- *And this reminds me of…* this is the time-travel to your past, past life memory and depending on the strength of your psyche, information telepathically picked up from others.

- *And this creates…* how your thoughts, feeling, and time-travel perceptions are and will affect your life.

How you "see" the world around you is
how you "see" yourself. And how you "see" yourself is
what you and the world around you become.

The way you perceive everything affects who you are. *Everything, therefore, is a reflection.*

Time for an example. Let's take a look at something you "see" every day. Pick something: A TV show. The TV itself. Your bed. Your best friend, your job, your obsession, your struggle.

1. *Dear _____,*
   When I look at you I see...
   And I feel...

2. Now turn the "you's" into "I's," "me's" and "my's." (Remember, if, in the original writing, you use the word "I" or "me," those words stay and you add the word "others").

3. *I just learned...and I feel...*

Now rinse this image. Take out your racket and vent about the object/person that you just wrote about. Get all your internal crazy voices out. Own as many angles as possible.

Now do this next exercise with a situation instead of an object or a person. Treat the "situation" as if it were a person.

Example: *I feel "triggered" at Christmas.*
           Since Christmas is a "situation," I'd write...

   Dear Christmas,
   When I look at you I see...
   When I look at you I feel...
   And I remember when...
   And I felt...

1. *Dear _____ (person or situation),*
   when I look at you I see...
   and I feel...
   and I remember when...
   and I felt...

2. This is owning how their reflection is you. Now rinse and own. This is a processing exercise to see and understand.

3. Now turn the "you's" to "I's," "me's" and "my's."

This is how you can use things, people, movies and actors or situations to help you "see." Your eyes can't "see" yourself, as you walk around all day, unless you're carrying a mirror. You're busy watching everything and everybody else. So everyone and everything becomes how we "see" ourselves. Everything and everyone become reflections of ourselves.

Visualization is "seeing" without the use of your physical eye. As you look straight ahead, are you aware of how much you are picking up peripherally? There is a psyche peripheral vision too. You can sense and see subliminals from other parts of your home or area. Where is that information going and what is it stimulating, subconsciously?

 First write your definitions and then we'll write Webster's New World and my definitions.

1. *Blind means... And feels... And creates...*

2. *Deaf means... And feels... And creates...*

3. *Mute means... And feels... And creates...*

4. Now take "blind," "deaf" and "mute," and change these words to "I's," "me's" and "my's."

Blind: lacking sight, heedless, random, dim, closed at one end, concealed, deprived of sight, something cutting off light, screen for a window

Blind can feel patterned, solitaire, scary, sad, overly accepting, lost, confusing, and livable

---

New paragraph to write!

When I'm **blind** spiritually, mentally, emotionally, physically, sexually, financially or psychically, I *lack sight*. This condition makes me *heedless* and *random* (out of control). Everything is *dim* which *closes* me off *at one end* (putting me in tunnel vision). When I am *concealed* (isolated) and *deprived of sight* (can't understand), **blindness** is *something cutting off* my *light* (wisdom). I need a *screen* (to filter) *for a window* (eyes).

My **blindness** makes me feel *patterned* (robotic). I feel *solitaire* (alone), *scary* and *sad*, yet *overly accepting* of being *lost* in *confusion*. I find it *livable* over time (ghost trance).

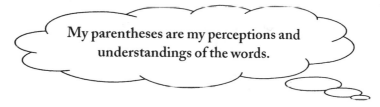

My parentheses are my perceptions and understandings of the words.

Deaf: wholly or partly without hearing, unwilling to hear

Deaf can feel closed off, lonely, angry, scared, and left out

---

New paragraph to write!

When I'm **deaf** spiritually, mentally, emotionally, physically, sexually, financially or psychically, I am *wholly or partly without hearing*. I am *unwilling to hear*, because I feel *closed off*. This makes me feel *lonely, angry* and *scared* of being *left out* (because I'm blocked, blaming and therefore a "victim").

Mute: dumb, silent, hired mourner, deadened sound of musical instruments

Mute can feel suffocated, frustrated, nervous, sad

New paragraph to write!

When I'm **mute** spiritually, mentally, emotionally, physically, sexually, financially or psychically, I come off *dumb* from being *silent* (speaking no truth.) I'm like a *hired mourner* for myself and others (which would be pity, or sympathy). I am *deadened* to *my sounds* internally and externally that are like a *musical instrument* (my voice and intuition). But I feel *suffocated, frustrated* and *nervous* whenever I feel *sad* (I deny my own sadness).

Someone cannot see, hear or speak, who is fearful, judging, confused, denying or lying. If you or someone else is talking in this state be aware: no one can connect or understand with any depth or achieving any wisdom.

The only way out of this blind, deaf, mute state of being is to own and forgive yourself and others!

1. What truth can you admit?

2. What do you understand?

3. How can you de-personalize?

4. What is the truth or story that created the behaviors in you and others involved, can you empathize?

5. What are your preventions and actions?

6. What is your celebration and learning?

Owning and forgiveness is what being humble is. Humble does not mean shaming yourself or putting yourself down. Being humble means to see mistakes, accomplishments, hurts and celebrations with intuition, awareness and wisdom. There is no shame or hierarchy. Being humble does not put anyone above or below another; otherwise, shame transforms humility to humiliation. Careful!

The Reflection
Pick someone who drives you crazy or use yourself as well. Write:

1. *Dear _____, When I look at you I see... And I feel... And you remind me of...*

2. Rinse Paper

3. Now change the "you's" to "I's," "me's" and "my's." Visualize how you can connect with this person's thoughts, feelings and behaviors and "see" another hidden part of you.

4. If the story doesn't fit exactly, make it fit by altering the story to match your truth somewhere.

5. _____ (name from above) *became this way because...* (find a truth of why or how this other person became the way he or she did, or make up a fictional, compassionate story for de-personalizing and understanding. Everything happens for a reason, whether we know the exact reason or not).

6. *My prevention is...*

7. *I just learned... And I feel... I am grateful for...*

Equally important with owning your anger, fear, guilt and shame is owning your talent, intelligence, accomplishment, patience, growth, and compassion.

Pick a person you think is amazing or talented and write:

1. *Dear _____, When I look at you I see... And I feel... And you remind me of...*

2. Rinse Paper

3. Now change the "you's" to "I'," "me's" and "my's." Visualize how you connect with this person's qualities and "see" another hidden part of you.

4. If there is a part of that person that is not developed yet in you or is not your truth let it develop because you now see it. The talents do not have to match exactly.

5. *My plan to integrate these qualities into my life is...*

6. *I just learned... And I feel... I am grateful for...*

Implanting these visual images into your subconscious mind allows them to automatically start to evolve and develop! A picture and/or feeling will drop new ideas and thoughts into your psyche. When the psyche grabs it, changes happen and miracles begin. Your conscious mind cannot make changes at the same rate of speed or precision as the psyche. Trust yourself and let it go! Revisit your old visuals and then replace them with your new pictures as much as possible!

Everyone has to struggle with the low- and high-ego in the beginning of learning to see oneself. That's why I say practice. Seeing yourself stops hurting when the self-beat calms down after owning and forgiving become a habit and a way of life.

It's My Turn!
By Mona

When I was sick and numb from the waist down, my holistic doctors wanted to "see" inside my mind. I called this a "voodoo trick." They wanted to "see" what my subliminal pictures were. They felt these subliminal pictures were keeping me weak.

These doctors believed the mind and body had created a type of comfort zone in being weak. These doctors believe all illness has a psychological aspect to it. Meaning, my life traumas, fears, or hurts had affected my mind, heart, and body. Over time and with the suppression of my truth and feelings I wore my immune system down. Soon, my body collapsed. The x-ray capabilities in the mid-to late-1980's were not what they are today.

The holistic doctor had me lie down on the table, covering my eyes so I couldn't see. How do you like that one? Anyway, he started to touch different parts of my leg. Of course, I felt nothing.

After I started to relax and just play "the game," my judger energies got out of the way. Soon I saw a quick picture flash in my mind. I stopped the doctors and said I saw Pac-man (the arcade game) going yum, yum, yum on my shin. The doctors said, "Great! Now see yourself as you wish. So I said, I saw myself at Yosemite, California, near a waterfall, with long, blonde, curly hair, running around in a white dress. The doctor said, "Beautiful. Now in your mind, take the picture of Pac-man out and put the picture of the girl in the white dress" in it's place. So I did.

The strange thing was, as I was in rehab, the girl in the white dress flashed in my conscious mind many times. It was part subliminal and part conscious now. I've learned there are many picture frames per second in your subconscious mind and we, as a human race, can't catch them all consciously. But, I was catching this one, because I was so aware of it in rehab.

As time went on and I became stronger, I forgot about the "girl in the white dress" until many years later. I was in the mountains. I believe I was at Lake Arrowhead, California, in a white dress, by the water, with long blonde curly hair, running to fetch a ball. True, it was not literally correct. It was not Yosemite, but definitely close enough.

> How powerful is the mind?
> How much do visualizations affect our lives?

When you visualize your memories, and rinse your subliminal pictures and programmed self-talk, you get to re-program yourself.

You may remember we did a similar version of this exercise in the chapter about time-travel. Can you "see" why these exercises are so revealing?

Catching the Subliminals in Your Subconscious Mind

1. Take a situation that is upsetting you, and sit or lie down in a quiet place.

2. Begin to breathe slowly and deeply from the diaphragm. When you inhale, the lower abdomen rises and when you exhale the lower abdomen goes inward. The chest remains still. Allow yourself to sink into the floor, couch or bed as you continue breathing. Let your mind go.

3. Picture the memory in your mind and ask yourself, "What do I see?"

4 When a picture comes forward into your consciousness, be aware that some memories can cause you to feel upset. This does not mean you will get upset, but it is possible. There may be many emotions that get triggered. This is not a "bad"

thing. Relax and don't judge your memory or your feeling/re-actions. Keep breathing. Slow down. These pictures can move very quickly, so just keep breathing. Let yourself be confused yet aware. It will pass.

5. The slower your conscious mind and body go, the faster and more efficiently your psyche works.

6. Open your eyes long enough to draw or write down a de-scription of the memory that you have in your head. Ask yourself as many questions as possible concerning this visual, like "When did this happen?" and "How old was I?" "What was I wearing?" "How did I feel?" "What could I hear?" "What did I smell?" Let this image be "seen" and felt and make sure you answer these questions.

7. Go back to deep breathing to relax your body, mind and soul. Now, let the next picture come to your mind; and go through steps four and five again.

8. Keep coming up with pictures until your intuition tells you that you have enough pictures to truly "see" whatever you needed to "see."

9. When the pictures and feelings subside, more may come. Just lie still. Don't push them away. Don't judge them. This exer-cise may result in almost falling asleep.

If you have enough energy, do a physical rinse! If not, make an ap-pointment with yourself for a rinse later. Please keep that appoint-ment, or you may lose self-trust. Losing self-trust while asking your-self to open up is not advisable.

10. Get your rinse papers out and take each picture through the rinse, one at a time. Don't try to process them all in one day. One picture at a time. If a couple of pictures naturally enmesh together, that's okay. Don't force yourself to stop or to keep moving in one sitting.

11. After you have finished rinsing, lie back down. Come up with your wish to replace your visuals. What do you wish? How do you wish you could have behaved differently? How would things look if you were in a spiritual state, an empowered state? How would it have looked if you had confidence? Happiness? Love?

12. Pick a visual that represents the thoughts, feelings and behaviors you want to have. This is a chance to create; use your right brain, allow for feelings and inspiration. For me, to create a visual from a feeling, I need to "see" something that represents the feeling I want to feel. It doesn't have to be a human picture. For example, if I want to be strong and playful, I might visualize a tiger. If I want to feel free, I might visualize a bird. If I want to visualize strength returning to conscious awareness, I might visualize a cripple getting out of a wheelchair.

13. Ask yourself questions about the visual to make it real. Involve your senses. You can hold these visuals in your mind, draw the visual or write out a description of the two visuals. Let the old visual and the new visual connect, so the new visual replaces the old one. Do not control this process. Stay out of your own way. An immersion process will automatically begin.

14. Now stay in that new visual. Breathe deeply. Allow this wish to become part of your subconscious mind. See and feel the image. You can influence and affect yourself. This is subconscious self-empowerment.

You are on your way!

How does visualization become an active subconscious subliminal? The more feeling and visual detail you create, the more engrained the image becomes. The more you feel connected to your visuals, the stronger and faster your visual will drop into your subconscious mind. Create the visual, paint it, feel it, then let the psyche take it and go.

Visual Replacement vs. Positive Affirmation

Many of us have been taught to believe that positive affirmations will change our thoughts and behaviors, but I have rarely seen positive affirmations work on their own. An affirmation can enter the mental realm and remain there as a logical piece of information if it has no feeling or visual attached. You need the affirmation to attach itself to a visual that relates to you and/or connects to your feelings. If you have a subconscious internal disagreement with a thought, feeling or picture attached to your affirmation, you may have just cancelled out the affirmation. The negative thoughts, feelings or behaviors can accidentally become stronger than the positive affirmation. This is a negative and positive mix creating a neutral or negative outcome.

When I was a little girl, I remember having to write, over and over again, "I will not talk in class." (Surely you can tell by this book that I never learned that one). Why didn't it work? Didn't I do it often enough? Well, if I think about it, every single time I wrote, "I will not talk in class," I was confused about it. In my mind's eye I was picturing all kinds of reasons why talking was fun and good. Some of those positive pictures even came to me from my teachers and fellow classmates. So, for every time I wrote "I will not talk in class," my visual mind conjured up dozens of defiant, expressive, and energetically charged subliminal images against it. Therefore, I did not change this behavior. The positive and negative energies cancelled each other out and sometimes I even talked more.

Mental affirmations are no different from writing "I will not talk in class" over and over again. The idea and concept of the "do not talk in class" affirmation might have helped me to learn more and grow, but where are the feelings and the visuals needed to deposit this concept of not talking into my subconscious?

Here's an interesting thought. Why do you think negative reinforcements work? Well, negative reinforcement includes the message "don't do that!" along with a negative visual and/or feeling that matches, consisting of: "Pain! Suffering! Humiliation!" This may not be spiritual, but it's a thought with strong feelings, which connects to a visual. And that's the formula!

This formula can be used to program or de-program yourself.

Take, for example the habit of smoking.

Take a negative thought and feeling, such as "Smoking can kill me and it makes my hands shake," which feels scary and embarrassing.

This negative thought and negative visual can equal a positive result.

Then mix the negativity with a positive idea, such as: smoking curbs my appetite so I stay thin and I can't quit smoking, especially if I really want to be thin! Now the negative and positive energetic mix cancels the goal. Negative wins. I will continue smoking because my big feelings and visuals are attached to being thin.

If a negative picture was, "I smoke, I am burning my inner layers from the inside out, which is horrible looking," and the truth is, nicotine will deplete my system of oxygen and weaken my immune system, causing me to develop illnesses not even directly related to smoking—and if I "see" or feel this image, these negative thoughts and feelings create ugly, upsetting pictures and I can begin de-programming myself.

Now breathe. Really "see" the pictures in your mind, until the picture becomes upsetting.

And the psyche has it!

Visually, the negative habit is attaching to a negative picture and the negative feelings are awakening and can begin canceling out the habit with no conflicting thought or feeling interrupting your new creation.

If a negative picture grows and is attached to a so-called positive thought ("smoking keeps me thin") and thin is the goal, the recovery is over before it begins. The desire to be thin cancelled out the threat of disease with smoking.

And the psyche's got that.

Concentrate on the negative picture and feel upset as much as possible. When you want to smoke, talk and visualize yourself with your new-found concept (negative habit x negative picture + negative feelings) and see the subliminal emerge. You have just begun to de-program yourself.

All repeated thoughts, feelings, visuals and behaviors eventually become habits. Keep repeating this process until you have stopped consistently. Don't play with this new habit by going back and forth.

The old body memory can still be stronger and take you over.

So in order to create habits that we consciously want, we need to use our formula to re-create our choices. We need to be as consistent as we can for body memories to unite with our mind and wishes. That means involving both our left and right brains. We need our logic, and we need our feelings. We need our conscious and our subconscious. All our team members get to play!

How Visualization Works!

If I have a glass of pure, clean, fresh water and
I put just a drop of dirty water in the glass,
is the water pure and clean anymore?

That is how Visualization works. Rinse, then
create; rinse, then create.

Visualize a Wish

Pick an image that inspires you and stimulates feelings. Use as many senses as possible.

1. *I " wish"...*

2. *I "see"...*

3. *I feel...*

4. *My questions to myself are...* (Feel free to use the question words on any piece of information. Who, what, where, when, why, how, could, would.) Examples are: Who am I? What am I doing? What do I see?

5. Answer the questions.

6. *My new actions are...*

Create a Feeling Through Visuals

1. *I "see"...*

2. *I feel...*

Now, go through the process of implanting this visual into your subconscious by writing and/or drawing the picture. Then breathe as you see and feel it.

The following energies can easily enter our subconscious mind:

1. Memories
2. Thoughts
3. Feelings
4. Judgments
5. Perceptions
6. Psyche
7. Dreams
8. Pictures
9. Subliminal Messages

Awareness of these energies is one thing. "Seeing" these energies in truth, love, and understanding is another.

How you "see" affects how you "hear."

How you "hear" affects how you "speak."

How you "speak" affects how you and others "react."

Have you ever heard someone who is physically deaf speak? Since they can't hear sounds, they can't copy sounds. So, their words are distorted. When hearing is distorted, speaking is distorted. If you perceive the world in a manipulative or distorted way, how will you see, hear, and speak?

How Do We "See" What We Are Learning?

First we learned how we are killing ourselves. How our self-perception creates our realities. Then we saw how the way we love or don't love ourselves can energetically kill our neighbors. No one escapes our idea of good, bad, right or wrong.

When we start to realize that we are imperfect, even though we know we are supposed to be imperfect, we get engulfed in guilt and shame and then deny any of this is happening. So the denial becomes a liar, creating an image that can cause us to feel depression from the see-saw game.

The loss of clarity and truth has no hope without the skill of asking questions of ourselves and others. If we can't find a picture of what to be, do or say, this becomes our Hell on Earth!

The fear of truth and the guilt for lies coupled with the shame of being imperfect makes us so incredibly frustrated and angry, who can see straight? Love is so distorted with care, worry and control of ourselves and each other. Human love has turned into a fearful war zone of protection and codependency. This human version of love has created such insanity from projections, paranoia, and phobias that we don't know what we are doing or what time zone we are in. How did truth and love become so complicated?

We need to rinse the confusion and brain washing from the generations before us who were confused, traumatized and upset. We as humans are conditioned before we know we are separate beings from those around us. Our psyche holds our inner knowledge consisting of our past, present and future existences, but it is invisible. How do we see what we are doing? If we step outside what we know to look at our lives in a different way, we can be attacked and shamed immediately. Wisdom has become a joke. The ridicule can scare us easily.

Understanding the past can scare and upset everyone you love, causing back-door invisible guilt. This makes living in our own skin claustrophobic. The powerful create and dominate whoever they can, creating a powerless society. Nothing but shame and abuse here. Empowerment is almost impossible to find because without an ego, empowered people have no desire to step out into the power struggles. Empowerment doesn't judge and doesn't fight.

Our intuition knows all of this and can help if we will pull ourselves through the ditches of anger, fear, guilt and shame to hear it without judgment. To own without self-beating is the way out.

The left brain's logic needs to hear the right brain's feelings without judging the right brain's feelings. Then the right brain needs to listen and adhere to the left brain's logic and boundaries without freaking out. These parts of the brain speak two totally different languages, so how is understanding going to happen there? The prefrontal cortex keeps us empathetic, so hurting ourselves and others becomes impossible. Concentration and focus give us mental strength and endurance to carry on.

We come into this world alone and we go out alone, so why do we care what someone else thinks? Is someone going to die for us so we are immortal? If not, who cares? The fear of death is the fear of wasting our lives because we live in a pre-programmed ghost trance doing what has been done before and we didn't like it the first time.

The ego is the false god killing our soul's awareness. We know this, but do not change because change makes us self-beat. Change means someone we love or even our very selves were wrong and that is not allowed, although it is expected.

To see all of this without shutting down or becoming hysterical is a miracle with our contradictions and brainwashings. But we need to see "what is" before we can **go beyond what we know** to see and create something new! A wish! Visualization! An enlightened person is awakened from within ourselves.

This, in a nutshell, is what we are talking about in this book—consciously understanding the subconscious.

Becoming conscious of how our subconscious works is a big step. Learning to connect and communicate directly with the subconscious is another big step.

The language of choice for the subconscious after the rinse, time-travel and owning is subliminal meditation. By visualizing with meditation, we learn to watch the inner workings of our mind, as if it is a movie and we are the audience. Visualization and meditation have miraculous power. They require a quiet mind, free of fear and judgment. Faith in the understanding of universal truth is the way in.

Meditation & Visualization

(Play music, dim lights, light candles, sit in a tub with running water or have no noise at all. Whatever stimulates your mind, heart, body and soul. Set your environment to "let go.")

1. Sit or lie down quietly.

2. Begin breathing, deeply.
   Inhale—the stomach goes out, the chest does not move.
   Exhale—the stomach goes in, the chest does not move.

3. Close your eyes. Use them to "see" within your mind.

4. Begin to release your anger, fear, guilt, shame, and control.
   Let go... Breath... Go slowly. Let the psyche come forward.
   The slower the body and mind, the faster the psyche. Empty
   your conscious mind.

5. Say these sentences to yourself out loud and internally. When
   you finish, write these out. If you get stuck on one, skip it and
   go to the next one. Do not control. Take your time. Be
   patient.

   I do not need anger because...
      Letting go of this anger feels...
   I do not need fear because...
      Letting go of this fear feels...
   I do not need guilt because...
      Letting go of this guilt feels...
   I do not need shame because...
      Letting go of this shame feels...
   I do not need control because...
      Letting go of this control feels...

6. Being grateful for our struggles and lessons gives hurts and mistakes worth, which brings peace. Thus, we create wisdom instead of trances. Being grateful and self-beating don't go together. Pick one.

    I am grateful for my anger because...
        And it has taught me...
    I am grateful for my fear because...
        And it has taught me...
    I am grateful for my guilt because...
        And it has taught me...
    I am grateful for my shame because...
        And it has taught me...
    I am grateful for my control because...
        And it has taught me...

7. Now identify and "see" what you "wish" to be, feel, believe, create, or become...

    I wish to be...
    I wish to feel...
    I wish to believe...
    I wish to create...
    I wish to become...

8. Now pick a visual and "see" yourself through your wishes; use natural images, colors, animals, and your imagination.

    I "see" me as... because... and I feel...

9. Keep breathing. Feel free to use your soul's language by chanting, praying, humming, or singing in a way that conveys the thoughts and feelings deep into your mind.

10. Open your psyche by listening to and feeling yourself. Can you hear a little voice? If this voice is true, it is your intuition. Listen carefully to what it says; "see" the images your psyche plays. Do not think.

11. Ask questions of your intuition, and "see" what kind of re-sponses you receive. Some questions may end up with no an-swers at this time. It is amazing how many times responses to those questions will just pop into your mind, later.

12. Can you telepathically receive or send a message while medi-tating? Don't judge, care, or worry about these messages.

13. Open your eyes. Move slowly and come to a sitting position. Reach for your computer or notebook, and write "I learned... and I feel..." This is very important. And if there is anything to own, own!

Come back and do this meditation as much as you can.

Chapter Review

I just learned...
I feel...

Summary

Visualization is described at the end of this book, but it is truly the be-ginning of creation. Many times it is when our eyes are closed that we truly "see." We "see" our thoughts, our feelings, our memories our pain and beauty. From these visions come our wishes and dreams. Every-thing comes from within.

The understanding of our subconscious subliminal mind is crucial. Creation begins with a thought, feeling, visual and then behavior.

Childhood brain-washings become a part of our belief system be-fore we've had time to develop an awareness of our true psyche's wish-es. If there is no good, bad, right or wrong, according to the psyche, we will create and re-create from these childhood teachings. We may even forget we are here for a purpose. The goal is to know who we are by ex-periencing who we are not. This book is just a way to uncover who you really are, no matter what you have done. If you have been a murderer, you can pop out of that trance any time you wish. These act-outs, if turned around by owning and then transforming, teach us so much. So, transform and teach us. Don't let the Earth trick you into believing these illusions are the end and that there is no way out.

The goal is to "see" yourself in everyone and everything with no self-beat. The more you "see" and understand, the more you can create consciously. What is your motivator? Anger, fear, guilt, and shame—or truth and love?

To own and forgive is to admit, rinse, time-travel and take responsibility for all your thoughts, feelings and behaviors, and then create a prevention to celebrate that your life just became a choice, from the inside out. Even prison can't touch you this way. Prison is "out, in" and you are now "in, out"!

To rinse and then meditate, through your own form of prayer, visualize your "wish" and create. No shut-down, flat, vibeless energy, whether it's your own or that of others, can be connected with the soul, and be expected to move forward.

Visualize the past, present and future. Breathe from the diaphragm, feel, "see" and move. Welcome the opportunity to "see" the past and create a "wish" for your future. Visualize and begin changing.

WARNING
Careful of this cause and effect:

What you "see" affects how you "see"

How you "see" affects what you "hear"

What you "hear" affects how you "hear"

How you "hear" affects what you "say" or "don't say"

What you "say" or "don't say" affects how you and others "react"

P.S. Are you seeing, hearing, speaking internally and externally with truth and love, or with anger, fear, guilt, shame, victim and blame? Careful!

How do you "see" and "feel" *now*?
You do matter! A picture is worth a thousand words!

Dear Reader,
Thank you for going through this process with me.
I hope it has touched you and stimulated even one
new idea. I have learned so much just by writing and
re-reading these thoughts, feelings and ideas. If you
have any comments, log onto www.monamiller.com,
or www.communicationartscompany.com to contact
me.

Thank you,
Mona Miller

Glossary

APPROACH: A welcome invitation for information to enter in question form with an openness to understanding. Every answer triggers another question with no attempt to control the outcome. Based on peace, full of understanding, with an openness to see from as many perspectives as possible, there is openness, understanding and clarity.

BACK-DOOR GUILT: A heavy feeling, hopelessness. Being overly responsible from carrying others' disowned thoughts, feelings, judgments and truths with no self-boundaries.

BELIEF: A belief is a thought or feeling you deem true and therefore real. Because you believe it is true you have manifested it as real. Just as we can program a computer to run a certain way, we can program what we think and feel. Over time, programmed thoughts and feelings become beliefs—regardless of whether they're true. What we believe affects the way we live. Our beliefs become our reality.

BLIND: lack sight, heedless, random, dim, closed at one end, concealed, deprived of sight, something cutting off light, screen for a window.

CARE: Anxiety, pain, heed, charge, oversight, has regard or liking.

COMING INTO YOUR OWN: Have you heard the phrase "coming into your own?" It happens when we begin to open up and see ourselves and the world through self-awareness and self-responsibility. See the word "own?" When we come into our "own," we have *learned* to own our truth and change our lives.

CO-DEPENDENT (CODA): Loving or caring with no self-awareness, self-boundaries and no truth.

CONFRONTING: An intrusive, aggressive attack on your thoughts, feelings, judgments and behaviors stimulated by fear and anger. Statements or loaded questions that are open-ended, usually based on fear, full of righteous, egotistical opinions. Confrontation creates more anger, fear, guilt and shame.

DEAF: Wholly or partly without hearing, unwilling to hear

DESIRE: To wish, request, long for, or have an appetite for.

DE-PERSONALIZE: Understanding that your action and another person's actions are separate from each other. Look at the circumstances from every angle, without becoming reactive. Understand yourself and then the person that upset you. Whoever was upsetting you was an off-center person. Do not disconnect from your truths, thoughts, feelings and intuition in the process. Stay aware and connected to yourself and maintain an understanding of people involved. Hold on to the truth that belongs to you and let go of the rest with no judgment.

GUILT: A double-edged sword consisting of a shaming self-beat, stabbing inward and a blaming attack, stabbing outward, which continually repeats.

HIGH EGO: The false god we read about. It is an arrogant perception of being superior to others. It is a survival skill for blocking one's shame and guilt. It does not own or understand. It is a state of condescending control and arrogance, created from a lack of acceptance due to painful and embarrassing truths. When a part of you feels injured, the high ego arises to dominate and save you. The goal is to be powerful.

INFERIORITY: Seeing yourself as less than, in a state of shame; self-beat and low ego.

JUDGMENTAL: Holding and expressing opinions, positive or negative that cause a "better than" or "less than" perception. Creating low- and high-ego modes for yourself and others.

KARMA: The sum of all that an individual has done and is currently doing. The effects of what you think, feel, believe and how you behave actively attract and create your present and future experiences, making you responsible for your own life. In religions that incorporate reincarnation, karma is believed to exist through one's present life and past and future lives as well. In several eastern religions, karma comprises the entire cycle of cause and effect. Karma is not about right and wrong or good and bad; it's about experiencing what you understand and do not understand. It's about what you think, feel and believe—and, therefore, play out.

LEFT BRAIN: The logical, rational and intelligent part of your brain.

LIGHT: A natural agent where things are visible; a window; bright and pale, not dark.

LOW EGO: The concept of slavery that develops from a feeling of insecurity, worthlessness and failure. It is a perception of being inferior to others. It is a survival skill, for protection, to remain invisible or to obey others in order to not be judged as wrong. It is a camouflage of weakness so dominators will not notice you and will leave you alone. Full of self-beat and personalization this is created from a lack of self-responsibility and effort for painful and embarrassing truths. When a part of you feels injured, the low ego suppresses your inner strength to hide you and keep you safe. The goal is to be powerless.

MISTAKE: An experience that happens when truth is not clear.

MIRACLE: A change in perception.

MORAL: Right conduct or duties; ethical, virtuous, chaste, discriminating between right and wrong, verified by reason or probability; the underlying meaning; fables.

MUTE: Dumb, silent, hired mourner, deadened sound of musical instruments.

OWN: To admit and understand with feeling what happened or is happening and finding a prevention or new behavior that will change your path for your future. Owning is remembering the past and understanding why and where something originally happened. Owning leads you to truth and understanding of the past, present and future. This is called taking responsibility for pain and wishes, no matter who is at fault.

PERSONALIZATION: Personalization has two processes. One is a perception of how to see and feel someone or something and use it as an an example and picture, to see an aspect of yourself. This type of personalization is an ingredient for owning, as a way to teach yourself about yourself, as a reflection.

The second is to personalize through judgmental eyes, you will see someone or something as your reflection as a way of blaming yourself or others for your thoughts and feelings, creating paranoia. This causes a negative self-perception that will trigger anger, fear, guilt or shame, causing self-beat and self-abuse internally or externally. This type of personalization creates a negative self-absorption or a projection of your denied thoughts and feelings and life experiences onto others. This causes you to view everything in fear, which causes you and others pain.

PITY/SYMPATHY: Feeling sorry *for* yourself or someone else, not processing and taking an action for the anger and sadness concerning you or someone else. You're carrying yours or others' sadness with no self-responsibility and no change. Others' sadness does not belong to you; yours does. Therefore, it can become very heavy, like a weight, and cause depression! Sympathy is feeling *for someone else*. Not to be confused with empathy, feeling *with* someone, not for someone.

PREFRONTAL CORTEX: The part of the brain that holds concentration, focus and empathy.

PROJECTION: To throw; plan; cause to appear on a distant background; stick out.

REAL: What we perceive and believe is true.

REALM: A circle of self-processing. Used as a road map, it shows us where we are and where we are lost. It is a direction for self-awareness of our different aspects of self. There is an order to the realms for our alignment like a spinal column. If the spine is out of order it needs an adjustment and a re-alignment. The order is… spiritual, mental, emotion, physical, sexual and financial.

RIGHT: Conformable to justice and morality, in accordance with the truth; appropriate; most favorable; in satisfactory condition; and in good health or order.

RIGHT BRAIN: The feeling and creative part of the brain.

RINSE: A technique and processing of our thoughts, feelings and memories—spiritually, mentally, emotionally, physically, sexually, financially and psychically—by writing things down, or physically rinsing.

SELF-BEAT/SHAME: Every thought or feeling that is topped by judgment creates a self-beat. The self-beat voice is telling you to become aware and to understand something. If the self-beat is not heard and understood, it can manifest self-hate, insecurity, depression, addiction, mutilation, suicide, insanity or criminal act-outs. You don't fight or try to get rid of the self-beat; you go to it, understand it and open your mind to new thinking, feeling and behavior. A self-beat keeps us in a spin of self-judgment.

SPIN: A thought, feeling or behavior that repeats with no change of thought, feeling, belief or behavior, topped with a self-beat that spirals uncontrollably. A spin happens when you put anger, fear, guilt, shame or hurt on someone or something and repeat those thoughts, feelings or behaviors with no change. You are in a spin because you are not understanding the lies and truths of the situation. There is no owning here. If no awareness or behavior comes, you can begin to feel crazy. If you get stuck in one thought, feeling or belief with no processing or understanding, your spin will turn you into a shut down or depressed, out-of-control, emotional person rather than a sensitive, feeling one.

STUBBORN: A false sense of strength which is a centering for fear to exist.

SPIRIT or ESSENCE: "What is." It represents the understanding of all truth and struggle. It knows the importance of flipping to the high and low ego to develop understanding. Before you can experience a balance from the middle, you need to be able to recognize the opposite energies on each side. Spirit sees all as equal and full of purpose. Spirit is the perception of truth and lies with love for both. It is your own personal Higher Power or God energy of awareness. It speaks to you through the intuition, which reveals truth. It shines its light through the understanding of your confusions and mistakes. It does not push or control; it listens with wisdom and compassion. Of an age beyond Earth years, it is faith. Faith that when you are ready, you will come to it and listen. It waits patiently for you to not project the judgments learned from this planet onto this energy. It is here to heal, through deep understanding, the injuries of pain and embarrassment, as it already knows why these injuries exist. It knows your magic and talents and is there to remind you of who you are. If you choose to remember. Reaching this understanding is where the struggle stops. This is empowerment!

TRIGGER: A trigger is a psychological mechanism causing a thought, feeling and memory to awaken from your subconscious mind that affects and influences your thinking, feeling or behavior in present time. When a trigger is activated, it can cause an irrational response, an over-reaction, or a reverting to past behavior, even that of a child. Don't be surprised if an instantaneous shutdown can turn into a crazy feeling or a freeze from all movement, ending with you feeling depressed. Having a reaction totally unrelated to the circumstances at hand is very common when you are triggered into a memory that was upsetting. This is why the addict is so prevalent in our world. Addictions help to block feelings and awarenesses from triggers.

TRUE: What is! As it has been and always will be.

SUFFERING: Undergoing or sustaining, experiencing, enduring, and permitting.

SUPERIORITY: Higher in place, position, rank, quality; surpassing others, above, beyond, power of influence; too dignified to be affected by snobbery.

UNDERSTANDING: Understanding has no anger, fear, guilt or shame in it. If I can "see" all of myself—the good and the bad and everything in between without judgment, then I can "see" and feel the same in other people.

WORRY: Seize or trouble, harass, utterly concerned, with useless care or anxiety.

YIN YANG is a symbol that represents the ancient Chinese understanding of how energy works. It has an outer circle that represents "everything," with black and white shapes within the circle that represent the interaction of two energies—"yin" (black) and "yang" (white), which cause everything to happen. They are not completely black or white, just as things in life are not completely black or white, and they cannot exist without each other. While "yin" is dark, passive, downward, cold, contracting and weak, "yang" is bright, active, upward, hot, expanding and strong. There is continual movement between these two energies, yin to yang and yang to yin, causing everything to happen, just as things in life expand and contract, and temperature changes from hot to cold.

According to this theory, when we evolve to the point of understanding and accepting all opposites, we lose any desire for righteousness, war and ego. Accepting and understanding opposites is the beginning process for peace and balance.

Appendix A

The First "Invisible" Lesson

The realms (in order)
1. Spiritual
2. Mental
3. Emotional
4. Physical
5. Sexual
6. Financial

The Sub-realms
1. Psyche
2. Intuition
3. Telepathy

The Second "Invisible" Lesson

The Forgiveness and Owning Rules (an easy to-do process to forgive anything!)

1. Admit
2. Understand
3. De-personalize
4. Empathize
5. Prevent and Act
6. Celebrate

Appendix B
Feeling Rinse Paper

Dig For Feelings

I am angry because...

And that makes me feel...

You (the object of my anger) ruined my life because...

I hate you because...

I hate me because...

I am scared because...

I am afraid because...

I feel bad because...

Fuck you because...

I am guilty because...

I am ashamed because...

I am embarrassed because...

I am disappointed because...

I feel sad because...

I am hurt because...

I feel sorry for myself because...

I feel sorry for you because...

I love you because...

I like you because...

I love me because...

I like me because...

I'm happy because...

This makes me feel...

Time Travel

This reminds me of the time when…

and I remember when…

and remembering this now makes me feel…

Create and Visualize Something New

I wish…

If I could do this over again, I would…

Realizations

Doing this exercise, I learned….

And I feel….

When you have completed the rinse, go back through, as your inner child.

Feel free to change any "you"s to "I" or "me" whenever possible:

Fuck ~~you~~ me…

When I look at ~~you~~ me I see and feel…

Appendix C

The Rules of Self-Love

1. Want to love someone? Love yourself first.
2. No blaming your thoughts and feelings on others.
3. Take responsibility for yourself. Nobody owes you anything, including a living.
4. You can't have clarity without sobriety.
5. Your goal is not to be right, it's to understand.
6. Your goal is not to fight over points that are not the point. Do not engage in point/counterpoint.
7. Do not choose an "air-head" routine. Face the truth.
8. Own your role in any situation.
9. Know your weaknesses and embrace them. Only by loving them through understanding will you be able to even see them.
10. Don't expect anyone to understand or accept your weaknesses before you do.
11. Learn to let go of control battles.
12. Don't fight over "stupid" stuff.
13. Avoid telling others how and what to do.
14. Accept people for who and how they are.
15. Develop your sense of humor.
16. Learn not to shut down.
17. Share thoughts, feelings, and beliefs; they lead to intimacy.
18. Don't save or protect others. Relationships should not be about rescuing and saving.
19. Don't go down with the ship. Preserve yourself rather than a relationship.
20. Nobody is better or worse than anyone else.
21. Gossip does nobody any good.
22. Understand and set boundaries for yourself.
23. Understand the good, bad, and ugly truths of your loved one, with no attitude.
24. Love your truths first. Love yourself second. Love others third.

CPSIA information can be obtained at www.ICGtesting.com
261453BV00004B/1/A

9 780978 665203